IN FOCUS

IN FOCUS
A Guide to Using Films

written by
Linda Blackaby, Dan Georgakas and Barbara Margolis

concept by
Affonso Beato

A Project of Cine Information, Latin American Film
Project and Neighborhood Film Project

Published by New York Zoetrope

IN FOCUS: A Guide to Using Films was made possible, in part, by grants from:

The Film Fund

The National Endowment
for the Arts, Washington D.C.,
a Federal Agency

The New York State Council
on the Arts

The Playboy Foundation

The Women's Division —
United Methodist Church

The Women's Fund —
Joint Foundation Support

Published by New York Zoetrope

ISBN: 0-918432-23-5
ISBN: 0-918432-22-7 pbk.

Book design by Marla Milne
Ilustrations by Tracy Garner
Printed in the United States of America
by Athens Printing Company, New York, N.Y.
First Edition: January 1980

ACKNOWLEDGEMENTS

Our own experience over years of working with film and film use, and the ideas we've developed through contact with many talented and committed individuals and groups, have made **In Focus** both necessary and possible. We would like to thank all the different organizations we have worked with over the years, and the people on the boards and staffs of Cine Information, Latin American Film Project and the Neighborhood Film Project, who have contributed in many ways to the realization of this project.

We particularly want to thank Rich Clark of Last Chance Sound, Philadelphia, for Chapter 13, "Sound Improvements," and for his many other suggestions. Nadine Covert and Marianne Chach of the Educational Film Library Association and William Sloan of the Donnell Film Library in New York City shared their expertise, their resource libraries and files and provided suggestions for other bibliographic references. Discussions with them and with Michael Miller of the Mid-Hudson Library System, Poughkeepsie, New York, gave us a clearer understanding and appreciation of the resources and services offered to film users by public libraries. Patricia Peyton, editor of **Reel Change**, and Kathleen Weaver of Reel Research were most generous in sharing with us information they developed.

The following people contributed to the production of **In Focus:** Gary Crowdus helped with the editing of the final draft, Marla Milne designed the book, and Tracy Garner did the illustrations. Dan Ochiva, Pam Cairns and Judy Schatz did additional research on resources. Lenny Rubenstein, Jiva Brooks Rankin and Lorraine Pederson assisted in the preparation of the various manuscript drafts.

We would also like to thank the many people who read and commented on the manuscript, those who contributed from their own experience, or supported this project in other ways. Mia Adjali (Women's Division, United Methodist Church), Jim Bradley, Anne Doley (Bread and Roses Community Fund, Philadelphia), Adisa Douglas (Interreligious Foundation For Community Organization), Judy Hoffman and Gordon Quinn (Kartemquin Films, Chicago), Kathy Kline, Valerie Lynch Lee (Sound and Print United, Warrenton, NC), Ralph Moore (Christian Association of the University of Pennsylvania), the National Congress of Neighborhood Women, David Palmer (Faith, Hope and Charity, Bethel, VT), Julia Reichert (New Day Films), Ruby Rich, David Michael Rosenberg, Ray Santiago (Farm Labor Organizing Committee, Toledo, OH), Michael Seltzer (Philadelphia Clearinghouse for Community Funding Resources), Tom Sigel, Star Film Library, and Pamela Yates.

PREFACE

In Focus is a how-to manual about using films. It discusses ways of dealing with the common problems and concerns involved in showing films, whether to a few people or a large audience. We have confronted these recurring issues in our own work and while working with other groups. Information for this book has also been developed by talking with resource people — including filmmakers, distributors, film librarians and exhibitors — and film users from all over the country.

In Focus is designed to help groups use film resources more effectively, especially local sources of films and information, such as public libraries. While we assume that you are working with other people to organize a film showing, we do not assume that you are necessarily familiar with film terminology, scholarship or exhibition. For someone who has never before publically shown a film, **In Focus** provides the basic information needed to organize and present a film screening. For people with more experience, **In Focus** will hopefully offer new ideas and suggestions for improving your current programs in specific areas, such as publicity, building an audience, or leading a discussion.

We encourage you to read the book through once in order to acquaint yourself with procedures and possibilities. Then, as you develop your skills, there may be sections you'll want to reread as they become more applicable to your specific needs. We have also designed **In Focus** as a reference tool to be used in planning and organizing sessions, during screenings, and in evaluations. Schedules, lists and diagrams can be photo-copied to use as worksheets.

While we have listed sources of information about films which are currently in distribution, many films are not cited in these books and filmographies, and even periodicals are not always up to date about new film releases. We have therefore developed a new mechanism, the **Film Users' Network**, to inform you about new films. By joining the **Film Users' Network** (simply fill out and return the coupon on p. 207), you can receive information from distributors and filmmakers about their latest releases. At the back of the book you will also find an evaluation form for **In Focus.** We welcome your comments and suggestions.

New York City
August, 1979

TABLE OF CONTENTS

1 | PROGRAM GOALS AND OBJECTIVES 1

Setting Goals 4
Program Planning 6

2 | FILM SELECTION 9

The Process 9
Films to Choose From 13

3 | PROGRAM PLANNING 23

Assessing Your Group's Resources 23
Plunging Ahead: Working with a Committee 24
Simple Organizational Schedule 26
The Bottom Line: Your Budget 28

4 | SPACE AND TIME 31

The Right Space 31
Checking Out the Space 33
The Right Time 36

5 | PUBLICIZING THE EVENT 39

Campaigns 41
Direct Mail and Mailing Lists 42
Flyers and Posters 43
Printing 48
Distribution 49
Networking 51
The Media 53
Public Service Announcements 56
Publicity Schedule 58

6 | DEVOTION TO DETAIL 63

Establish a Workable Time Frame 65
Assign Responsibilities 65
Start Your Program Close to the Announced Time 67
The Spokesperson 67
Introducing the Program 68
Introducing the Film 68
The House Manager 69
What to Do If the Film Breaks 70
Summary of Tasks and Responsibilities 71

7 | DISCUSSION FORMATS AND FACILITATION 73

Discussion Formats 74
The Role of the Facilitator 76
Starting the Discussion 76
Moving the Discussion Along 78
Sidetracks 79
Closure 81
Resource People 83
Working with the Resource Person 86

8 | ON PROJECTION 89

The Physical Properties of Film 89
Sight 90
Sound 94
16mm Projectors 96
Setting Up to Project 107
Running the Show 109
Troubleshooting 110

9 | EVALUATIONS AND FOLLOW-UP 115

The Evaluation Meeting 115
Topics for Evaluation 116
Basic Follow-Up 118

10 | FILM SOURCES 119

Distributors 119
Public Libraries 127
University Film Libraries 132
Other Film Sources 133
Buying Prints 134

11 | INFORMATION SOURCES 137

Media Arts Organizations 137
Smaller Organizations 138
State, Regional or Local Arts Agencies 139

12 | EXPANDED FILM PROGRAMS 141

Film Series 141
Press Screenings 150

Fundraising With Films 152
Going Outdoors 156

13 | SOUND IMPROVEMENTS 159

The Nature of Sound 159
Loudspeaker Improvements 161
Amplification and Multiple Speaker Arrays 163
Speaker Placement 168
Compensating for Room Acoustics 171
The Sound Check 173
Evaluating Existing Sound Systems 175

14 | RESOURCES 177

National Information Services 177
Resource Guides 178
Film Literature Indices 180
Programming Guides 181
Funding and Other Skills Guides 182
Independent Film and Video 183
Film and Video Making: Technical and Equipment 184
Distribution 185
Filmographies 185
Periodicals 193
Distributors 198

FILM USERS' NETWORK 206

EVALUATION FORM 209

1 | PROGRAM GOALS & OBJECTIVES

In Lumiere's THE ARRIVAL OF A TRAIN, one of the first motion pictures ever made, there is a moment when the train appears to leap out of the screen and hurl itself into the audience. The spectators of 1896 gasped, screamed, applauded, cheered, whistled, and stamped their feet, delirious with delight and amazement. Today, more than 80 years later, films still retain this hold on our imagination.

Increasingly, the power of the cinema is being used by groups and individuals in a variety of unconventional contexts throughout the United States. There is no one profile that fits all film users. They range from individuals in community or educational settings to program directors in professionally staffed national organizations. Throughout the country, we're organized into groups: we belong to church groups, block associations, parent organizations, citizens' action groups, community arts centers, unions, clubs, interest groups, and other not-for-profit organizations of all kinds. Our community life, our informal on-going education and much of our social life takes place within these contexts. We are volunteers, part- or full-time staff, and our groups are independent, federated in some loose alliance, caucuses within some larger organization, or branches in national structures. We all participate in these organizations in many ways, carrying out programs, activities, and events which affect and determine the quality of our lives.

Film can be used for diverse purposes in relation to a membership, a community, a constituency or the broader public. Many groups use films effectively as components of their programs. They may incorporate a film into a regularly scheduled meeting for variety, to attract more attendance or to supplement other information. A film may be part of a larger event such as a festival, exhibition, block party, or annual meeting. Films can contribute to quality childcare during a group event. Using a film can be a particularly effective way to present your group's concerns to a larger audience. It can provide a basis for lively discussion. Perhaps your organization has a speaker's bureau on a particular issue that could be augmented by showing a film. If your group has been working quietly but intensely on a project, you may want to use a film for a grassroots fundraising event or as a part of a celebration of your accomplishments.

A good film, selected with a specific purpose in mind, and presented well, can benefit a group in a variety of ways:

To educate, inform, or train. Wonderful films have been made about almost every conceivable subject, from the metric system to the workings of a nuclear power plant, from baking bread to safe driving skills. Films can show us places we have never been, jobs we might be employed in, introduce us to cultures unlike our own or offer a different perspective on familiar situations. You'll need to decide if you want your program to be a snappy attention-getter or to educate or train with some attention to detail.

To entertain, celebrate, inspire, and have a good time. Movies are traditional entertainment, and provide an opportunity for people to go out, get together, and share an experience. Going to a film is fun, and showing a film is a terrific way for your group's members to enjoy an evening together. In addition, the film content may relate to the work of your group, issues you are concerned with, human values you see as positive, and provide reinforcement, support, or new insights in a manner which is not escapist. A group's celebrations together are important, and showing a film as a social event can be great entertainment.

To organize around a particular issue. Many films are about issues of concern to us and have been made by people who also care about these issues. The additional information, dramatic impact, particular analysis, or national perspective of some films make them useful as organizing tools. A film can show how other people have worked on a problem similar to yours, can bring depth and life to a subject which has seemed abstract, can provide access to situations which may be physically remote, and can offer stimulus for discussion. Sometimes a film can be more effective than a speaker, an article, or a pamphlet in reaching people.

To gain visibility in the media, in the community, and to reach out to potential new constituents. A film showing can often be a good way of introducing or reintroducing your group to the media or of getting attention in your community. Do you want to strengthen or reestablish ties with people already familiar with your work or do you want to reach out to new people? If the goal is outreach, what people are you looking for and what do you want them to take away from your screening? It is easier to get publicity for a premiere of a new film than for your day-to-day efforts, and people can come to your film showing, see how your group presents a public event, pick up your literature and get acquainted. Many of the skills and contacts you develop presenting a film will also be applicable for other activities. If you publicize effectively, even people who can't attend may at least hear of your group.

To raise money. A film which has not been shown recently in your area, or a film with a speaker, filmmaker, musician, or refreshments can provide a good opportunity for grassroots fundraising.

People are used to paying money to see a good film, and they will be more than willing to attend and pay admission to see a film you are presenting, especially when they know that the money raised will be going to a good cause. Careful budgeting and volunteer effort is the key to using a film as a fundraiser, and you can raise money while providing information, cultural experience, entertainment and gaining visibility.

The group presenting the film may benefit intangibly from the very nature of the film experience—one of sharing, socializing, stimulating interest or activity, and entertainment. The following are examples of some of the many ways films have been used.

A church organization conducted an educational seminar focusing on Caribbean issues for the benefit of its clergy and lay leaders. The films were supplemented by speakers, educational packets, and other materials.

In San Francisco, a film society co-sponsored, with many other organizations, a premiere of a new film about Mozambique and raised $5,000 to contribute towards a medical center for that country.

A senior citizens group sponsored "Cycles: An Intergenerational Film Festival" in conjunction with a number of senior centers around the city. Speakers and discussions followed the films in the afternoon screenings.

A neighborhood group of artists in Philadelphia showed five programs of short experimental films in a parking lot late at night. The audience, composed of other artists and neighborhood people, watched from chairs and cars.

A series of films by independent black American filmmakers circulated last summer to museums and libraries around the country. The filmmakers accompanied the films, discussed them with the audience and helped provide images of Afro-American culture and life quite different from those portrayed in the mass media and exploitation films.

A children's librarian in a small town regularly uses films during her story hour. One morning the group of small children watched a film about giraffes, made animal finger puppets and created their own stories with them, and browsed through the library's books on giraffes.

A program of short animated, experimental and documentary films by women was selected by a Free Women's School for a spring fundraising event. They invited a fe-

minist filmmaker to speak, solicited $15 co-sponsor con-
tributions from sympathetic individuals and groups (including local merchants), and celebrated the end of their
school year with a standing-room-only crowd of supporters.

A Puerto Rican graphics workshop sponsored a Saturday
night event which combined a new film about Puerto
Rico, a nationally known folk singer, refreshments and
a dance. Over 300 people of all ages enjoyed this midsummer community party.

A women's goals and values clarification study group
at a settlement house used a film as a starting point for
a discussion of housework, male-female power relations,
and life experiences. The film had been previewed by the
group coordinators, who designed the discussion questions
based on previous sessions. They later went together to
see a thematically-related commercial film and discussed
it at another session.

A small group of former mental patients premiered a
film about the use of drugs in mental institutions. They
gained press coverage for the issue, talked with the
audience about the problem and, based on contacts they
made at the premiere, received several requests to speak
to university classes, church meetings and community
groups.

At the monthly meeting of a community food cooperative, the members were treated to a film about the life
and garden of a woman who grew her own organic
vegetables, and discussed the benefits of having such
produce available at their store.

A tenant's group planned a showing of a Hollywood
film about a blues singer which had received little commercial exposure in their city. They sold advance tickets,
put up a literature table and provided popcorn for this
family social event.

SETTING GOALS

Most of the groups who presented these successful film
screenings do not show films as their primary activity. In each case,
a specific film or program of films met their needs at a given time,
and showing the film in a particular context fit into their long-
range goals. Most will use films again. Each group considered its

screening a success, whether for ten or 500 people. Each success was based on an evaluation of the objectives a group had in mind for its film program.

The small screenings involved identifying and locating an appropriate film, preparing for discussion, setting up and operating the projector, and talking with friends. Additionally, the larger screenings involved organizing publicity (which ranged from simple flyers to complex campaigns), dealing with other groups and organizations, presenting the film in a competent manner, providing refreshments, backup information and, in one case, celebrities. Most of the work was done by volunteers, members of the groups who were convinced enough of the value of the program that they donated their time and enthusiasm to make it a success. In each case the screenings provided a unique opportunity for cultural, educational, or social experiences which otherwise would not have been available, and which were not being provided by commercial movie theaters or other institutions.

These examples demonstrate how film screenings can serve a variety of audiences, depending upon the goals set by the sponsors. For best results, goals need to be determined with as much precision as possible. It will not be enough to talk about seeking visibility, outreach or credibility. You'll have to ask yourselves: With whom? For what purpose? Is your target a small neighborhood or a broad geographical area? Do you want to get the attention of specific public figures or to raise issues for the general public? What is your objective in relation to other groups working in the same, allied, or different fields? Is your major publicity target exposure in the mass media or attention in the newspapers of a specific religious or ethnic group? How you respond to these and other such questions will determine what films you choose, how they should be advertised, where they are presented, and in what format.

Most people immediately define a successful program as one which fills a given room with many bodies. This isn't always so. The women's study group and the church people understood that for their purposes they wanted to reach a limited number of specific individuals rather than a large, amorphous public. In the case of the women's group, the coordinators wanted to use a film to attract other community women. The church group, on the other hand, wanted to share vital information with people already within its structure. In either case, large numbers could have been counterproductive.

Films have been used effectively by groups like yours, and there is a film for almost every purpose. Your group will want to decide first upon your purpose in showing a film, then survey the films that might be suitable—that are about that subject, appeal to that particular ethnic group, or relate to your particular audience and program—then go back and see if you can really meet the purpose you defined.

PROGRAM PLANNING

Since you and your group are not operating a commercial movie theater, your film showing can involve something more than just screening the film. While the goal of a movie theater is to have patrons return again and again for more movies, your goal might be to build a sense of community on your block, to initiate the exchange of ideas, or to break down racist stereotypes. The film showing may be just one event out of several which your group is planning for the year. There are many elements which can distinguish a film showing by a community group from the experience people have when they go to a movie theater or watch the same film alone at home.

Because you are interested in using a film to call attention to an issue, the film itself, or your group, your approach to publicity, the program itself, and any supplements will be more informational. Your publicity will often have more information about the film and your group than a theater's newspaper ad for a movie does. Having materials available for the audience to take home with them is also a good idea. A brochure about your group and its work can be a tool for outreach. An informative pamphlet about the subject of the film can give more detail about the issues raised in the film and list other resource materials. Program notes can provide background or information supplemental to that contained in the film, raise questions for discussion or further study, and answer questions about the film or those the film might raise. They may contain material which people can think about later. Program notes might include:

- Production data: year, country of origin, credits, cast, running time.
- Relevant quotes from critics or reviewers.
- Background material: historical, factual, cultural, or about the film technique.
- Quotes from the filmmaker or an interview.
- Biographies and filmographies of the director or performers.
- Lists of other films on the same subject, or related subjects.
- An original essay about your group, why you chose to show this film, or about the film.

- A bibliography of books and articles about the subject.
- Topics for discussion.
- Print source (for people who might also want to show the film).
- Acknowledgements.

An introduction before and a discussion following a film can help place it in a context for your audience. The exchange of ideas, information and views in a discussion session can pick up where the film left off, and round out the program. No film can be all-inclusive on any one subject or completely applicable to all occasions, and a discussion can help to supplement the film experience. When you think about adding the opportunity for discussion, consider showing two short films which present different views of the same subject, or a film which treats a subject generally along with one with a more specific focus. You could show a film which generally relates to your area of interest and supplement it with a discussion about specific applications. The chance to talk with other people about their reactions to the film can be immensely stimulating and rewarding for your audience. How to facilitate good discussions is covered in detail in Chapter 7.

As you refine your goals for presenting a film program, you may become less interested in films which have already received commercial exposure in your area. As you learn more about the films which are available, you will be able to custom design film programs for your particular audience. The audience for the Free Women's School program cited earlier not only appreciated the selection of innovative films, but also the opportunity to see them. Even if you choose a feature length film, you might consider showing a short or cartoon before it.

Films can be combined with any number of other events or activities to create a program to suit your needs. A coalition of grassroots groups in Philadelphia regularly shows an afternoon of new films as part of their annual day-long festival which also includes children's events, information tables for each group, musicians, refreshments, and a raffle.

Pittsburgh Film-Makers Incorporated presents these programs with the hope that they will increase the understanding of film as an art form, and of film-makers as artists.

☆ For information call: 412/681-5449
☆ Program Coordinator: Joan Cicak
☆ Presented at 205 Oakland Avenue
☆ Admission: $1.50 unless otherwise noted.

INAUGURATION OF THE PLEASURE DOME

CACTUS by Dan Kiacz

Photography at Pittsburgh Film-Makers

EXHIBITIONS

Contemporary Photo-Silkscreen Prints
November 3 - 30

David Gilmore   Dan Kiacz
Todd Walker   Sam Wang

PFMI Student/Member Show
December 8 - 29

Gallery hours are 11-8 Monday through Friday,
12-5 on Saturday.

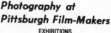

ALWAYS FOR PLEASURE

NOVEMBER

friday 3 — SABOTAGE (1936) by Alfred Hitchcock. The rarely screened British production that includes a superb performance by Oscar Homolka and the 'mistake' suspense sequence Hitchcock always cites in interviews.   8.00 and 10.00 pm

saturday 4 — FILM-MAKER LES BLANK will be present with ALWAYS FOR PLEASURE in 'Smells Round' and other films about Cajun and Tex-Mex music. Tonight's program will be a unique visual and olfactory delight.   8.00 pm

monday 6 — THE SANTA CLARA TAPES (1973) by Doug Davis and FRAGMENTS FROM WILLOUGHBY'S VIDEO PERFORMANCES: PART I (1973-74) by Willoughby Sharp. Co-sponsored by the Film Section of Carnegie Institute and UCIR, University of Pittsburgh. Presented at UCIR (ground floor. Hillman Library). No admission charge 4.00, 6.30, and 8.00 pm

monday 6 — SEVEN CHANCES (1925) by Buster Keaton inherits a fortune, on the condition that he marries by a fixed date, the day he learns of the inheritance! A classic race to the altar. Also Sincerity, Part I (1973) by Stan Brakhage, the beginning of his elaborate, and still-in-progress, autobiographical project.   8.00 pm

friday 10 — NEW FILMS BY THE AVANT-GARDE: Roslyn Romance (1977) and Valentin de las Sierras (1968) by Bruce Baillie; Inferential Current (1971) by Paul Sharits; Mongoloid (1978) and Valse Triste (1978) by Bruce Conner, and Burial Path (1978) and Sluice (1978) by Stan Brakhage   8.00 and 10.00 pm

saturday 11 — FILM-MAKER MOLLY DAVIES will present her multi-screen film/performance piece, entitled Sage Cycle, a portrait of dancer Sage Cowles, who will also be present.   8.00 pm

monday 13 — You Only Live Once (1937) by Fritz Lang. Based on the lives of Bonnie and Clyde, this film more significantly questions the nature of illusion — in life and on film. Also Sincerity, Part II (1977) by Stan Brakhage   8.00 pm

wednesday 15 — FILM-MAKER KENNETH ANGER will be present to screen and discuss his complete ANGER MAGICK LANTERN CYCLE (1947-74) which includes Fireworks, Puce Moment, Rabbit's Moon, Eaux D'Artifice, Inauguration of the Pleasure Dome, Scorpio Rising, Kustom Kar Kommandos, Invocation of My Demon Brother, plus an excerpt from his most recent work, Lucifer Rising. (Anger will present a program of Rex Ingram films on November 14 at Carnegie Institute.) Co-sponsored by the Film Section of Carnegie Institute   8.00 pm

friday 17 — PHOTOGRAPHER STEPHEN SZABO will lecture on Platinum Printing and discuss examples of his work. (Photography event.)   8.00 pm

saturday 18 — Platinum Printing Workshop. If interested, call 681-5449. (Photography event.)

saturday 18 — DIRIGIBLE (1931) by Frank Capra. With Fay Wray and Jack Holt. Great special effects, flights over the Atlantic, and a spectacular crash at the South Pole make this one of the most impressive early sound action pictures.   8.00 and 10.00 pm

monday 20 — SINCERITY, Part III and DUPLICITY, Part I (both 1978) by Stan Brakhage. The autobiography continues, changing name in mid-course as Brakhage questions his own perception of himself and his experience. Also One Week (1920) by Buster Keaton, with Buster assembling a do-it-yourself electric house in the wrong order, leading to catastrophe   8.00 pm

friday / saturday 24-25 — A MIDSUMMER NIGHT'S DREAM (1935) by Max Reinhardt and William Dieterle. With Mickey Rooney, Olivia de Havilland, James Cagney, Joe E. Brown and Kenneth Anger.   **Note time change.** 8.00 and 10.00 pm

monday 27 — THE ADVENTURES OF THE EXQUISITE CORPSE, Part I: Huge Pupils (1973) by Andrew Noren. The beginning of Noren's erotic autobiography. Also Sheffield Diary and Laporte Diary (1972-73) by Howard Guttenplan.   8.00 pm

DECEMBER

friday 1 — ABEL GANCE: THE CHARM OF DYNAMITE (1968) by Kevin Brownlow. A mini-biography of the relatively unknown (in America) French pioneer, with excerpts from his Napoleon, J'Accuse, and La Roue. And The Fall of the House of Usher (1928) by Jean Epstein, and The Fall of the House of Usher (1928) by James Sibley Watson — two expressionistic interpretations of the tale by Edgar Allan Poe.   8.00 and 10.00 pm

saturday 2 — A DAY WITHOUT SUNSHINE (1975-76) by Robert Thurber, and The Brick Makers (1972) by Marta Rodriguez and Jorge Silva. Two stirring documentaries, the first of migrant citrus workers in Florida, narrated by James Earl Jones; the second of landless Latin American peasants forced to migrate to the cities in search of employment.   8.00 and 10.00 pm

monday 4 — DIALOGUE FOR CAMERMAN AND DANGER (1974 video) by Amy Greenfield. Fases (1967) by Carolee Schneemann. Munchen-Berlin Wanderung (1927) by Oskar Fischinger. Two autobiographical films and a videotape — all with the camera as an active participant in the 'discourse'.   8.00 pm

wednesday 6 — CETA FILM-MAKERS GREG GANS, AL MAHLER AND ROGER JACOBY. In 1978 three film-makers living in Allegheny County received federal grants through PFMI to work on film projects. This screening presents extensive fragments from the works-in-progress of each of these artists.   8.00 pm

friday 8 — FILM-MAKER JIM VALE will present a solo program of his personal film projects, direct cinemas, and other party movies.   8.00 pm

saturday 9 — THE SOUTHERN SAMPLER, short independent films from our Southern neighbors: Dreamstealer by Eric Durst. Maybe Next Week Sometime by David Boatwright. Mississippi Delta Blues: Give My Poor Heart Ease by Center for Southern Folklore. Nature's Way by Appalshop Films. Polar by Peter Bundy. and Seasons by Bill Olsen.   8.00 and 10.00 pm

friday / saturday 15-16 — I NEVER SANG FOR MY FATHER (1970) by Gil Cates. With Gene Hackman and Melvyn Douglas.   8.00 and 10.00 pm

friday / saturday 22-23 — NO FILM but HAPPY HOLIDAYS TO ALL!

friday / saturday 29-30 — THE SHOOTING (1971) by Monte Hellman. With Jack Nicholson, Millie Perkins, Warren Oates, Will Hutchins. A woman persuades an ex-bounty hunter and his partner to accompany her on a strange journey.   8.00 and 10.00 pm

THESE PROGRAMS FUNDED IN PART BY THE PENNSYLVANIA COUNCIL ON THE ARTS AND THE NATIONAL ENDOWMENT FOR THE ARTS

2 | FILM SELECTION

THE PROCESS

When your group first starts thinking about showing a film either to your own members or to some larger audience, you usually have some sense of purpose, even if it initially may not be very well defined. Perhaps someone from the group has seen or heard of a particular film that relates to a current theme or concern of yours. If this is the film you want to show, then all you will need to do is locate it, determine the rental fee (if any), and organize the screening. If your intent in showing a film is more general, think about the different types of film you might use, clearly define a theme for the film program, and then make a specific selection. Chapters 11 and 14 include information on catalogs, reviews, filmographies, evaluations and other tools of film research.

Realistically speaking, however, the first few times you are likely to pick your film through less formal means. You will know you want to use a particular film that is familiar to someone in your group, one that you've read about, or one that has been recommended by a respected person or organization. A good way to begin your research is to collect suggestions from everyone in the group. You'll be surprised by the number of films that made a lasting impression—films seen in school, at a conference, or a film someone read about in a journal. It would be useful to discuss the film's merits with someone who has seen or used it and can describe what happened. While every audience is different and each group has its own specific goals for a film program, a concrete example of a screening of the film may allow for some useful comparisons.

Early on in the process you will want to start keeping an annotated list of recommended titles. At a later stage, go through this list and discuss how each film relates to the goals you have set and what kind of experience it would provide. Will this film communicate with the audience you have in mind? Is it a film you can publicize well? Has it been shown recently at a conference, in the community, at a museum, or on television? Does this work for or against you? In some cases, a previous screening can build interest in your program. People who missed the earlier screening may be especially interested in seeing it. Others may want to see it a second time or bring friends along. On the other hand, a recent screening could temporarily overexpose that particular film and you may want to consider something else. Along the same lines, check with the distributor to make sure the film is not scheduled to be shown elsewhere in your area when you plan to show it. Perhaps a local community or arts center keeps a calendar of upcoming cultural events which you would be wise to check.

Before making a final decision, you will certainly need to know about the film's cost and where to find it. If you have learned about the film from another group, call them and find out where and how they obtained their print. When in doubt about the distributor of the film, consult your public librarian who can direct you to the appropriate reference materials.* Do not make the mistake of thinking a small town library doesn't carry this kind of information. Even if the branch is open only once a week, it is likely to be connected to a state or county network that can provide the materials you need on an inter-library loan. In larger cities, a neighborhood library can always draw on the resources of the main branch. Others you might consult include people in university film departments, information officers of media arts centers, programmers at local film societies, filmmakers, and anyone else who is responsible for showing films on a regular basis.

During the selection process, you may find yourself reconsidering the goals for your program or the film you want to show. You may discover your original selection is not appropriate to your needs. The film may be too difficult or too simple or just not have the right tone. Costs may be more than anticipated. Finding the film can be an open-ended process that allows you to refine your goals as you think through the various aspects of a successful film program. You may end up with a much different program concept and a far different film than you first thought. But you should set a definite time for reaching a decision. Five things to always keep in mind as you discuss possibilities are: **

- The availability of the film.
- The film rental cost.
- The running time of the film and how that relates to your planned program.
- The content, style and technical quality of the film.
- The experience provided by the film.

---

* Pages 127-132 contain detailed information on libraries and pages 119-127 contain detailed information about distributors. A distributor directory begins on page 198.

** In this book we are primarily concerned with the use of films with adult audiences. Programs for children and young adults require just as much care, and some of the chapters, such as on technical or publicity matters, are applicable to groups programming films for these constituencies. There are many aspects, however, which are particular to young audiences. We refer our readers to the resources provided by the Media Center for Children, which has tested many films, screening situations, and activities with the kids themselves. Media Center for Children, 3 West 29th St., New York, NY 10001.

When planning a screening, your group may want to consider programming two films together. For example, you might select a short animation or experimental film to show with a documentary or a feature. Or you might create an interesting program by showing two documentary films together, or a short documentary with a feature. The selection of these films, of course, depends upon your programming goals. You'll want to consider any special relationship between the two chosen films or the effect of relationships created by showing them together. In some instances these relationships may not be all that direct, but it will be important to think about them.

The order in which you show your films is another consideration for your planning sessions. A shorter film, if it is 5-10 minutes, would usually be shown first. Otherwise, because attention is highest at the start of a program, when showing two films show the longer one first unless historical sequence or some other logical consideration prevents you from doing so. If you have a particular activity or discussion scheduled, be sure to end with the film, regardless of length, that most directly relates to the activity or discussion.

The experience of the ad hoc film committee of the Free Women's School provides a good illustration of how a creative film selection process can work. The women's goal was to raise money while creating some attention for the school. They knew they wanted a film that had something to do with women's experiences and which reflected the objectives of their organization. They planned to have their screening shortly after the end of the spring session, before everyone went away for the summer. Among early considerations were feature films like Ingmar Bergman's FACE TO FACE, John Cassavettes' A WOMAN UNDER THE INFLUENCE, or Frank Perry's DIARY OF A MAD HOUSEWIFE. As they discussed these titles, they realized that they wanted to show films made by women, and wanted to do something that was fun and innovative.

The first group of films was discarded because they were directed by men and had been shown commercially at a local repertory theater. Through discussion and looking at catalogs, another group of films emerged, all made by women. Among the new possibilities were NOT A PRETTY PICTURE, JANIE'S JANIE, ANYTHING YOU WANT TO BE, and THE EMERGING WOMAN. Eventually, however, these films were passed over because most of them were readily available through the public library and had been seen by a large percentage of their constituency. This meant that they were not prime material for a benefit showing in that city.

The selection committee then decided that their best choice was GIRL FRIENDS, a feature film by Claudia Weill which had just opened in New York. Unfortunately, it was not yet available for nontheatrical showings. If they wanted to work with that film, they would have to wait until it opened commercially in their city and sponsor a benefit at the theater.

There were further discussions and more looking through catalogs until the women came up with the idea of a program of short (2-28 minutes) experimental, animated and documentary films created by women. They ultimately put together eight films about a variety of feminist concerns—a program which was fun and could lead to any number of interesting discussions—and they invited a filmmaker who lived nearby to speak after the films. Not only did the selection present independent and noncommercial films that had never been shown together in that city, but it was so attractive to their constituency that they sold all the tickets and had the painful task of turning away about 200 people. They are busy planning another film program for the fall.

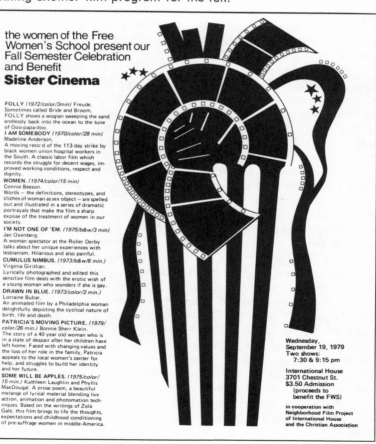

the women of the Free Women's School present our Fall Semester Celebration and Benefit
Sister Cinema ★★★

FOLLY (1972/color/3min) Freude.
Sometimes called Bride and Broom, FOLLY shows a woman sweeping the sand endlessly back into the ocean to the tune of Ooo-papa-doo.

I AM SOMEBODY (1970/color/28 min) Madeline Anderson.
A moving record of the 113-day strike by black women union hospital workers in the South. A classic labor film which records the struggle for decent wages, improved working conditions, respect and dignity.

WOMEN. (1974/color/15 min) Connie Beeson.
Words — the definitions, stereotypes, and cliches of woman as sex object — are spelled out and illustrated in a series of dramatic portrayals that make the film a sharp expose of the treatment of women in our society.

I'M NOT ONE OF 'EM. (1975/b&w/3 min) Jan Oxenberg.
A woman spectator at the Roller Derby talks about her unique experiences with lesbianism. Hilarious and also painful.

CUMULUS NIMBUS. (1973/b&w/6 min.) Virginia Giritlian.
Lyrically photographed and edited this sensitive film deals with the erotic wish of a young woman who wonders if she is gay.

DRAWN IN BLUE. (1973/color/2 min.) Lorraine Bubar.
An animated film by a Philadelphia woman delightfully depicting the cyclical nature of birth, life and death.

PATRICIA'S MOVING PICTURE. (1979/color/26 min.) Bonnie Sherr Klein.
The story of a 40 year old woman who is in a state of despair after her children have left home. Faced with changing values and the loss of her role in the family, Patricia appeals to the local women's center for help, and struggles to build her identity and her future.

SOME WILL BE APPLES. (1975/color/15 min.) Kathleen Laughlin and Phyllis MacDougal. A beautiful melange of lyrical material blending live action, animation and photomation techniques. Based on the writings of Zola Gale, this film brings to life the thoughts, expectations and childhood conditioning of pre-suffrage women in middle-America.

Wednesday,
September 19, 1979
Two shows:
7:30 & 9:15 pm

International House
3701 Chestnut St.
$3.50 Admission
(proceeds to benefit the FWS)

in cooperation with
Neighborhood Film Project
of International House
and the Christian Association

FILMS TO CHOOSE FROM

There are many categories for classifying films and we are by no means presenting an exhaustive list. Films may be categorized by:

Length. Features are 75 minutes or more, shorts less than an hour.

Subject. There are no standard subject categories. There are filmographies and indexes on various subjects films deal with. Libraries are the most systematic in categorizing by subject.

Genre. Categories based on elements such as structure and style, including the science fiction film, the disaster movie, Film Noir, the Western, musical comedy, the personal film, newsreels, screwball comedies, the Biblical epic, the blue collar movie, to name just a few.

Content and style. General categories include:

Narrative — a complete story with a beginning, middle and end which is portrayed by actors, puppets or animation.

Documentary — a term with broad meaning, but basically used to describe a film primarily nonfictional in nature.

Experimental film — does not use conventional structures or techniques, and is more concerned with communicating mood, feeling, motion or structure than information or a story.

Other categories used for classifying films include intent, recommended age level, production history, and funding sources. For example, a "sponsored film" is one where the person or company putting up the money for the film has complete control over its style and content, while an "independent film" is defined as a work "that is created by persons who are not regularly employed by any corporation, network, institution or agency which determines either the form or the content of the materials which he or she produces." *

Films can be analyzed in terms of the development of national cinemas or individual directors, international cinema movements, movements in other art forms, aesthetic theories or technological innovations. They can present individual fantasies and creations, record historical or contemporary events, interpret works of literature or mathematical principles, and reflect the sensibilities of a particular time and place.

Films can be dramatic, abstract, poetic, avant-garde, and can star great actors, ordinary people, moving blobs of light and color, computer-generated images, machines, puppets, drawings, or the formal elements of the medium itself. Much has been written about

---

* From the Association of Independent Video and Filmmakers' **Recommendations for the Future of Public Broadcasting 1/25/78.** AIVF is a not-for-profit national organization of almost 1,000 independent producers, directors, writers and other media technicians. AIVF, 99 Prince St., New York, NY 10012.

film in all of its manifestations. The resource section at the back of this book lists some of the materials available. Film scholars, historians, critics, theorists, and reviewers are constantly commenting on and redefining the field and the categories, and fine film programs can be developed from exploring this literature.

We will make only some very simple and utilitarian distinctions among kinds of films, based on present systems of distribution, production and, primarily, how they can be used by groups. Because most groups and educational organizations do not usually have access to 35mm (commercial gauge) projection equipment, we will be discussing films which are available in 16mm, the gauge most commonly used in educational and nontheatrical settings.

THE FEATURE FILM

What most people think of as a movie is the feature-length fiction film which tells a story. Made for showings in commercial movie theaters, its primary purposes are usually entertainment, escapism, or profit. Nevertheless, some narrative feature films can, through the characters, their relationships and their behavior, take us beyond the story line, the plot, and the exoticism of people and places to a deeper understanding of issues, attitudes and ideas.

When we speak of the feature film made in the United States, we are talking essentially about those made in Hollywood, considered to be the backbone of the American commercial film industry. Hollywood dominated world cinema from the mid-thirties to the mid-fifties and is made up of major financial institutions, large studios, national distributors, theatrical operators, risk capital entrepreneurs, and famous performers. By and large, their interest in creating films is a financial one and their product is characterized by trying to appeal to the largest possible audience. The technical quality of these films shows the work of large numbers of highly skilled artists and craftspeople.

Before the television stations, networks, and cable companies began purchasing films for regular broadcast, the 16mm reduction of a feature film was a favorite among small screening groups. Almost every feature is now available in 16mm within a year after its commercial release. They are still also shown in settings that became very popular from the sixties onward: repertory movie theaters, film societies, museum or university programs, and Media Arts Centers. The film society movement in the United States not only showcased important Hollywood films and started looking at them in a serious way, it also grew out of the desire of its members to see international feature films which would not otherwise receive much exposure.

Consequently, even such ever-popular classics as CITIZEN KANE and CASABLANCA, if they are regularly programmed on television or in repertory, can no longer provide an automatic full house in most urban or university areas. If your region does not have such showcases, however, then the presentation of a classic feature film on a large screen in your own location might be the cultural event of the season. While Hollywood feature films can be successfully employed in a variety of contexts, they are not as easy a way to raise funds as they once were.

One advantage of showing a recent Hollywood film is that you have the benefit of the industry's multi-million dollar national publicity campaign, so people most likely will have heard or read something about that film. One disadvantage is that the rental fees for new releases are rising, and now are often from $150-$500 for one showing. The newer and more popular a film is, usually, the higher the rental will be. There are, however, many excellent feature films that are specialized or for some reason never become big box-office successes. They are known in the trade as "difficult" or "cult" pictures and, along with older films, are often available for a low rental. Many classic films are now in the collections of public libraries around the country and can be taken out with a library card for free showings. If your primary purpose in using film is to raise money, you should consult Chapter 12, where there is a discussion of how to stage premieres, benefits, and special events. In using a feature film, you should carefully consider how that film ties in with your goals in sponsoring the showing.

In the United States, as abroad, there are independently produced feature films. Historically, independents have had a difficult time raising the money needed to make a feature length, fictional film, and there are many more independent documentaries and short films than features. While even a modest commercial feature made in the seventies would cost several million dollars to make and the commercial documentary hundreds of thousands, most independent films are made on budgets in the tens of thousands. Like all professionals, the independents have to make a profit in order to exist and to continue their work, but their primary motivation in making films is usually not financial. Many of these films, in fact, could never be completed without the donated or deferred-payment labor of performers, technicians and other persons motivated by aesthetic or social concerns. Because of limited budgets, the technical quality of independent productions can vary greatly, but most look as if they cost 2-3 times the actual budget. Special effects, costly retakes, and extensive shooting on location are not generally possible. What gives the independent production its flair and power is the artistic freedom enjoyed by its creators. Whether a documentary, narrative or other type of film, the filmmaker feels a responsibility and commitment to the point of view expressed, bringing to it the kind of integrity, passion and innovation one expects from a serious author or painter.

The feature films produced in this country by independents are not generally as well-known as those produced by the studios. Yet a few years ago an independently produced feature length documentary, HARLAN COUNTY, USA won an Academy Award. After the film won its Oscar, some of the commercial theater owners who had been reluctant to show a documentary, much less one with a position on controversial issues, were willing to screen it because it could be advertised as an award-winner in the same manner as commercially produced films. Independents have existed for as long as there have been films, but in the sixties and seventies there has been a tremendous upsurge both in the quality and variety of their work. Independent features produced in this country range from SALT OF THE EARTH (1950's) to more recent examples such as GIRL FRIENDS, HESTER STREET, NORTHERN LIGHTS and BUSH MAMA, each produced under very different conditions.

A group considering the use of a feature film will usually think first about well-known Hollywood films, either recent or classic. One of these films will often meet their purposes nicely. If you are looking for a feature film which treats a particular issue, you might look for information about independent productions. Another possibility for selection might be from among feature films produced in other countries. They may not be as well-known and immediately accessible as Hollywood films, but they often present dramatically unique and different points of view.

The distinction between art and entertainment established in the United States is not so prevalent around the world. In other countries, films are often a highly respected and popular art form, and many countries provide generous governmental and private support for young filmmakers' experimentation and risk-taking in terms of aesthetics, issues, and forms. This means that the films can take on social, cultural, aesthetic, and personal subjects through innovative film forms — endeavors which do not generally find ready support here. The results of such support are the interesting and valuable contributions of national cinemas as diverse as their countries of origin.

The mid-sixties heralded an upsurge of foreign features coming into the United States. Film societies, repertory theaters and other film showcases developed in response to the growing interest in these films. For many people, seeing Bergman's THE SEVENTH SEAL or a film by Fellini in a high school or college auditorium was the first exposure to anything different from a Hollywood film. While many people were at first resistant to foreign films with English subtitles, subsequent technical and artistic improvements in subtitling methods have greatly enhanced the general accessibility of foreign language films. Today, international features are shown throughout the country. With an increasing global consciousness and awareness of our ethnic roots, we can see and enjoy films from all over the world.

Currently, there are many exciting international feature films available in the United States, providing opportunities for important cross-cultural experiences. For example, the Museum of Modern Art in New York recently presented retrospectives of films from Senegal and from Quebec. Japanese films were among the first to be of interest to film societies here and some works of the New German Cinema are now receiving wide distribution. Films from Latin America have been appreciated by audiences here for years because of their innovative forms, use of popular culture, and direct treatment of social problems. Through these films we can see different cultures, histories, methods of analysis, and ways of dealing with problems and issues. It is also educational for people in the United States to see how they are viewed by people in other countries. Feature films are only the tip of the iceberg in terms of exportable production from other countries. There are international films in all of the categories we are discussing.

DOCUMENTARY OR NONFICTION FILMS

Documentary films are more easily identified as "being about" a specific topic or subject than either fictional or experimental films. This is a broad term which is used for films ranging from network journalistic reports to very personal subjective statements. Since the early sixties, the documentary film has been influenced by technological innovations which made lightweight, portable cameras and sound equipment available.

One of the most inclusive and still applicable definitions of the documentary film was endorsed in the late 1940's by 14 nations at the first (and only) meeting of the World Union of Documentary:

> . . . by the documentary film is meant all methods of recording on celluloid any aspect of reality interpreted either by factual shooting or by sincere and justifiable reconstruction so as to appeal either to reason or emotion, for the purpose of stimulating the desire for, and the widening of, human knowledge and understanding and of truthfully posing problems and their solutions in the spheres of economics, culture and human relations.*

---

* Quoted in Paul Rotha, **Documentary Film**, forward to the 3rd edition (London: Faber and Faber, 1952).

Some documentary techniques have been developed from or influenced by the methodologies of other disciplines such as anthropology, journalism, sociology, history, creative writing and political science. Some stylistic conventions include: the use of non-actors or "real-life" interviews with people, unstaged sequences, location shooting, and a naturalistic look. Documentary films range from those which record a process, orderly presentations on a subject structured like an essay, and newsreels, to open-ended films which do not resolve problems but provide material for discussion, and films which take a strong stand or present a definite point of view on issues. On one hand, a documentary can be a totally acted film which has evolved out of or re-creates actual events, or, on the other, actual events may be filmed and used by the filmmaker for totally personal purposes. Some documentaries appear to be largely observational in nature, while in others the filmmakers and their equipment may appear.

Documentaries and other nonfiction films, because they do not always use obvious actors or dramatic forms, often have an atmosphere about them of objectivity, truth, and reality. They give the impression that they are accurately portraying incidents, activities, contexts, and relationships. Yet most documentaries, like fiction films, have been made by people with highly subjective interpretations of reality. What they can record on film is limited by time, light, and where they can be. They can not and probably do not film everything spontaneously, as it happens.

The filmmakers select what to include in a shot, the particular camera angle, who to interview, and whether or not to move the camera. The choice of a lens can change the appearance of a scene or a person — a wide-angle or fisheye lens can produce comic or unflattering distortions and a telephoto lens can flatten distances. The filmmakers can hardly ever include everything they have shot in the finished film. They choose what to put in and what to leave out, and the order in which the material appears. Some documentaries feature a "voice of god" narrator, either on or off the screen, who explains to the viewer what is happening, provides a context for seeing the images, gives tips to limit or clarify their meaning, and generally tries to create the illusion of reality and objectivity. Other filmmakers acknowledge within the film that they have a point of view. People thinking about using a documentary should also consider who made it and from what perspective in order to determine its appropriateness for their program. It is sometimes very interesting to show together on the same program two documentaries about the same event or subject made by two different people.

Documentaries use the techniques of fiction films for optimal

black film institute

A Film and Lecture Series/Fall 1978

- Programs during the month of October will be held in the Dunbar Senior High School Auditorium, New Jersey Ave. and N streets, N.W.
- Programs during November and December will be held at Minor Auditorium, 2565 Georgia Ave., N.W.
- Programs are FREE. • Films marked R not recommended for children.

November
Independant Black Film Festival

Just as the Black American experience is unique, the films produced by the growing number of Black independent cinematographers are quite distinctive. Unlike commercially produced films, it is a Black-for-Blacks cinema attempting to speak to specific needs of its audience.

NOVEMBER 2   Thursday 7:30 P.M.

Passing Through

An eloquent and powerful testament to the spirit of Black music. Once released from prison, a young promising musician (Nathaniel Taylor) tries to organize his band outside the syndicate. He is motivated through his spiritual relationship with his musical mentor (Clarence Muse). Directed by Larry Clark. 105 min.

Guest Speaker: Bill Quinn, music critic.

NOVEMBER 9   Thursday 7:30 P.M.

Black Women Filmmakers

VALERIE: A WOMAN! AN ARTIST! A PHILOSOPHY OF LIFE! — Explores some of the attitudes and insights of an extremely gifted sculptor. Directed by Monica Freeman. 15 min.

. . . BUT THEN. SHE'S BETTY CARTER — Excerpts from a film in progress about the famed jazz vocalist. Directed by local filmmaker, Michelle Parkerson. 10 min.

MISTER MAGIC — Shot in Mexico, this is a film about "actual dreams" of children reenacted by the children themselves. Directed by Edie Lynch. 30 min.

JUST BRIEFLY — A young woman meets a man with whom she has a short-lived involvement. Through her bittersweet reflections of their encounter she is able to gain insight and hope for the future. Directed by Louise Flemming. 15 min.

Guest Panel: Monica Freeman, Edie Lynch and Michelle Parkerson.

NOVEMBER 16   Thursday 7:30 P.M.

Pass/Fail

A drama depicting an independent Black filmmaker's struggles to secure funding for a documentary. His everyday reality and dream life are explored. Directed, written and produced by Roy Campanella, Jr. 30 min.

Street Corner Stories

The film spends several mornings with a group of working men who congregate at a corner store each day to socialize before work begins. Through their stories, the men give their own critique of their lives and the society in which they live. Directed and produced by Warrington Hudlin. 63 min. R.

Guest Speakers: Roy Campanella, Jr. and Warrington Hudlin

NOVEMBER 30   Thursday 7:30 P.M.

Killer of Sheep

Stan works in a slaughterhouse killing sheep. This inhuman work results in insomnia and strained relations with his family. In spite of his social conditions, Stan maintains a high inner moral attitude which keeps him afloat. Directed by Charles Burnett. 90 min.

POINT OF CHANGE — A family moves into a new neighborhood and their teenage children must make new friends. Made by District high school students in the Black Film Institute's Young Filmmakers Workshop. 15 min.

I COULD HEAR YOU ALL THE WAY DOWN THE HALL — The Classic confrontation between a teacher determined to keep order and a class determined to defy. Directed by Robert Gardner. 15 min.

THAT FABULOUS FACE — Various film techniques are used to create colorful effects with the graceful face of a Black dancer. Directed by Joe Zinn. 3 min.

effect. They can often be quite entertaining. They may reorder real life situations into a conventional dramatic story structure. Speeches can be chopped up, reordered, combined with other material, and an argument or case may be built up from the relevant footage, leaving out anything contradictory to the intended point. Our emotions can be manipulated. Conventions readily accepted in the feature fiction film, which are in fact the very components of the art of filmmaking, are less obvious to us when we are watching a documentary. We tend to be less aware of the involvement of the creator. On the other hand, there are filmmakers who have learned to imitate the conventions of the documentary film. Thus there are completely fictional or dramatic films which give the illusion of being "real", accurately portrayed incidents. A good example of a dramatic film based on real events but totally re-enacted is BATTLE OF ALGIERS, which even uses black and white newsreel-style cinematography to add to its effect. Many filmmakers, interested in demystifying the power of film, include elements which are intended to alert their audience to the very process involved in making the film.

Documentaries are usually primarily intended for nontheatrical use. Many well-known documentaries do not receive most of their showings in commercial theaters, but have been seen by great numbers of people in small groups. They are often used in educational settings, purchased by libraries, shown by groups interested in a particular issue, and shown on television. They range in length from short to feature. A great deal of information can be conveyed by a documentary film, and often they are the products of intensive research into a subject. Public libraries, university film libraries and distributors all have documentaries. Rental rates tend to be lower for documentaries· than for the more commercial feature films, but their titles are less well-known to the general public. Documentaries are good films to provide stimulus for a discussion, background for a speaker, or to encourage follow-up activity. A documentary about a subject of interest to your group will not take the place of a course, book, or article about the same subject; it is a different (and equally valid) kind of information and will provide a different experience.

Like other independent films, the independent documentary is characterized by the filmmaker's sense of responsibility and commitment to the subject, ideas and point of view expressed. A filmmaker, as well as the other persons involved in a specific independent project, may want to make a strong statement on an issue of importance to them. The best independent documentaries are characterized by an immediacy and vitality that are the result of such commitment.

Commercial documentaries may also be of use to groups.

Usually made for educational contexts or for television, they range from reporting and explaining to pictorial or poetic evocations of moods and places. Many fine commercial documentaries deal with technical or scientific subjects. Nature study films are particularly good examples. Training and how-to films are often well done and extremely useful in providing needed information. The commercial documentary will generally not argue explicitly for any particular point of view or posit solutions, but most often presents the issues simply and gives a "balanced view." When done poorly, this can result in documentaries that are too bland or documentaries with hidden or unstated assumptions.

Other films which fall loosely into the documentary category include educational films developed for specific curricula; industrial films which illustrate and sometimes glorify the use of a particular product; sponsored films where a filmmaker is hired to make a film about an institution, city, agency, individual or product as a subtle and expensive public relations device; and news reports.

ANIMATED, EXPERIMENTAL, AND AVANT-GARDE FILMS

Animated films, whether commercial or independent, are another category film users should consider. They can be employed as companions to other films, or to make entire programs. Although most people think of animation as a series of cartoon figures given the illusion of movement (e.g., Bugs Bunny and Betty Boop films), the art of animation has many different techniques. In the glossary to **How to Read a Film**, author James Monaco defines animation as:

> ... methods by which inanimate objects are made to move on the screen, giving the appearance of life. These methods include drawing on the film itself, photographing cells (drawings) one at a time, and photographing concrete objects one frame at a time while adjusting their positions in between frames (pixillation).*

Particularly in the seventies, many graphic artists have been attracted to animation. Animated films can deal with many different subjects, and should not be considered simply as entertainment. They are often used to make serious statements. The range of animation has grown so diverse that there is now an international animation festival held annually in Zagreb, Yugoslavia. In the United States, there is a growing interest in festivals of animated and other short experimental films which feature new releases, historical surveys and international films.

A traditional use of animation is as part of an informational

---

* James Monaco, **How to Read a Film**, p. 396 (New York: Oxford University Press, 1977).

film to illustrate subject matter which would be difficult to photograph. For example, trade unions such as the United Auto Workers
have found animation useful in graphically demonstrating the
phenomenon of inflation in terms the non-economist can deal with.
Another organization produced a cartoon which explains how
penicillin works within the human body. There are entire companies
whose work consists mainly of transferring popular children's books
to film through simple animation.

The experimental or avant-garde films are usually the work
of independent filmmakers. To stretch an inaccurate metaphor for
the sake of illustration, if feature and documentary filmmakers are
the novelists, essayists and journalists, then artists who work with
shorter films are the poets, painters and sculptors of film. The films
are often wondrous, humanistic, highly personal, lyrical, poetic, and
look at reality in new ways. They are referred to by various labels
such as conceptual, formalist, structuralist and materialist. Often
they emphasize and experiment with the physical elements of the
film, camera, and projector so that the elements of the medium or
the artist's relationship to the art form become the primary subject
matter. They are sometimes characterized by a concern with form
instead of content, and with creative manipulation of space and
time. The resulting images may be stylized, non-representational,
magical, and mythic. Like other independents, they are concerned
with using film as a medium of expression. A number of museums,
festivals, distributors, and exhibition showcases specialize in screening and promoting experimental and animated works. They may be
combined in many ways with each other and with documentaries
and fiction films for effective programs.

When selecting films for your program, a primary criterion
should be your objectives and how the particular films will help
you achieve them. Keep in mind your intended audience, how you
want to structure the program, what films have received exposure
in your area, and how your group wants to follow up on the screening. All the kinds of films touched on in this section can be used
effectively in a variety of programs, combinations, and for a wide
range of audiences.

3 | PROGRAM PLANNING

ASSESSING YOUR GROUP'S RESOURCES

It is very helpful in evaluating your screening plans and budget if you make a realistic assessment of your group's resources for this event. A film showing intended to attract a large audience will logically involve much more work than one which is for your group's membership meeting. Keep these questions in mind as you start to plan your film program and make sure that you don't try to do more than is realistic and necessary.

- How many people are active in your group? Who among them can take responsibility for the screening? Who else can help?
- Are there people with good organizational skills in your group who can give leadership and take on responsibilities?
- What activities and time commitments do you have as a group during the same time period?
- What other activities or major events are occurring during the time you are planning your event? the same week? the same date?
- Do you have funds for this program?
- Does your group have its own space for the screening or easy access to one?
- Who is your target audience? How many people?
- Do you have regular meetings, a mailing list or other effective ways of communicating with people within and on the periphery of your group?
- Are you in touch regularly with other people who might be interested in this screening?

Basically, your resources will break down into people — their time, energy, skills and contacts; time — for planning, preparation and publicity; and money — either you have enough to pay for the expenses or you feel confident that you can raise it through the event. The skills and organization you will develop by putting on a film screening are applicable to many kinds of presentations. Conversely, if you have organized any events for your group, you probably already know a lot which will help you present a film well.

PLUNGING AHEAD: WORKING WITH A COMMITTEE

Even if you are planning only a small screening for your group, it will be to your advantage to organize a committee to deal with it. This allows the skills of more experienced members to be passed on to others, and involves more people in the process from the beginning. This committee would be made up of people interested in working on the screening, and its first tasks will be the resource assessment outlined above, developing a plan, and defining responsibilities. If you are planning a large screening which entails publicity, an initial committee of at least four people is essential.

There should be one person who acts as convener and is responsible for calling meetings, checking on tasks and centralizing information. The committee will probably need weekly meetings leading up to the event, and a phone list in order to be in close contact throughout the preparation period. People on the screening committee will have primary responsibility for organizing the various tasks — arranging for the film, equipment and space, publicity, outreach, mailings, distribution of flyers, organizing volunteers, guests, introduction and discussion, food, childcare, the building, and so on. While everyone must be clear about their responsibilities, the full membership can be called on to carry out the work. It is a good idea to pair more experienced people with less experienced people on some of the large jobs such as publicity so that the skills can be shared.

Your screening committee, its meetings and communications about the film event will be formal or informal as needed for the scale of the event and will fit your organizational style. At the meetings, people give progress reports, ask for help if needed, work out logistics and set tasks for the next week. The meetings are particularly useful if someone is having difficulty and needs advice, assistance or reinforcement. For example, if one person is getting nowhere contacting an institution for use of its space, or trying to get a particular reporter to return calls, others might try their luck or contacts. The person preparing the flyer might ask the group to make sure all of the important information is included. While this committee becomes the steering committee for a large event, they should always be able to call on the general membership for people and resources, and check back with the entire group about the refined plans.

The people taking responsibility for the screening will, for example:

- Assess your group's resources — people, time, money.
- Make arrangements for getting the film and the projection equipment.

- Assess the spaces available and make a decision or recommendation about the best one.
- Investigate and organize any additional information you might want to present at the screening in the form of resource people, program notes, background for discussion, your organization's brochures, supplemental literature, etc.
- Organize, assign and carry out the tasks for the screening (see Chapter 6).
- Make lists of other groups who might be interested in your event and delegate responsibility for contacting them.
- Organize your group's mailing list, think of other mailing lists and arrange to borrow them.
- Get together a mailing party.

With The Cuban Women

Art is one of the Cuban people's most powerful means of building a new society. Cuban women not only gain in the new society, but are particularly active in its creation.

Discussion with Margaret Randall

Margaret Randall, noted American author who has lived in Cuba since 1969, records Cuban women's experience through her oral histories and biographies, and communicates her own life as a woman in Cuba through poetry, prose and film.

Film: "With the Cuban Women"

d. Octavio Cortazar, Cuba, 1975, color, 48 minutes, English subtitles. A tribute to the Women's Liberation movement in Cuba.

Monday Oct. 16 7:30

Christian Association Auditorium: 36 & Locust Walk
free
For more information, call 386-1536.
Co-sponsored by the Penn Women's Center and the International Cinema, Series 5 (Latin American Cinema).

SIMPLE ORGANIZATIONAL SCHEDULE

Below is a schedule for a simple screening intended only for your membership. Little publicity is involved, but you still have to plan ahead long enough to allow for the time it may take to receive the film and to make the other arrangements. A more elaborate schedule for a larger screening can be found at the end of the publicity chapter. A good rule of thumb is to plan backwards from your screening date.

First Week
- Select film, space and date.
- Outline program.
- Assess group's resources.
- Make up budget.
- Make up screening committee to coordinate event.

Second Week
- Telephone to book film. Have alternative date in mind. Usually you will have to book the film at least six weeks in advance to allow time for shipping.
- Send written confirmation to distributor, confirming film title, date, cost. Most distributors will require payment in advance (see Chapter 10 on distributors and other film sources).
- Telephone to confirm your space if necessary. Also send a written confirmation reaffirming particular arrangements.
- Make sure that you will have projection equipment and a projectionist for the screening.
- Make arrangements with special guests for the program.
- Announce film at your monthly meeting.

Third Week

- If you have not received a confirmation from the distributor within two weeks of when you sent your confirming letter, write or telephone them.
- Start any research on the film or the topic that will be necessary for the discussion, program notes, or literature table. Order any literature well in advance.

Fourth Week

- Include notice of the film in your mailing (first class) about the meeting. If you don't regularly send out announcements of the meetings, this might be a good time to begin. (If you are using bulk rate mail, do this two weeks earlier).

Fifth-Sixth Week

- Finalize specifics of the space, when to pick up equipment, who is bringing the literature, etc.
- Learn how to set up and run equipment.
- If the film has not arrived at least two working days before your scheduled showing, call the distributor. They can still usually get another print to you.
- Preview the film with the discussion leaders. Finish and type up program notes, xerox or duplicate them.

THE BOTTOM LINE: YOUR BUDGET

Making your film program a reality is going to cost time and money. Everything you want to do will be affected by these considerations. A budget needs to be prepared well in advance rather than as a last minute report after the group has become committed to a specific course of action. Most of your expenses will need to be covered before the night of the event and unless your group has credit with the distributor or other providers of expense items, you will need a cash reserve. The sample budget given here will help you to determine your costs. After working out your prospective budget, you may want to replan some items or economize by getting some of the items donated. When people are delegated a job, they should be told the amount budgeted for that item and it must be impressed upon them that they cannot spend more than that amount. Receipts should be obtained for **every** expenditure.

Program Expenses

Not all of these items will apply to all programs and some of the items may be covered by donations.

_____ Film rental (if rental is charged this probably will be required in advance).

_____ Film shipping and insurance (you pay both ways).

_____ Space rental.

_____ Custodial, heating, or other space fees not included in your rental or asked for in place of rental (could include overtime for personnel working evenings).

_____ Equipment rental or purchase (could include a projector, speaker, screen, public address system, microphone, amplifier, and extra projection and exciter lamps).

_____ Projectionist (generally charged on an hourly basis).

_____ Staff salaries.

_____ Production of promotional flyers, posters, brochures.

_____ Other printing or xerox (program notes, press releases, information about your group).

_____ Materials and supplies for art work.

_____ Purchase or printing of tickets.

_____ Telephone calls (long distance).

_____ Paid advertising.

_____ Postage for your flyers and press releases.

_____ Fees, travel costs, and lodging for guest speakers.

_____ Refreshments (include cost of paper plates, napkins, etc.).

_____ Costs of literature to be sold.

_____ Total Expenses

Projected Income From Program ▬▬▬▬▬▬▬▬▬▬▬▬▬▬▬▬

Be realistic in making these projections. Calculate on the basis of your anticipated **minimum** attendance rather than the maximum. Better to be pleasantly surprised than caught short.

_____ Admissions (number of people times ticket price, if any).

_____ Program funds allocated from your treasury.

_____ Anticipated donations or sponsorships.

_____ Income from refreshments.

_____ Income from literature table (if applicable).

_____ Total Income

_____ Total Income

_____ Minus Total Expenses

_____ Equals Total Profit (Loss)

EVALUATING THE BUDGET

Showing a film will not necessarily be profit-making in the narrow financial sense. Attracting new members, getting a vibrant community image, presenting an issue to the media, or raising the consciousness of the audience are primary goals for most groups. Consequently, you should not be alarmed if your budget shows that the anticipated minimal revenues fall short of anticipated outlays. You should be satisfied that the cost is worth the objectives you have decided upon. You can also rethink certain items. Perhaps you can get a free projector instead of renting one, or you may be able to have someone donate printing, space, or one of the other larger budget items. Clearly, your treasury has to be able to handle the cost of the program without disrupting the other work of the organization. Most screenings should produce a modest profit or cover costs, but evaluating your budget gives you realistic foresight on what any specific program may require in terms of advance outlay of cash and anticipated income.

OTHER THAN $ BENEFITS

Evaluating your budget beyond an elementary dollars and cents approach is extremely useful. We got valuable insight into this aspect from a rank and file caucus operating within a larger trade union in California. After a year of steady weekly meetings, the members of the caucus decided to show films with a labor focus once every month as part of an internal educational program and to give variety to the meetings. They soon found that film nights were particularly popular with prospective and marginal members. Without consciously planning it, the caucus had discovered a way to combine modest outreach, entertainment, and the strengthening of its own group spirit. The amount of film-related money that had been set aside for education and entertainment proved money well spent even though no admission was charged. Their selections included Hollywood feature films of the 30's like BLACK FURY, independent features like SALT OF THE EARTH, and contemporary independent documentaries.

A similar experience was reported by Sound and Print United, a black group located in rural North Carolina, which operates a community radio station. The group was loaned a print of LAST GRAVE AT DIMBAZA by a church group. Sound and Print arranged for a free space and paid for the modest publicity in addition to announcing the film on its radio programs. The first time the film was shown, fifteen people attended. In Raleigh or a college town like Chapel Hill, this might have been considered a small turnout but in Warrenton, North Carolina with a population of one thousand it was an important breakthrough. If Sound and Print had not sponsored the film, no one else would have and an important issue might never have been raised. As it was, there were important ripple effects. Discussion of the film led to interest in having additional screenings which drew larger numbers of people.

4 | SPACE AND TIME

THE RIGHT SPACE

Where you choose to show your film is extremely important because different kinds of spaces are more or less appropriate for, and accessible to, different kinds of events and audiences. Obviously, if you intend to show an educational or how-to film to a dozen people, they would feel lost in an auditorium. A free classroom with a screen, a living room with a screen or sheet, or your regular meeting place with a table and screen would do fine. Your concerns should be that everyone can see, hear, and be comfortable during the film.

When you want to attract a large or more general audience, a more public space would be better. Good first choices are places where people are accustomed to seeing films, like a school auditorium, a local movie theater, or the public library. Just as good are other public places associated with social or cultural events. These can include church halls, union halls, arts centers, art galleries, coffee houses, community recreational or educational centers, settlement houses, grange halls, day-care centers, program or conference centers, and neighborhood bars and parking lots.

Consider the alternatives in terms of where your intended audience would feel most comfortable, congeniality for the sort of program you are planning, accessibility to public transportation, availability of equipment and chairs, and the history of other activities which have taken place there.

People in smaller towns and rural areas often have access to more effective spaces than urban dwellers. Public institutions may be more accustomed and open to dealing with small groups and individuals and can be flexible in providing free or low cost space and equipment. Grange and other service organizations often have halls available on specific nights. Many times all that is needed to use the space is to approach them or another public institution like a school, library or fire house with a reasonable request. Another consideration in rural and suburban areas is the distance people will travel for education and entertainment. Film users in rural New Jersey report that a screening may draw people from as far as fifteen miles away, although the primary audience comes from a radius of about five miles.

Urban groups have to be somewhat careful in their selection of public program sites. Numerically, there are many halls, basements, store fronts, Y's and auditoriums in a city. The problem is to locate one that really serves your needs. Shifting the location even a few blocks can make an enormous difference in who and how many people will attend. Tight budgets and security considerations may make schools, libraries and other public institutions difficult to work with for evening events unless they are normally open during those hours. They should always be considered, however, as they may have space available on given nights or have other free or low cost services. Institutions which have as their own goals serving the public might be very pleased to assist a program which brings people into their facility.

One service that people should familiarize themselves with is the Public Building Cooperative Use Act of 1976. This statute provides for the free use of federal building space by individuals and organizations involved in cultural or educational activities. Contact the General Service Administration Building Supervisor in your area for details. The number can be found in the government listing section in your phone book. In some cities, public service institutions like a cultural association, arts council, or civic association publish lists of spaces available to groups, usually noting the rental rates, if any. Banks, corporations and restaurants may be willing to volunteer space if the program offers them some good publicity or relates directly to their interests. Churches and community organizations working on projects around specific issues similar to the topic of your program could be enthusiastic about letting you use their space. Even if they are not directly involved in the same issue, they tend to be generous and cooperative, through their sense of public service. It's always a good idea to think about places where similar events have occurred, or about spaces used by similar groups.

Think carefully before coming to a final decision, and don't ever accept space sight unseen. Free isn't always best. Certain shapes, obstructions such as pillars, low ceilings and lighting pose difficulties for a good film showing. Each space also has its own ambiance. If you want to reach youth offenders with a film about prisons, a church center might not attract them. Senior citizens might be put off by a recreational center for teenagers or a screening room at the top of three flights of stairs. A union hall might be an unknown location to an audience of middle class professional people. A great university auditorium might be surrounded by invisible but real barriers for community people. Neighbors might be delighted at finding yet another use for the large room in their community center. There are many variables in deciding upon a space. Remember that others may have different standards than yours about language in a film or positions on controversial subjects, and you may want to ask them another time for help. You'll want to avoid a falling out over a film that will provoke their displeasure.

CHECKING OUT THE SPACE

Even if it is free, a space costs too much if it does not suit your needs. Some people from the committee will have to go and check out the site, with your intended audience and program in mind. It is important that the projectionist go along on this visit.

Physical requirements are primarily matters of common sense. You need a room that can easily be darkened, and that is large or small enough to accommodate your anticipated audience and program. It's better to have a smaller room almost full than a larger one 3/4 empty. If you are anticipating a lot of people, however, you might pay for a larger room, and figure that the admissions from the additional people you can get in will more than cover the expense.

Other questions to answer include: Where are the electrical outlets and circuit breakers located? How many and what type of chairs are available, or will you have to bring in your own (no easy task)? Ventilation, air-conditioning, and heating arrangements must also be evaluated. Hot, cold, or stuffy rooms are not comfortable and people who have suffered once are not likely to want to repeat the experience. If you are planning to have refreshments, provide child care or have a discussion, make sure appropriate facilities, space, tables, chairs, and other furniture are available.

When you rent or are loaned a space, you generally make these arrangements during normal business hours. Be sure that you know who will be opening the building for you or where to get keys if you are using it in the evening. In large institutions custodial help will probably be included (do you pay extra?). Find out the names of the custodians who will be there and how to reach them. Do they have keys to all of the rooms you expect to use? Talk with them before the day of the screening to find out exactly what they will do for you and what you will do on your own. Arrange to get into the space about two hours in advance of your scheduled starting time. As long as you think ahead and remain polite and reasonable in your requests, you are not going to put anyone off and all should go well. In fact, your thoughtfulness and foresight may reinforce the feeling that whoever has provided you the space has made a good decision.

SIGHT AND SOUND

The reason you want the projectionist or another knowledgeable person along on the site visit is that the room should be evaluated for sight and sound. The size and shape of the room will have implications for the projection equipment you will plan to use. In general, the larger the room, the more powerful your projectors will have to be to provide adequate illumination and understandable sound. Equipment that works fine for a classroom or living room of ten to thirty people usually will be inadequate for an auditorium which seats 500 (for more on technical matters see Chapter 8). If you are considering a basketball court, a 500 seat auditorium, a movie theater which does not have 16mm equipment, or a park, you will probably have to make arrangements for special projectors which use powerful arc lamps and supplemental sound equipment. You may find that the proper equipment is provided with the room. Or you might save money by looking for a smaller space if you don't really expect 500 people. The projectionist should also locate the working electrical outlets (will an extension cord be needed? a three prong adapter?), the circuit breakers, sturdy tables, and measure the distance from the projector location to the screen to determine image size and the amount of sound cord which might be needed.

Image

The best places for showing films are rooms which slope down as they approach the screen. If the room is flat, the ceiling must be high enough (often over 15' for audiences numbering over 60) so that the screen can be raised. This is necessary so that people in the back seats can see more than a field of necks. A balcony often makes a perfect place from which to project.

First determine where you would put the projector, the screen and the people. Certainly the room should not include pillars or other obstructions that ruin the sightlines (check the tables in Chapter 8 for room size/audience/screen sizes). The size of the image will be limited by the size of the screen, but the further the projector is from the screen, the larger the image will be. The exact image size is determined by the focal length of the lens. The idea is to have an image which is large and bright enough so that the people in the back rows can see clearly. In flat rooms, both the projector and the screen (if it has legs) can be put up on tables. If you can get the projector up high enough to clear the audience's heads, you can often avoid having to set up the chairs with a center aisle (the prime viewing area). Often the legs on even a large (7'×7') screen are not high enough so that the bottom of the screen is visible to people 10-15 rows back.

Sound

The acoustical properties of the room itself play as important a part in sound quality as do the components of the sound system. There are two variables in reproducing the sound track well: to select a room with good acoustics in the first place, or to try to minimize the room's bad effects through proper speaker placement, signal processing with additional equipment, or temporary modifications of the room. (See Chapter 8 and sound section Chapter 13 for problem solving).

Generally, a room designed for amplified sound rather than un-reinforced public speaking is best. If the room is cavernous or tunnel-like it may distort the sound. You should also check for noises that may come from adjacent spaces (a dance class overhead), passing subways or buses, or nearby construction sites. An initial evaluation of a room's acoustics can be done just with your hands, ears, and eyes. Some acoustical problems will not show up until you test for them with your equipment and film. Every room sounds different, and these are only guidelines.

In order to produce audible sound for the people in the back row, your system must be producing that much volume everywhere in the room. If the room has a very high ceiling, much of the sound will just bounce above the viewer's heads, at best to be absorbed up there, at worst producing a lot of unwanted reverberations, muddying up the sound. The closer a room is to a cube in shape, the more suspicious you should be.

How to Assess

While you stand near the center of the room, have another person stand at the front. Close your eyes, face front, and have them speak in a fairly loud voice, varying from low to high pitched tones, and from a slow to a fast pace. Can you understand the words? Keeping your eyes closed, try to point at where you think the speaker is standing. Is it easy to locate the direction? Still with your eyes closed, have your helper walk around, clapping hands. Can you follow the movement? With your helper speaking from the front, move from the front to the back of the room, and from side to side. Are there places where intelligibility seems to fall off, where the loudness is appreciably less?

If, in the course of these tests, you find that you can always tell what direction sounds are coming from, and the words are always clear, there is a good chance that your film sound (given a decent amplifier and speaker) will also be clear. If you had problems during these tests, you'll have to evaluate whether the problems can be corrected. Lack of intelligibility or clear directionality can usually be traced to excessive reverberation or echo — common in rooms which are very "live" because they have hard wood floors, panelled walls, glass doors, wood or metal furniture. The sound bounces around these hard surfaces. If low frequencies (like footsteps or low male voices) or high frequencies (like high female voices or "whooshing" sounds from fans or air conditioners) are over- or under-accented, the room may have "standing wave" or other frequency-response problems. Rooms have frequency responses of their own. This means if you feed a "flat" signal — one containing an equal amount of acoustical energy at every point, from low bass to high treble — into a room, the room will lend a shape of its own to that once flat signal. If, as you walk around, the volume of sound drops in a particular location, you've found a "dead spot."

Always keep in mind that the human body is a first-rate sound absorber. A room full of people will always be deader, less reverberant, but this effect diminishes as the proportion of filled to empty space decreases, which is why rooms with very high ceilings can be problematic. These tests will let you know what sort of problems you may be in for. If you have no choice in a screening space, or like a space that is problematic for sound, see Chapter 13 for some ways to correct these problems through speaker placement, artificial barriers and supplemental equipment.

THE RIGHT TIME

Effective scheduling of events is an art in and of itself. Our suggestions here should be taken only as general guidelines rather than as strict rules. City and country people, for instance, have different daily and weekly work routines. Different cities have different routines. Different groups in the same city have different routines. Starting times may be earlier in the winter (it gets darker earlier) than the summer when people tend to stay outside later.

Your first decision is whether to hold your screening during the day or in the evening. Nightime is most effective for a general adult audience, especially if you wish to attract working people, but there can be exceptions. For example, young people or retirees may have more flexibility in their schedules and you might consider weekday or weekend matinees. After school and weekend mornings are good times for children's programs. Day or night, in scheduling your event be aware of religious or secular holidays when people may be away or want to be in family situations. Yet you may want to time your screening to coincide with significant historical dates or times set aside locally or nationally for special attention, such as Sun Week, Black History Week, Gay Pride Week, International Women's Day, independence celebrations, birthdays of important people, anniversaries of significant local events, all of which can provide a context for your film screening. Also determine if there is major competition like the annual state fair or an important sporting event which would attract your constituency. University programmers may want to avoid exam periods and other times that are inappropriate in the academic calendar.

To attract people who work from nine to five, allow time to get home, eat, and get to your screening without feeling rushed. You also have to finish early enough so that the next morning they do not regret attending your screening because they are tired.

Monday, Tuesday and Thursday are generally quiet nights, even in the largest cities. There is much less likelihood of competing events and a greater possibility of finding attractive free space. Although these may not be the best nights to try to reach out to a large audience, they may be suitable for lower keyed programs. Some people consider Thursday the start of the weekend and are "itching" to do something, so this can be a good choice.

Wednesday is a traditional meeting night. This is an advantage although there may be competition from the regular meetings of other groups. Keep in mind that in some areas this is a night when department stores may have late hours.

Friday and Saturday are nights when people are accustomed to "going out." Friday is a good choice for meetings and special events of all kinds. However, if you choose it, be aware that you are in for competition. If you hope to draw couples to an evening event, Saturday may be a better choice. Saturday afternoons, in most cases, are not good because this is a shopping, fix-up, and loafing day. College sports may also provide formidable competition.

Sunday is usually a day when people get out of the house and when families are most likely to do something together. Midafternoon programs can be attractive as long as they break up early enough for dinner. Given that meal times tend to be more flexible on Sunday, it is possible to schedule events in the early evening, which is an advantage since Monday is a working day. In general, Sunday can be a good day for educational programs.

Check around early to see what other events are being planned. You may discover that other groups are planning programs on the same night or close to the date you are considering, and you may have to adjust your date. This can be turned into a mutual advantage. Confer with the group and see if it is appropriate and feasible to do joint programs or joint publicity for the separate events. This would cut costs and expand the potential audience at the same time. Minimally, each could announce the other's programs at its meetings and events and make promotional materials available. The simple act of some members of each group making a point of attending the other's screening may help lay a foundation for future cooperation. Don't get caught up in trying to outdraw another group for the same audience or become rigid about a specific date for strictly personal or subjective reasons. Working cooperatively is far more advantageous.

LAURA MULVEY

VISITING FILMMAKER
will present her film
RIDDLES OF THE SPHINX (1977),
made in collaboration
with Peter Wollen,
**TUESDAY APRIL 25,
8:00 P.M.**
Museum of Art Theater,
Carnegie Institute
Admission $1.00

A synthesis of feminist politics
and avant-garde technique,
RIDDLES OF THE SPHINX
offers the American avant
garde an explicitly political direction

design -- mana paul kyros

5 | PUBLICIZING THE EVENT

All the thought and planning which go into events will be wasted if yours is not publicized correctly. Publicity simply means devising ways of making the connection with your intended audience. Film-goers will not fall from the sky at the correct time and place just because you have thought up a wonderful program. They have to know about the basics of what is going on far enough in advance so they can plan to come, so you must publicize in a clear and attractive manner:

- What is happening.
- Where and at what time.
- Who is presenting it.
- Why they are doing it.

Good publicity assures people that the program will be productive and enjoyable and puts the event in a context. Sponsors do not need to hype or blitz people, but they do want to convey their honest enthusiasm. An obstacle you may face is the time lag between when you first discover and want to share a film and when you are able to organize a screening. Your publicity should try to convey your initial enthusiasm for the film and a sense of its importance.

Publicity methods most often used by groups include:

Direct mail. Postcards, flyers and other announcements sent to people on mailing lists.

Distribution. Flyers are left for people to take and posters are displayed at strategic locations.

Networking. Personal and mail contact with groups and individuals who might be interested in the event; announcements at meetings or other events and in newsletters; inviting other groups to set up literature tables or work as co-sponsors; telling friends.

Coverage in the media. Sending press releases to the print media to get listings in calendars or have stories published. Public service announcements (PSA's) to the broadcast media to be read over the air.

A key to effective publicity is, of course, knowing your "target audience." Make sure the scale of publicity is appropriate in relation to your audience and program. If you are trying to reach neighbors to encourage them to see a film in a neighborhood church, you will not need a full page ad in the city's major newspaper. You might, however, want to put a small notice in the local paper to reach those who might not see your poster in the corner store.

The more people and the broader the cross-section you want to attract, the more elaborate and sophisticated your publicity campaign will have to be. This chapter discusses most methods used by non-profit groups to get the word out, with the exception of paid media advertising which is usually beyond modest resources. These publicity methods depend on willing volunteers who are informed and enthusiastic about the event and the sponsor and who become representatives of both.

No matter how simple and inexpensive or elaborate and costly it may be, all good publicity should not only convey information and present a persuasive and favorable image of the event and sponsor, but, above all, generate excitement, create enthusiasm, get people to talk about and ultimately attend the event — in short, get it on the grapevine. Word of mouth is probably the best connection to your intended audience. If someone you know and trust tells you, as a potential viewer, "Oh, I saw that film, it's great, you have to see it," or "That film was really important," that can be more persuasive to you than the recommendations of a reviewer. Movie theaters and companies spend a lot of money to create good word of mouth. Your group can do this in a more intimate way. After all, you wouldn't be presenting the film if you didn't think it was worthwhile. Reading about a screening in their own newsletter can be more meaningful to people than a paid ad, and it may be more effective in encouraging their participation.

The grapevine varies from place to place, from community to community, and you should consider, when planning your publicity, how people hear about things. You want people to be talking about your event when they are making their plans for the week or the weekend, and you want them to be talking enthusiastically about why they are going. Word of mouth is the most powerful publicity, and most of your efforts should be designed to initiate it. If you have the grapevine working for you, then your flyers, posters, and media announcements serve to further encourage the talking, pull in new people, and validate the fact that the event is taking place.

One example of the success of an elaborate campaign is instructive in this regard. An alternative fund in Philadelphia, along with two other groups, found out on very short notice that it could do a benefit premiere (the first night of a commercial engagement) of HARLAN COUNTY, USA, a film which had received a lot of national publicity, was being eagerly awaited in Philadelphia, and which all three groups thought their constituents would find enjoyable. They had only 14 days before the show-date, but decided to plunge in since they felt they could raise a lot of money. A flyer was designed, printed and blown up to poster size (the quickest job in the community print shop's history). Series tickets were run off. The flyers and tickets were mailed out first class and hand delivered to about 50 groups to distribute and sell. A press screening was arranged, press releases and public service announcements went out about the film, the sponsors, and the concert following the film. A non-profit radio station made a cassette of the PSA using music as background. Somehow, posters went up all over the city. Volunteers started making telephone calls. On the night of the premiere there was standing room only, and hundreds of people had to be turned away. The community organizers did such a good job of publicizing the premiere through their grapevines that most people thought the film was playing only that one night. In fact, the theater had also been advertising its own two week engagement. The groups raised enough money to justify all the hectic activity.

Your membership, constituents and friends will usually make up the core of any audience, no matter how "general public" it is. As soon as you have made the decision to show a film, you should start including it in your regular notices to them. If you are organizing the screening with a committee who reports back to the membership on their progress, your word of mouth campaign has already been initiated. Particulars can be added as you move along in your publicity and organizing schedule (see end of this chapter).

CAMPAIGNS

Good publicity often means calling people's attention to the event in more than one way. Most people need several reminders. Any newsletter, newspaper or written minutes of a meeting sent to your members should contain announcements about your film programs. Of course, there is always room for innovation. Postcards announcing the next two scheduled programs have proven very successful for a professional historian's organization based in New York City. Members of this particular group are very schedule- and print-oriented. The officers learned that postcards arriving two to three weeks in advance was sufficient notice to insure a good turnout. When they showed a film, they moved their meeting to an auditorium in the same university building where they usually rented a classroom. For a membership, postcards alone might be enough; if you are expanding your audience, postcards might prove useful in augmenting other means of publicity. For instance, early "save-this-date" postcards to key people can be a good way of starting a word of mouth campaign. They can go out quickly, before you have your flyers designed and printed.

There are two standard devices most groups use for communication — a mailing list and a telephone tree. The regular organizational mailing list can and should be supplemented by additional names. The historians had a short mailing list consisting of people who paid dues or otherwise had a formal association with the group, plus a long list made up of anyone who had ever come to their meetings or sent a letter of inquiry. The short list is the backbone of their ordinary mailings for meetings and regular membership business. For films and other special events for which they want to attract more people, they use the long list. Long lists can be built by getting the name and address of anyone who comes to any given screening or public event your group sponsors, and by saving names and addresses of people who ask you for information.

The telephone tree is used for rapid intra-group communication. It is basically a tree diagram of people and their phone numbers. Initiators call the 5-10 people on their list, who have lists of people they are supposed to call. This can have as many stages as necessary. It is a sort of formalized grapevine, and assignments can be arranged for people who tend to be in regular communication anyway.

DIRECT MAIL AND MAILING LISTS

Your group may need to be in touch regularly with members, supporters, and other people interested in your work, meetings, and public events. A direct mail campaign can be one of the most effective ways of communicating information about your film screening, or any other event. Direct mail solicitations are often used as fund raising devices. Effective direct mail depends on the mailing piece (see following section on flyers) and on your mailing list. If you have over 200 names on your list and you mail things to them several times a year, you can save money by getting a "bulk third class" mailing permit. A non-profit organization is eligible for even lower rates (approximately 3¢ / piece) the "special non-profit bulk third class." Call your post office for an application form and the current rules and guidelines. You complete the application and pay an annual fee. Bulk third class rates are cheaper because you sort the pieces by zip code before taking them to the post office. Bulk mailings must consist of at least 200 copies of the same material. The Post Office has all the rules and will be happy to explain them to you.

To do an efficient bulk mailing, it is best to have your list already in zip code order, and add new names in order. Scriptomatic cards, xerox labels, index cards, and computerized storing and printing are some ways of organizing mailing lists. The best processes allow you to keep the list so you don't have to retype it each time you want to use it. You can have a mailing party to address and sort the pieces or, if you have a huge list, there are professional mailing companies which for a fee will prepare and mail your material.

Keep in mind that the post office does not provide the same instant service as the telephone. Your audience should receive the announcement at least two weeks in advance. Bulk mail delivery times vary for different zip codes in the same city, and for different times of the year. Allowing two weeks for the mail to arrive might be enough. This is one instance, however, where it is better to be a bit early than to be late. More than one group has been embarrassed when told its announcement came a day or even a week after the event had been held.

You can add names to your mailing list in several ways. The best method is to have a mailing list sign-up form at all your events. Some like-minded groups in your locale might be happy to exchange mailing lists with you (just check for duplicate listings of the same name). Or they might loan you their list for a mailing for a special event. Other groups who are more possessive about their lists might include your flyer in one of their mailings or put a notice in their newsletter. You can find some names by doing a little research, or simply mail to departments — for example, to reach all the high school art teachers in the area, or all the social service agencies who relate to senior citizens. If you ask a favor of another group — such as the use of their mailing list, the inclusion of information in a newsletter, or an announcement at a meeting — you should be prepared to respond in kind when they need assistance for an event.

FLYERS AND POSTERS

The simple and inexpensively produced flyer is the mainstay of many groups' publicity efforts. The cardinal consideration in all publicity material is that the sponsor and the event will be associated with whatever image is projected. First impressions can be important here. The flyer and poster are calling cards; well conceived, attention-getting materials appropriate for your program can give your group a boost. Conversely, if the flyer looks silly or boring, the stigma will attach to the sponsor; if the piece lacks critical information, the sponsor will come off as careless or stupid. Five color printing, fancy paper, and other expensive printing techniques are not necessary. A good design on white paper printed in black ink can be very effective, and even one colored ink or color paper can add a feeling of elegance. If you are sponsoring a film benefit for your group or have a small program budget, you don't want to spend a lot of money on printing. Cultural and educational groups may find that local corporations and businesses will donate the printing of publicity materials.

A concern for artistic quality does not mean that you have to be a Toulouse-Lautrec to design a good flyer or poster. Anyone with minimal art skills can turn out attractive materials. Being careful about art work does not mean curbing creativity either. Quite the opposite. A good flyer grabs and holds the readers' attention long enough to pass along essential information about the event. As long as you observe basic design guidelines, you can be as imaginative as you wish. A good line drawing, a graphic, or a photo can help a lot, but well conceived and logically placed lettering can be very appealing on its own or in combination with art work.

SUPPLIES AND TECHNIQUES

Presstype. Stationery and art stores now carry a wide variety of presstype in many sizes. It can be professionally applied without any special tools (using the grid printed on each sheet) and is inexpensive. For a few dollars per sheet, your group can have a variety of sizes and typefaces on file to use for any event and thereby greatly increase the attention-getting ability of your publicity. Avoid mixing too many different styles of type on any one flyer.

The blue pencil. Buy a (non-photo) blue pencil in any art supply store and you can rule and write all you want in preparing your design. The printer's camera doesn't photograph the particular light frequency of the blue pencil so all your marks will disappear on the final printed piece.

The grid. You can make a grid of vertical and horizontal lines which helps you keep the letters straight as you place down type or add artwork. You don't have to purchase a T-square. Using a ruler, just mark off equal increments (every inch or half inch, or whatever you need for the size of the design) on all four sides of the paper. Using your blue pencil, join those lines together. You can also buy a packet of readymade grid paper.

Free art. Some film distributors provide posters with a space for you to add the date and place of your screening. You may use them as they are, or cut out and rubber cement graphics from them onto your own layouts.

Rubber cement. Rubber cement is much better for sticking down material than tape, which often shows up on the finished flyer.

Typesetting. Your options for type are hand lettering, presstype, cut out pieces of copy, typewritten copy, or typeset copy. Typesetting looks the most professional, and will be clearer than typewritten copy. Typesetting machines space letters to different width units which saves a lot of space. They also have different typeface styles and sizes from which to choose. Most professional publications are typeset. This process is more expensive than typing the copy yourself. If you are going to print a large number of pieces, however, or if you want a particular piece to really look good, you might consider it.

If you need ideas, start by analyzing the materials other groups have put out, advertisements in the newspaper, the relationship between copy and graphics in magazines, and other publicity materials. You can adapt a lot of them for your needs.

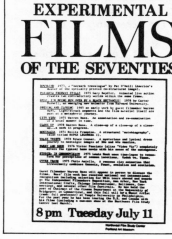

SIZE

Given how most flyers and posters are used, the following physical considerations should be kept in mind. Posters are large (17"×22" is a standard size), printed on one side on heavy or stiff paper, and designed to provide high visibility from a distance. Flyers generally are either typewriter (8½"×11") or legal paper (8½"×14") size. They may be folded and sent through the mail, handed out, and left in stacks at public meeting places. Most are printed on one side only, but when they are used as self-mailers, the reverse side may carry additional information on the program as well as allowing sufficient space for a return address and a mailing label (see sample). One way to save money on artwork is to print the same design on both light and heavy paper and use the heavier paper as a poster. Flyers can also be blown up in size by a print shop to serve as a poster. You'll have to plan a design that will work well either large or small.

All good flyers and posters should include the following:

- The name of the event should be in the largest type. This may be the title of the film. Near it should be one or two sentences describing the film which will help generate interest in seeing it. You can also add the name of the filmmaker, the film's running time, when and where it was made, whether it is black and white or color, and other pertinent information.
- The date, the day, and the time of the screening should be in the second largest type.
- The place of the screening should be prominent. This means providing an address and, possibly, directions on how to get there. Specific entrances and room numbers may be helpful if you are screening in a big building or educational complex.
- The name of the sponsor is important because people want to know who is responsible and you want visibility.
- A phone number for additional information is important. Be sure the person handling these calls can answer all reasonable questions.
- The price of admission should be stated, or indicate if admission is free or by donation.
- If it is a self-mailer, include the return address. If you are sending the flyer bulk rate, your bulk rate permit number should also be on the flyer (either printed or rubber stamped). The return address must be that of the registered permit holder.

Most good flyers and posters will include some of the following:

- A graphic or photo to attract attention.
- An endorsement of the film. This may be a quote from an authoritative figure such as a national film critic, a statement from a local person known for their good judgement, or a statement by your group about why it is showing the film.
- Note any awards or honors accorded to the film like, "Best Documentary — Mannheim, 1978," or places where the film has been shown, like "Recently seen on Public Television Station WNET" or "Exhibited last year at the Pacific Film Archive."
- The name of any co-sponsors or cooperating groups.
- If the flyer is a self-mailer, the space on the back can be used for additional promotional material.
- If appropriate, coupon for advance-sale tickets or sponsorships (on flyers only, not posters).
- Statement on child care.
- Statement on refreshments.

On any given flyer you will have to balance the design's need for space with your need to provide information. Don't try to cram too much onto one piece of paper, but do give all the necessary information. In cases where the film is not extremely well known, you should always include two to three sentences of description, so people will know what to expect. Design the flyer for a double hit. The larger, bolder elements will catch people's attention, and they will take it home and read it if there is interesting copy as well.

SIDE A   SIDE B

One of the most important things to consider is who you are trying to reach. Try to be objective about the description of the film, the event, your group and look at the flyer as if you were a stranger to the whole thing. While you want your copy to sound natural, you also want it to convey information. Check the pictures and graphics in a similar manner. Many publicity stills are simply straight-forward pictures of the performers, while others have a little more graphic interest. If you are writing copy for a publicity leaflet, you might want to read about the film — in books, reviews, and other descriptive materials — instead of just using the first blurb you find.

If you are trying to reach a particular constituency, consider the kind of language they use. A group from Dayton describes an important learning experience. They had identified particular constituents they wanted to reach, among them working women. They planned to show BLOW FOR BLOW, a film about French women workers in a garment factory. For their publicity effort, they targeted several women's centers and four or five factories with a large number of women employees. They prepared a nice looking leaflet with both a picture and a description of the film. When they went to hand out the leaflet, they watched people read it. After all their efforts they were surprised when "the women looked at the leaflet, looked at us, and threw it away." When the group later analyzed what had happened, they realized that the leaflet they had so carefully prepared was totally wrong for that particular audience. They had taken the description of the film directly from the distributor's catalog, which they now realized had as **its** primary audience teachers and college students. The language and the syntax were simply not appropriate for their target audience.

PRINTING

Fortunately, getting materials printed in multiple copies is not too expensive. Instant offset machines make hundreds of copies inexpensively and mimeographing done with care is even cheaper. Because of the poor quality of reproduction, ditto machines which print in purple are not very effective and should not be used except for "in-house" notices. A good quality xerox would be cheaper if you are only making a few hundred copies. Always maintain a high standard. If, as sometimes happens, a professional printshop turns out a poor job, you have every right to reject it and ask for it to be done properly.

If you are going to spend money on professional printing, be a good consumer. Call a couple of printshops for estimates. You may be surprised at the various prices for the same job. You should be prepared with the following information:

- Final size of piece.
- Printing on one or both sides.
- Kind, color, and weight of paper (60 pound offset paper is good for a lot of purposes, but different printers have different sources. You might need some discussion with the printer on this, and if you are not familiar with the various papers available it would be worthwhile for you to look at samples).
- Ink color (colored inks usually add to the cost).
- Photographs which will have to be screened (there is an additional charge per screen).
- Number of times and where you may want the piece folded. There are standard folding patterns and sizes.
- When you will have the final (camera-ready) layout of the design completed and when you want the printing done (this will vary with printers' schedules).
- If you will pick up or if you want them to deliver (extra charge?).

Some printers will also recommend people who do typesetting or design work or have staff themselves to do it. Both will cost.

DISTRIBUTION

Posters and flyers should not be thought of in isolation. They are a one-two publicity punch. The posters can go up early and serve as a long range reminder while the flyer arrives in the mail to jolt the memory into the realization that the big night is coming soon. A reverse strategy (and better in rainy places) would be to send the flyers out in advance and then put up a poster barrage the last week before the screening. Always send several leaflets to any organization that is a meeting place for groups. Film users in Dayton have found two rubber stamps extremely useful. One reads, "Please Post," and the other, "Please Distribute." Stamped with one or the other, flyers can serve a double function with a minimum of effort.

Printed flyers and posters will be the most important items in any large promotion effort. Think about how and where they will be used and design them accordingly. Each organization will have to experiment to find what is most effective in its context.

The Sound and Print group in North Carolina, for instance, learned through experience that 25 large posters would cover their needs nicely. These were placed in store windows, at the post office, in supermarkets, on community bulletin boards, in churches, and 20 other places where people regularly congregated. Because the group had a radio station at its disposal, they did not mail flyers for film programs. For some events, however, Sound and Print found it useful to have volunteers take flyers from door to door. Giving them out by hand led to informal chats, similar to the kind of contact that canvassers have. It was an informal way to find out about particular interests and generate excitement about the event. The Sound and Print volunteers soon learned that their major competition was not big public affairs but the informal networks most people related to like garden clubs, card nights, social organizations, and other small gatherings which command high loyalty. They also learned that weekends were not good times for programs unless they were primarily perceived as entertainment. The exception to this was that educational or political events seemed appropriate for Sunday afternoon or evening. What was most creative in the door-to-door approach was that the flyers opened a two-way communication which provided valuable feedback useful in planning future activities.

A similar experience was reported by a group called Faith, Hope, and Charity in rural Vermont. In nine years the group had grown to have a staff of six, including some people working for governmental agencies. The area serviced included about 15 small towns, each with a population less than a thousand. Faith, Hope & Charity had established health centers, co-ops, tenants' groups, senior citizen clubs, a rural bus service, and thrift shops. They found that personal contact was the most effective mode of publicity and many events were held in homes over coffee and donuts. Like the North Carolina group, they too had gone door to door with materials. Generally the canvassers were paid or volunteer senior citizens who were respected and well known. The group also used the New England tradition of town meetings to coordinate or centralize larger activities.

The urban situation presents different kinds of distribution challenges. Door to door work is not usually so feasible, because of high population density, urban paranoia, and the lack of cohesive neighborhoods. If you are planning a true block or neighborhood event, however, then going door to door might be exactly the right approach. While giving away flyers on a street corner or at a supermarket may be effective in a small town, it is pretty much a waste of time and paper in a city. Many of the people passing any particular corner live in other parts of town or outside the city limits.

Groups would be wiser to think of a particular neighborhood or community as an urban village and try to determine where people in that area normally go for social activities and day-to-day needs. This will lead to mom and pop stores, bulletin boards in supermarkets, community centers, activist churches, bookstores, record stores, other film programs, places which have music, dance, theater or other cultural performances, restaurants, Y's, art galleries, offices of organizations, and many other places where leaving a poster or stack of flyers will be effective. Storekeepers who let you use their windows and counters are particularly helpful.

Urban groups which present public programs regularly or want to reach a broad public often assign distribution routes. Sit down with your committee, map out the city, and have different people take responsibility for different areas. Be as specific as you can. You'll soon learn that one bookstore on a street has a policy against putting flyers on its counter or in its window, while the restaurant next door likes flyers on top of its cigarette machine for customers to look through. Ice cream stores are great in the summer, but flyers don't move quite so rapidly there during the winter. If you're enthusiastic, you'll find you always load up on flyers whenever you go out, and that you also encourage your friends to take some.

You should not just leave your posters and flyers in any place that strikes your fancy. People will get a negative impression of your group if they perceive what you are doing as littering. It is usually against the law to use any private or public property not specifically designated for posters. Local customs vary about such use of telephone posts, construction sites, and so on. More damaging to you than any potential fine are offenses you may commit against local attitudes and customs. There is a certain etiquette involving a sense of fair play when it comes to posting on bulletin boards and kiosks. It is not polite to cover up another group's announcement, nor to monopolize all the space. It is fair to cover up or remove announcements for events which have already taken place.

By establishing regular routes you will begin to develop personal relationships with various community people. The taking down is as important as the putting up. Each distribution squad should carry lots of flyers, masking tape, scotch tape, a good staple gun, a few thumbtacks, and a staple remover.

NETWORKING

Personal contacts and relationships with other like-minded groups are a key to publicizing an event effectively within a particular community or among people with common interests. We have already suggested some networking ideas for direct mail. In the long run, cooperation and support between groups contributes to the audience development efforts of everyone.

EVENTS CALENDARS

When scheduling your film event, you should contact other groups and check cultural calendars to find out what dates and times would not conflict with events other groups have already planned. Identifying those groups and making initial contact about their events is the first step. Tell them a little about the event you are planning, discuss how it relates to their work and interests, and let them know you'll be back in touch when the program is set. Keep a list of the groups, the contact person, and their scheduled events.

An events calendar is simply a listing of the important community cultural and social events which are occurring between the time you schedule your film and when it will actually take place. Your committee should assign someone to go to each important activity to ask the sponsors if they will announce your program and ask if you can distribute your flyers. Don't just start leafletting their audience, but check with them first about the most appropriate way to distribute your information. Perhaps you can leave it on their literature or registration table, on the chairs in the auditorium, or some other place where people will pick it up.

NEWSLETTERS AND MAILINGS

Many groups publish monthly or quarterly newsletters for their membership and, if you tell them enough in advance, they will be happy to include a notice of your event. You can call them first, then send them information in the appropriate written form. Some groups mailing out minutes or announcements of their event will be happy to include your flyer in their envelope, but you should probably offer to help with the stuffing.

Other ways of networking and involving related groups in your event include: telling them about it so that they can announce it at their event; inviting them to have a literature table or information display at your screening; asking someone from the other group to be on a panel or to be a resource person for the discussion following the film. You might ask them to co-sponsor the event with you. This is an effective way to present large film screenings and, if three or four groups are working on the program, you have increased your chances of success. Co-sponsorships range from simple endorsements by other groups to a coalition where the groups make joint decisions, divide up responsibilities and split expenses and proceeds. In most cases, it is to your benefit to involve other groups or individuals working in the areas related to your planned program, whether you just check with them to coordinate plans or develop a more elaborate relationship.

THE MEDIA

Media exposure is another way of getting publicity, credibility and visibility for your event. Reading about your film showing in the calendar listings in the paper, or hearing it announced on the radio may provide that extra bit of excitement needed to get some people out of their houses.

Media choices include:

The mass media. The major newspapers and magazines (print) and radio and television stations (broadcast) in your area.

The intermediate size media. The community-oriented, weekly or monthly newspapers, small FM stations, public television, cable television and specialized publications.

The non-commercial media. The many newsletters and bulletins which circulate within communities, and the newspapers and stations serving university, ethnic, political or artistic constituencies or subscribers.

Large or small, all of the media have specific deadlines and formats that must be observed. If a newspaper goes to press at noon on Tuesday, your copy arriving at 12:08 might just as well have never arrived. It is to your advantage to quickly learn local media deadlines and formats. Groups that do get a lot of free publicity, while those which do not, lose out. If you read the newspapers and follow radio and TV shows it is easy to identify logical people to contact. Call their offices, introduce yourself, request the guidelines, and ask who should be receiving your releases. Start a media mailing list in a file or on index cards in which you record the deadlines, contacts, and formats for each.

Women Make Movies, a women's filmmaking group in New York City, developed two approaches to getting an audience, since it was concerned with reaching residents in the immediate neighborhood, but also wished to interest the greater women's community of the city. Bulk mailing of flyers was more successful in drawing immediate neighbors, while mass media press notices helped to draw outside people. They made up a press list with contacts' names, deadlines, and addresses, so it became a very simple process for them to send out notices for their public screenings.

If you are unclear or hesitant about dealing with the media, try to get the assistance of someone who has done it before. Many cities have local media guides that are available in libraries, from organizations that do a lot of public relations work, or from agencies which provide services to cultural and grassroots groups. In Philadelphia, for example, the Cultural Alliance publishes a **Guide to Getting Cultural Publicity** which includes local guidelines for releases and the addresses and phone numbers of some of the key media contacts. In other areas this service might be provided by the local arts agency, a women's media group, or a technical assistance agency.

PRESS RELEASES

The purpose of a press release is to get a notice or listing in the print media and perhaps to interest a reporter enough to do a feature story. A press release is, quite simply, written information given to the press for publication. The press release should:

- Be a typewritten, double-spaced statement on 8½"×11" paper with wide margins. Do not use onion skin or other fragile paper and do not use unusual type faces like italics and script. Organizational letterhead is most commonly used.

- Be typed clearly in a professional manner—free of grammatical errors, misspellings or other mistakes.

- Use short, clear sentences and paragraphs.

- Always include the release date, usually in the upper left hand corner, (e.g., FOR IMMEDIATE RELEASE). Other reference material would go in the upper right hand corner, such as the name of the organization, address, and name and phone number of a person to contact for further information.

- Detail the who, what, where, when, why and how of your program in a factual rather than promotional manner. The most important information should come first, since copy is edited from the bottom up. Opinions

may be given in quotes and attributed, but avoid descriptive adjectives and never editorialize.

- Include all the important details, e.g., the name of the speaker and the topic.
- Preferably be on one page, ending with a typed ## or -30- (a habit carried over from the days when the telegraph was a major form of communication and -30- was used to indicate the end of a message). If you continue on another page, include all of the reference material again and end the first page with "(more)".
- On the second page or another page you might want to include a brief, single-spaced background paragraph about your group and its major activities.

The press release and your self-description should be mailed in accordance with the established media deadlines. Mailing your material too early is almost as bad as sending it in too late. Should it arrive too far in advance, your release may be forgotten.

TELEPHONE FOLLOWUP

A telephone followup can be made as soon as you think your press release has had time to arrive. Since media people tend to be extremely busy, you must be brief and informative, taking only one to three minutes for your entire presentation.

"I am (your name) from (group) and we sent you a press release about (event). We wanted to be sure it has arrived and we want you to know we can answer any additional questions you may have."

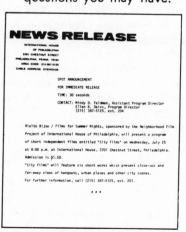

If you have stills from a film, don't include them with the press release, since they will be thrown away most of the time. Do put on the press release, "PHOTO AVAILABLE". You might offer to send over a still during the phone conversation. Try to give the reporter a "hook" or "peg" on which to hang a story. Perhaps you have had some last minute news such as the planned attendance of a celebrity. Your major purpose at this juncture is to provide the reporter with an interest in the event and an orientation around which to build a story. Don't try to convince them of their responsibilities, their duty to cover your event, or tell them their job. Always be factual. If you're asked a question you cannot answer, do not bluff. Say you'll get the needed information and call back, or say "I can't answer that right now." Reporters are professionals and if you treat them fairly, you will get professional treatment in return. If you mislead them even once, you will lose credibility for a long time.

Your relationship with the media is not a one shot affair. The first few times you talk with a reporter, radio station announcer, or an editor, you are laying important groundwork for future contacts. Always get the name, phone number, extension, and address of whomever you talk with. This becomes part of your local press and media file. Don't worry about completing such a media list overnight. In time you will know which contacts are favorable to you and which are a waste of effort. If the person you first talk with is not interested in your event, ask if there is another department or person more appropriate to contact. Your event may come under Entertainment, Community Affairs, Features, or News.

When you do find a good media contact, hopefully they will try to list your organization in the calendar section or bulletin of community events. This is your minimum expectation. You may find someone who will want more information, a photograph from the film, or be interested in doing a feature story about your group or an interview with your guest speaker or filmmaker.

People living in smaller towns or ethnic communities will discover that their weekly newspapers may be happy to receive material about a local group sponsoring cultural events. Whereas the mass media will generally only be able to give you a listing in the community affairs section, the smaller media are more likely to give your group more coverage.

PUBLIC SERVICE ANNOUNCEMENTS

Under current law, radio and television stations are required to donate a specific amount of air time to public service announcements (PSA's). A PSA is usually from 10 to 60 seconds in length. This service is legally available to all non-profit organizations and is often extended to other groups. PSA's on radio and television can have immense drawing power and prime time announcements on Public Broadcasting System stations are not unusual. If the station thinks your event is interesting enough, you might even be asked to appear on a local talk show. They will not do free advertising. They will, however, announce events of interest to the community. This service is often called the Community Bulletin Board.

Like newspapers, broadcast media will have procedures and specifications concerning how your information must be presented to them. To find out the preferred format and schedule, request their guidelines by calling or writing the station's public relations person (sometimes known as Community Affairs).

In some situations you can go to a radio station to assist with the editing or you can submit graphics, slides or tapes to TV stations. If this is possible, and it often is in rural areas or smaller communities, take advantage of the opportunity. When dealing with FM stations, you might ask if you can participate in the preparation of the PSA tape. You might offer to bring in music that is particularly appropriate, for instance, or a person to read your written copy who you feel will be especially appealing to your intended audience. Many stations will be pleased to have your input, since if you come prepared, at a scheduled time, you actually save them effort. The more directly involved you are in the process, the more likely you are to get across your intended message.

Your general aim is to get as many free listings and announcements as you can, but you should be practical and put your greatest energy where it will do you the most good. If you are living in a Polish neighborhood in Chicago, a listing in the **Chicago Tribune** may not be nearly as important to you as a story in a Polish language newspaper or on the Polish radio program. When you do go for the larger media, always ask for the public relations department. Find out what they provide free of charge.

Occasionally you may find that the publicity department will call you back and attempt to sell you a paid advertisement on the basis that it will be more effective for your group. This generally is not true for groups with limited space and modest budgets, but rather than being abrupt, turn the situation to your own needs. You might answer, "No, thanks, but would you brief me on any free services you provide for non-profit educational groups". Such an approach often results in either free services or substantial discounts. If your event requires more elaborate media involvement, consult Chapter 12 on premieres, benefits, and special events for additional suggestions and examples.

PUBLICITY SCHEDULE

This schedule is a guide to an elaborate screening with an extensive publicity campaign. Don't think that because your screening is simpler you can move much faster than this plan indicates and still be effective. Even a simple public screening requires advance planning. You may be doing only some of these tasks, especially those related to publicity. Always find out costs or fees for services, space, equipment, and so on. Throughout the weeks, get continual reports on progress.

Preparation (* Indicates items you may need to budget for.)
- Select and locate film.*
- Evaluate available spaces, select the best one.*
- Consider where you will get projection equipment.*
- Line up outside projectionist if needed.*
- Locate artist (if available) to work on publicity flyers and posters.*
- Make sure your printer will be available when the publicity materials are designed (get time estimate).*
- Form screening committee to coordinate the event, assign responsibilities and establish meeting schedule.
- Make up and evaluate budget, program (speaker, literature, food, child care, etc.) and group's resources.
- Choose date and alternative (check with other groups for possible conflicts, check space for availability).
- Make any changes in plans (budget, location) and then stick to them.

First Week
- Telephone distributor or person who has the film to book it for your date or alternate. Confirm price, finalize financial matters, including advance payment policy. Ask for reviews and graphics you can use in your publicity.
- The same day you phone, send a written confirmation on letterhead to distributor. Confirm date, price, number of showings, where they should send invoices, correspondence, and the film. Film should be shipped to a place where someone is in during normal working hours. Keep a copy.
- Telephone confirmation of space for that date.
- Send a written confirmation of the space reservation, also on letterhead (keep a copy). Make sure you include the day, date, hours you have confirmed, the particular room(s) you will be using, equipment for the room(s) agreed upon (e.g., chairs, table, kitchen

First Week (continued)
facilities, etc.), arrangements for access to the building, agreed upon rental or utilities charge, any other arrangements.

- Phone and confirm in writing arrangements with speakers or special guests, including promised honorarium, travel and housing, dates, topic, etc.*
- Recheck budget against reality.

Second Week

- Decide on flyer details (see p. 43).
- Gather information about the film for your flyer and press releases, including graphics.
- Write copy for flyer.
- Write copy for press release (see p. 54) and have it xeroxed or printed.
- Meet with artist to discuss flyer/poster layout and production schedule as soon as you have material assembled.
- Prepare your mailing list, see if there are other lists you might want to use.
- Prepare your press list, check deadlines.
- Start mailing out press releases (first class) to publications, key persons and other groups which need a lot of lead time.*
- Mail out "save this date" postcards to key organizations and people.*
- Order or purchase tickets (if planning paid admission).*

Third Week
- All materials like flyers, posters and tickets that must be printed should go to printers as early as possible (bulk mail may take up to two weeks to arrive).
- Write or call film distributor if you have not yet received written confirmation for your date.
- Make up an events calendar up until the date of your event. Assign people to cover major events to make announcements, distribute flyers, sell advance tickets.
- Follow up on press contacts with a phone call (a week after mailing the press release). Offer still photographs or additional information.
- Make up a list of key people and groups to contact and assign people to network with them.

Fourth Week
- Mail out flyer to mailing lists.*
- Distribute advance flyers and tickets to group members for distribution and sale.
- Plan and prepare literature and child care.
- Go through checklist of tasks with entire group and confirm responsibilities and tasks.
- Begin to put up posters.

Fifth Week
- Continue publicity. Make sure someone knowledgeable about the event is available to answer phone calls. Start checking monthly publications for media coverage.
- Visit site to check out particulars. If possible, take your projectionist along so you will be appraised of any additional equipment that may be needed. Locate wall plugs, circuit breakers, etc., and do a thorough evaluation for sound (see p. 34).

Sixth Week
- Continue publicity campaign, especially outside posting.
- Get a report on advance ticket sales.
- Determine if anything has been overlooked or if people assigned to a particular task need help.

Seventh Week
- Continue publicity campaign.
- Make sure your friends are coming.
- Check with guest speakers to make sure they know when to arrive and what you expect of them.
- Prepare background for program notes, prepare evaluation forms of the film.*
- Make sure people are prepared for tasks at the screening.
- If appropriate, have your press screening.*

Eighth Week
- Telephone barrage to make sure people are coming.
- Film should arrive. If you don't have it two working days before the screening, call your distributor.
- Preview the film (with discussion facilitator and guest if possible).
- Write and print program notes (after seeing the film if possible). Include background information.*
- Clip newspaper coverage.
- All unsold advance tickets should be turned in the day before the screening.
- Pick up small change for the night of the screening.
- Return the film the day after the screening.*
- Return projection and other equipment.
- Deposit your earnings and pay your bills.

The Week After
- Review budget and evaluate the event.
- Send thank you letters.
- Do any follow-up that is necessary.

References

The Grass Roots Fundraising Handbook: How to Raise Money in Your Community by Joan Flanagan
The Youth Project, 1555 Connecticut Ave. NW, Washington D.C. 20009, 1977.

Contains a section on publicity oriented towards grass roots fundraising and a number of additional bibliographical listings.

We Interrupt This Program: A Citizen's Guide to Using the Media for Social Change by Robbie Gordon
Citizen Involvement Training Project, University of Massachussetts, 138 Hasbrouck, Amherst, MA 01003.

Designed to help groups and individuals get access to the media, design press releases and public service announcements, and make effective contact with the press.

How to Do Leaflets, Newsletters and Newspapers by Nancy Brigham
The New England Free Press, 60 Union Square, Somerville, MA 02134, 1976.

A clear and thorough manual covering production and editorial procedures from start to finish on leaflets, newsletters and newspapers. Provides many examples.

"Film Festival" by Clyde Taylor
Essence, August 1978, p. 55.

Describes scheduling of a Black Film Festival and includes programming and organizing suggestions.

6 | DEVOTION TO DETAIL

Watching a film, people share a common stimulus. While the same film is experienced differently by each individual, each has heard and felt the reactions of others in the audience. This provides a jumping off point for potentially interesting discussions, and it helps people communicate by readily providing shared references and concrete examples.

We have all gone to the movies with friends or run into people we know after a film. A simple "What did you think?" can turn into a short discussion in the theater lobby. Even in an unorganized setting, a provocative, moving or informative film generates spontaneous discussions on the street. For example, groups leafleting audiences after THE CHINA SYNDROME found that this random audience was eager to discuss the issues raised in the film and wanted more information; some people asked questions or were anxious to take leaflets.

Successful film programs result from good planning and presentation. Your goals for the screening and discussion might be met spontaneously, but you are more likely to be successful when you plan for what you want. If you have most of the details well under control, you have a better chance of creating an atmosphere where productive and pleasant things can happen.

For example, a filmmaker spent a weekend screening films and presenting a workshop at the University of Kansas to students, teachers, librarians, filmmakers and community people. Because the groundwork had been done, out of these screenings and discussions came much activity — a mailing list, a Latin American Solidarity Committee, and a committee to coordinate film programs between the university and community. This committee later organized other events, brought in filmmakers, and presented their own day-long training workshop on film use.

This weekend was productive because the organizers were prepared. Different university departments sponsored parts of the program. The organizers had identified constituencies, contacted them early, planned their publicity and outreach, and thus brought interested people together. The mechanical and technical aspects of the programs were under control. With basics down, the organizers could spend their time dealing with their objectives in showing the films rather than with missing equipment or poor projection. They could participate in the stimulating and exciting parts of the programs, enjoy the interactions and connections which developed, and follow up on spontaneous suggestions from the audience.

When you have done the proper planning and preparation, your program can sometimes exceed your expectations, and the enthusiasm generated by word of mouth about a good event can work for you to continue everyone's interest and involvement into the future. When a screening does not go well, the reasons are often obvious. It started late and everyone was already cranky and bored. The film broke, no one could fix it, and half the people left. The guest speaker was uninspiring or defeatist. The event went on for an hour too long and people were tired. On the other hand, when a screening is successful, what seems to a satisfied audience an effortless and smooth operation is really the payoff from hard-headed planning, preparation, and attention to details.

The intent of this chapter and the ones that follow is to call your attention to the many details that can improve your programs. The more experiences you accumulate, the more quickly you will be able to evolve a style that is effective with your constituency. Details about equipment and projection are in Chapter 8.

As we begin to talk about the more humdrum aspects of putting on a film program, you should not think of them simply as ways of avoiding disaster, but as guidelines for successes which you can select and adjust for your particular circumstances. There is no better way to insure that things will go well than logistical planning.

Many film users and theater managers, however, have learned the hard way. Most believe in Murphy's Law — if anything can go wrong, it will.

> The one screening when you don't bring change, all 100 audience members will show up with nothing but $10 bills in their hands.

> The one time you fumble and blush your way through an unprepared introduction, the local paper will have sent someone to cover your event.

> The night you arrive to set up only 15 minutes before the announced starting time, someone will have hung banners from the ceiling which fall between the projector and the screen, the janitor will be away eating dinner, and the ladder will be locked in the basement.

There are things you can't worry about until they occur, and most situations can be pulled out of the fire with patience, lots of time, good humor and a calm demeanor. But, if you want your screening to go well, it is better to be aware and prepared.

ESTABLISH A WORKABLE TIME FRAME

Plan the time for an event the same way you plan an agenda for meetings. Assign a running time for each part and stick to it. The length of the film is a given. Discussions can run from at least 30 minutes up to 90 minutes. Introductions, crowd control, announcements, all can be assigned times. If you want a two hour program, plan accordingly. When considering your options, it is better to plan for a shorter rather than a longer program, since the different parts of the evening might take longer than anticipated. If not, let the audience leave feeling excited and with interest running high, rather than feeling that the evening has dragged on too long.

ASSIGN RESPONSIBILITIES

The screening committee can make this as simple or as complex as the event and the space require. Make sure everyone knows when to arrive, what to bring with them, and what to do.

Set up crew. Depending on the elaborateness and size of your screening, you need volunteers to help set up, carry in tables, equipment, food, literature. One person should help the projectionist unload equipment, get the table for the projector, set up the screen, the speakers, other sound equipment, and tape down cords and wires. Others should set up the chairs, put out garbage cans if you're having food, arrange ticket and literature tables. This group can also make and put up signs outside indicating the entrance, and signs inside for the restrooms, child care, and drinking fountain. If you are having refreshments, this should probably be a separate committee. Some of the set up crew should also help clean up following the screening, since they will know where tables and ladders came from in the building, and who is taking what home with them. Masking tape, paper, marking pens, garbage bags are standard set up items.

Ticket seller. This person should be competent and relaxed since they will set a tone for your guests. The ticket seller should have change, a cash box, a roll of tickets, 3"×5" cards or a tablet for the mailing list, paper and masking tape. They will greet each guest, sell tickets, make change, and remain friendly in the face of repetitive questions. Most of the information about the screening should be known to the ticket seller: whether there are different prices for children, senior citizens, or people with series tickets; where the restrooms are located (signs always help in an unfamiliar building); when the film will start; basic information about your group. They might also encourage people to sign the mailing list or to take literature. If you are charging admission there should be only one, clearly marked entrance, and the ticket table should be right there, so that people will naturally stop, without blocking the door. Put up a sign with the admission price on it. If the organization's mailing list, literature and program notes are also on this table, place them so they can be filled out or picked up after the ticket purchase — this is easiest and keeps the line moving. Rolls of numbered tickets can be purchased at stationery stores, or you may want to print your own and number them by hand or with a numbering stamp. Make sure the ticket seller has all of the unsold advance tickets before the sales begin and that they know how many have been sold and how many seats you have left. Before the first ticket is sold, the ticket seller should always count and write down how much start up cash is in the box for making change. They should write down the number of the first ticket. Whenever you want to know how many people have paid, just subtract the first ticket number sold from the number of the first ticket remaining on the roll. At the end of the program, this will allow you to figure your total paid attendance and exactly how much money you should have collected.

Greeter/Ticket taker. If you expect a real crowd and want to keep the line moving rapidly, or if you want to chat with the audience, you might have someone greet people and take their tickets. This would relieve the ticket seller of all duties except selling tickets. The greeter should also know all information about the screening, have more time to talk with people, and direct people to the literature table and mailing list (in this situation a separate table from the ticket table). They can help people locate seats, and also provide security if you are collecting a lot of money. Even if you are not charging admission you probably need a greeter.

Literature table person. If your group has enough literature to distribute or sell, a person should be at the separate literature table. If you place it so that it doesn't create congestion at the entrance, people are more likely to stop, browse and talk. If you do set up such a table, it could also have the mailing list cards, program notes, or programs which print the agenda, thank people who have helped, describe your group, and provide other pertinent information. It is always wise to have several free things for people to take home with them: a sheet about your group's activities, supplemental information on the subject of the film, etc. Program notes and other handouts can also help set the audience up for a good discussion. The person at the literature table should consider this an outreach job, and expect to be friendly and able to talk to people about the literature, the group, and the film.

START YOUR PROGRAM CLOSE TO THE ANNOUNCED TIME

You should be set up and ready for the program 30 to 15 minutes before the announced starting time. One advantage of giving yourself enough time is that members of your group can then relax, welcome the audience, chat with guests (especially newcomers), answer questions, introduce people to each other, ask how they heard about the screening or what convinced them to attend, and enjoy the sociability which a film gathering offers. When you were organizing this event, you may have spoken on the phone to groups and individuals about their calendars, newsletters, or invited them to participate. If you convinced any of these people to come, this is a great time to introduce yourself, to put a face on that telephone voice, and to thank them for their help. On the negative side, if you are not ready in advance, people who have arrived on schedule will not be entertained by watching you test equipment, set up chairs, and do other things you could and should have done before.

Unless there has been unusually bad weather, start your program no more than five minutes past the time announced in your advertising. If some delay becomes unavoidable, you should explain why to those who have arrived on time. Any audience will include people who have arranged for babysitters, younger people who may have a parental curfew, and persons who have to be up early to go to work. Don't inconvenience those who have come on time in order to accommodate hypothetical latecomers. You can set a precedent for starting your film programs on time which will be carried over to your other events and meetings.

THE SPOKESPERSON

Depending on whether you are having a membership event or one aimed at a wider public, you will want someone to more or less be the formal voice for your group. This person can greet people at the entrance, make the before-the-film announcements, urge people to take their seats, and make the explanation for a delayed start. These are important responsibilities and everyone should be clear about who is going to do them. It can help greatly to avoid confusion, especially if yours is a public event. The main responsibility of this person is to start the program. Before they stand up in the front of the room, however, they should check the ticket line, make sure the projectionist is ready, and have someone ready to turn off the lights and shut the doors. If something should go wrong during the actual projection of the film, this person, now a familiar voice, should be the one to announce what the trouble is and how long it will take to fix it. They may also be the facilitator for the after film discussion (see chapter 7).

INTRODUCING THE PROGRAM

Introducing a program always involves some housekeeping announcements which should be kept brief. Assuming that yours is a public rather than an intragroup event, the spokesperson should start with a self-introduction as a representative of the sponsoring organization, welcome the audience, and thank them for coming. A few sentences describing the organization are sufficient. People with questions who want additional information will generally sign up for the mailing list, or approach the spokesperson or another member of the sponsoring group. Very long statements may make people feel that you look on them as a captive audience to be talked at, not with. Be sure to present the program's entire agenda so everyone knows what is planned, and identify the discussion facilitator and any resource people. You can tell the audience what arrangements have been made for reel changes,* intermissions, refreshments, your policy on smoking, where your mailing list is, and how you intend to handle your post-film discussion. You may also ask people to sit closer to the screen or to vacate a back or side row so that latecomers will interfere as little as possible with the program.

If you have announcements concerning the activities of other groups, your spokesperson, rather than representatives of those groups, should make them, since you want to maintain the tone and time limits you have set for yourselves. For the introduction to the program, the film, and even for the after film discussion, you will find that written notes on 3"×5" cards are helpful. They are easily held in one hand, guarantee you will not forget to mention something important, and often the simple exercise of writing down the main points assures that your thoughts are organized and your talk will be relaxed and brief. Speak loudly and establish eye contact with your audience.

INTRODUCING THE FILM

An introduction to the film itself is always appropriate, and is logically made by someone who has seen the film or read about it, and who has given some thought to how it relates to the program's focus. A brief introduction can easily be built around why your group chose to show this film at this time, and what is special or

---

* If you have two projectors or a one reel film, the program should run without interruption. If you have one projector and more than one film or a film with more than one reel, you should tell the audience there will be a short pause for reel changes. The light from the projector, a flashlight, or a tensor lamp is the least disruptive to the audience during reel changes and should be sufficient for the projectionist to work by.

particularly interesting about it. Whether or not you are having a discussion, the spokesperson might want to raise issues for the audience to think about while viewing the film. If there are any technical difficulties with the film, they should be commented on now or much time could be wasted on the subject during the discussion period. You may want to identify an individual who appears in an anonymous interview sequence. Such comments should be factual rather than interpretive.

The introduction should not tell what the film is about or how it ends, but should establish a context for viewing the film and could refer to information on the program notes. It might be helpful in understanding some techniques used in a specific film to know that it was made under difficult circumstances, during a war or under a dictatorship. The year the film was made or the identity of the filmmakers may also be significant information. Occasionally you will be showing a film you don't agree with and you must explain why you are doing so. It may be that the film praises an organization or a political figure you do not approve of but still contains important information. Or you may have purposely selected a film that takes a position contrary to one held by your group just to see what others are thinking and saying.

If you have invited a guest resource person or the filmmaker to the screening, they may have interesting background or contextual information to present. Regardless of who makes them, any introductory remarks should be kept brief. Before formally opening a program with an introduction, make sure:

- The projectionist is ready to start and the spokesperson has the projectionist's attention.
- Someone is by the light switch and is prepared to turn it off as soon as the pre-screening presentations are completed.
- Everyone is seated or is moving toward their seats.

THE HOUSE MANAGER

One member of your group should have the role of house manager, and this role should be separate from that of spokesperson. If you are acting as house manager you must realize that you are not in the room to enjoy the show but to make sure that everyone else does. Instead of sitting with your friends, you should find a spot in the back where you have the best possible view of the audience and the screen and can move around without disturbing others. In fact, you may find that you don't sit down at all. One thing to keep in mind is that the projectionist may not be able to hear the sound the way the audience does. You will want to check it yourself when the film starts by standing in different parts of the room. Let the projectionist know if any adjustments are necessary.

You may also need to cope with:

- Checking the focus and framing of the picture.
- Helping latecomers find a seat (if you are in a large hall you should probably carry a flashlight).
- Adjusting the heat or ventilation.
- Directing people to restrooms.
- Asking someone to put out a cigarette (this should not be left to your guests to quarrel over).
- Dealing with unruly children or other distractions.
- Getting the guest speaker in time for the discussion if they have not been watching the film.
- Being a liaison between the spokesperson and the projectionist in case of a technical problem, and helping the projectionist if necessary.

WHAT TO DO IF THE FILM BREAKS

Should the film break or some other accident occur during the screening, it is the projectionist's job to figure out what is wrong and how to fix it. The house manager should find out what happened, how long it will be before you can proceed, and clearly and immediately inform the audience. Since you have established a relationship with the audience through the introduction, a statement about the situation will be readily accepted. Tell your guests how long the delay will be. If it is more than 30 seconds or so, the house lights should be brought up to half (if possible), since the audience will rapidly become uncomfortable in the dark. If the delay will be under five minutes, you should ask people to remain seated. If there is a major problem which will take longer to fix, call for a 15 minute intermission, invite them to stretch, browse at the literature table, sign the mailing list, or have some refreshments.

People will accept accidents if you let them know what is happening, that you are working on the problem, and how long the delay will be. However, you don't have to go into the gory details — they don't need to know that an entire reel of film unwound around a stool, that the projectionist is bicycling the mile home to get another exciter lamp, or that some bozo put two pieces of film together with a staple. Make sure the projectionist has light and someone to help out, and try to keep audience members away from the machine so the projectionist can concentrate.

SUMMARY OF TASKS AND RESPONSIBILITIES

Below are two lists of what to do before and during the screening. Of course, more people will be needed to put on a program for 500 paying audience members in a large auditorium than to show a film to ten in your living room. Two keys to running a program smoothly are to give yourself enough set-up time to handle any unexpected problems before the audience arrives, and make sure everyone is clear about their responsibilities.

Tasks	People Responsible
• Set up chairs, tables, podium	• Set up crew, helpers, everyone
• Set up ticket table (cash box with change, tickets, mailing list cards, program notes), sell tickets, answer questions	• Ticket seller, ticket taker/greeter, house manager
• Set up projection table, projector, speakers (equipment, extension cord, plugs, masking tape, film, take up reels)	• Projectionist and helpers
• Test sound and focus	• Projectionist and house manager
• Set up literature table	• Literature table person
• Provide information and directions	• Ticket seller, greeter, house manager, helpers
• Introduce program and film	• Spokesperson
• Turn off lights, close doors	• Helpers
• Troubleshoot during film (audience and projection)	• House manager
• Announce delays or problems	• Spokesperson
• Run projector, handle technical problems	• Projectionist
• Bring, set up and serve refreshments	• Refreshment committee
• Child care	• Child care committee
• Introduce and facilitate discussion	• Facilitator
• Clean up	• Everyone
• Return film, equipment, deposit money	• Appropriate organizing committee members

presents
FAMILY PROTRAIT SITTINGS (1975)

Visiting Filmmaker
Alfred Guzzetti
Tuesday, October 17, 8 pm

Museum of Art Theatre   Carnegie Institute   Admission $1.00   Film Section   622-3212

7 | DISCUSSION FORMATS AND FACILITATION

A discussion can distinguish a good film program put on by a group from the usual experience of watching commercial movies or television. Choices for this part of the program are: 1) a specific focus, 2) a facilitator and the appropriate resource people, and 3) a method and format which will best involve your audience.

A discussion can relate to the film in a variety of ways: it can focus on making cross-cultural points; move from an international point to a local one; from anecdotal material to principles; or from a general theme to a specific one. In one case, a lively small group discussion at a community education center followed DAGUERREO-TYPES, by Agnes Varda. DAGUERREOTYPES is about the filmmaker's own neighborhood on the rue Daguerre in Paris and the people who live there. The neighborhood where the film was shown had been the subject of much media attention. The film got people talking about their neighborhood and comparing it to Paris in terms of social stratification, how it would be represented in a film, and what they really liked about the place where they lived. The film stimulated a discussion about ways of seeing the community, reinforced their appreciation of it, and allowed those perceptions to be shared. The film selection, the screening location, program notes and the fact that the facilitator had previewed the film, all contributed to this result.

The exchange of views in a good discussion following a film is an active, participatory process and provides opportunities for information sharing, education, and growth. Discussions can develop and build on ideas raised in the film and serve to round out the program.

Goals for Discussions

- Answer questions.
- Provide supplemental information.
- Clarify aspects of the subject which might not have been understood.
- Focus attention on an issue.
- Allow people to share their ideas in an active way.
- Explore the relationship between the issues in the film and personal experience.
- Plan for the future.

In our examples, the discussion session in Kansas directly resulted in organizing activity. The neighborhood discussion following DAGUERREOTYPES left people with new perceptions about each other and the place where they live.

DISCUSSION FORMATS

Exactly how you organize your discussion depends on the size of the audience and space, your intention, and your preferred style. The amount of participation possible for the audience will be determined by your format choices.

No matter what the size and formality of the discussion, designating someone as a facilitator will help the discussion go forward, clarify points of view and help find a point of closure. The facilitator is there to make everyone present feel free to be active rather than passive participants, and to provide a structure in which this is possible. The facilitator may be the same individual who announced the program and film, or who greeted people as they arrived.

Several formats are basic options for after-film discussions. In each case seating arrangements are very important to the interaction. People can easily rearrange their chairs if you inform them clearly in advance.

Small group with a facilitator. Up to 50 people can have a fairly intimate discussion in this format. Some but not all of the people in the group will be able to talk. Here the facilitator simply tries to involve everyone present. Moving the chairs into a circle or semi-circle allows people to talk with each other rather than **at** the front of the room. If you can't move the chairs so that most people can see everyone else, your discussion will require a more formal style in order for everyone to hear and follow easily, and the facilitator's role will be more prominent. Questions may have to be repeated for the entire audience. Participants may need to raise their hand, be called on, and stand to make their comments.

Small group with a facilitator and resource person. The facilitator and resource person join the others in the circle, face them in the semicircle or stand in front of the audience. If the resource person has been properly prepared, the facilitator may have little to do besides introduce them, watch the tone of the discussion and the time, and help sum up and close the discussion. Again, the degree of formality will depend on the seating arrangement. If the chairs cannot be rearranged from their face front position, the resource person and facilitator will have to stand in front, or sit on a table or platform so that everyone can see. If they sit at a table in front of the audience, they are obviously set apart from it.

A facilitator and a panel of resource people. If you set up a panel to comment on the film and the issues it raises, you might seat all panel members at a table in the front of the room with the facilitator, who would introduce each guest, establish the ground rules for time, and help channel the questions. The panel members might present different points of view and respond to questions. Allowing each panelist to give a short statement first, to present their perspective, will help the audience to frame and direct their questions. A panel is often a good way to deal with an issue that is controversial, especially complicated, or that relates to a variety of constituencies. The more commentators, the trickier the dynamics, but even four people can be effective in this format. They may present different but not necessarily contradictory aspects of the question.

A structured debate. If a debate strategy seems more logical, the audience format can simply be maintained. Guests should be given an equal amount of time to speak on each side of the question and the facilitator must be certain there is ample time for both sides to respond to whatever questions come from the audience. Fewer people in the audience participate when you have a formal debate.

Small groups (5-15 people). If you have a large audience, but want to have intimate discussion and allow the most participation, you can break the audience down into a number of small groups. The audience could initially meet as a whole for a presentation, with questions directed to the resource person, and then break down into small groups to develop action plans or discuss the film and presentation more fully. Resource people could be divided up among the small groups, or the groups could decide questions to ask when they reconvene. If you wish to have everyone hear all of the ideas discussed in the small groups, each group can decide upon a spokesperson who will report back to the entire audience. The groups may simply cluster in a large room, or meet in separate rooms.

Whatever format you choose, think about it ahead of time. If you anticipate a large crowd or have an immense hall to deal with, you will probably need a microphone and sound system for the facilitator and resource person. If you want the audience to be able to respond and ask questions, you will have to consider microphones for the audience as well (either set them up in an aisle or at the front and let people line up, or have someone carry the mic to where people are sitting).

You do want to get people into the discussion quickly, so if someone suggests a small break after the film, remember that these breaks are usually not a good idea. They can stretch out and destroy momentum. Obviously there will be some shifting, stretching, and chatting when the film ends, but a facilitator who gives clear instructions will have few problems. Avoid rewinding the film when you are getting a discussion started, because the noise of the projector is distracting. Unless the projectionist is in an enclosed booth, the projector will have to be taken elsewhere or the rewinding of the film must wait until after the discussion.

THE ROLE OF THE FACILITATOR

The facilitator is not a speaker or resource person, but rather a member of the group who is responsible for seeing that the discussion deals with the needs of the specific audience and the focus of the program. They help the group clarify the various points of view presented. Since a certain amount of background information will be helpful to the facilitator, they may want to preview the film before the public screening. Using an index card on which they've written down any thoughts or questions raised by the film is always a good idea. They should also watch the film with the audience. By noting any specific reactions, the facilitator will be able to pick up important cues for the discussion.

Being a good facilitator and, in fact, being a good participant at any level in a discussion, is a skill that will develop with experience. There are surprises in every discussion and no matter how prepared you are, there are potential problems that inevitably crop up. However, running a discussion is not like a ten-yard dash. If you get off to a bad start, you still have plenty of time to recover. Here are some of the common things encountered by every facilitator and some suggestions for dealing with them.

STARTING THE DISCUSSION

When the film is over and as the lights are being turned on, the facilitator and any resource people should go up to the front of the room. Announce any furniture moving plans immediately, and get the seating rearranged before going over the agenda for the discussion, introducing the guest, or trying to talk about anything meaningful.

When a group is small or members know each other well, the facilitator does not always have to initiate the discussion, someone from the audience will just start. In a larger group, the best discussion starts come when the lead-off question is shaped by the overall focus of the meeting. If the facilitator poses the first question either to the group or to the resource person, the question should not be phrased to suggest that there is a right or a wrong answer.

Instead of saying something vague like, "Any questions?" or "What did you think?" or something sarcastic like "Now, don't everyone speak up at once," the facilitator should be specific: "Do you see any similarities between our neighborhood and Paris that you'd like to talk about?" "Are there any questions about women coal miners that you would like to ask the filmmakers?" "Why do you think Hamlet had so much trouble figuring out what to do?" Usually someone will take the bait of a well put question and you'll be off and running.

If the group is large and there is a resource person, the facilitator might do well to break the ice. An audience was very quiet after seeing IT'S NOT A ONE PERSON THING, a film about the work of the Federation of Southern Cooperatives. The facilitator quite honestly asked the filmmaker if the Federation was as unknown to most people as it had been to her before seeing the film and, if so, why. The filmmaker provided an historical analysis of the Federation as an extension of the Civil Rights movement. The activities of cooperatives were less attractive to television crews than demonstrations, and this lack of coverage was one of the reasons they had made the film. One simple question served to open up a lively discussion and the audience, it turned out, had a lot of questions about the Federation, its work, that region of the country, and the viability of economic self-determination projects.

Being prepared to ask the first question is one way around everyone's first fear about discussions: what if no one says anything? There are reasons for a silent audience. Maybe people are still deeply involved in their own thinking about the film — it may have been a very powerful experience and they need a moment to collect their thoughts. You might ease into a discussion by asking something concrete like "What was the most important point to you in the film we just saw?" Silence by some people might also indicate a lack of factual knowledge about the subject. In that case, you might pose a question that asks for an expression of opinion or feeling. Or you could ask a resource person who is present to provide additional information or an explanation of some fact or complicated idea in the film. If bewilderment and ignorance seemingly overwhelms the group, they could try to determine what they need to know if they are interested in pursuing the subject. If you are really afraid of silence, it might be helpful to have people ready to respond or ask a question in the event acute shyness suddenly engulfs everyone else in the room.

If you are facilitating a small group discussion, a good warmup is to go around the circle and ask everyone to introduce themselves. You might ask them to, in a few sentences, express what they liked about the film, what they hope to learn from the discussion, or what their experience has been with the subject. If the discussion is a workshop, you can ask them to state what is most problematic to them, then the group can use the discussion as a problem-solving session.

MOVING THE DISCUSSION ALONG

The facilitator can encourage maximum involvement by urging that comments be directed towards the audience, and asking for responses to comments made by members of the group. Listen to what the audience is saying and respond to where the discussion wants to go. The most effective facilitator helps the discussion group think for itself. People will bring a wide variety of experiences and opinions to any discussion and you want to make that element work for you. Everyone in the room should feel free to express themselves. The facilitator should emphasize that various ideas and points of view are being exchanged, so no one must ever be made to feel "wrong" for having an opinion which does not receive support from the group.

The facilitator's neutrality is central to the success of the program. Avoid words that have emotional or subjective connotations. Do not dominate the group, feel you have to respond to each comment, or favor particular factions within the audience when calling upon people to speak. If many people try to talk at once, identify them in order so they all know they will have a chance to express their views. If things get heated, you might say that you will not call on anyone twice until everyone who wishes has had a chance to speak at least once. You can also set a maximum time limit for any one person to have the floor. These are techniques for dealing with excited discussions when people start interrupting each other, or get into cross conversations which make general discussion difficult. Your job is to maintain orderly procedures so that everyone can continue to participate, and you should do this whether you personally agree or disagree with what is being said.

If you have a large group, set the ground rules at the beginning. In a large hall you might have to repeat questions from the floor for the entire group to be able to hear them. Paying attention to the expressions of people in your audience, particularly those who are quiet but seem interested, may help you identify people who would be stimulated to participate if you make eye contact with them and ask a specific direct question. Don't call on anyone who hasn't shown a desire to speak. Instead, you might make a general comment about the responses so far, and ask for agreement or questions from others about the points raised.

If the discussion falls silent, it may be because people are confused. Perhaps the discussion is moving too rapidly or is jumping around and some people are lost. You can help by quickly reviewing or summarizing the points so far. This should pull the group back together and allow the discussion to move on. People might just need a few moments to reflect. You could pause briefly and restate the last point.

After a time, you may see that without realizing it, people have agreed upon some point or clearly disagree with certain ideas. Point this out to them so you can move the discussion on to new issues. You may also note when people are repeating similar ideas. Summarize the points which have been developed, ask if anyone has anything new or different to contribute, and then go on to a different topic.

Occasionally, someone will use language that is not understood by everyone, be it excessive slang or professorial polysyllabics. Feel free to rephrase as long as what you say is an accurate reflection of the person's intent and not subtle editorializing on your part. If people have spoken in a confusing manner, the facilitator might ask them to rephrase their question, or rephrase it by asking, "I'm not sure I understood what you're getting at. Are you saying thus and so?" Many times you will discover that unclear questions result when someone wants to make a statement but feels compelled to put it into the form of a question. Another way to clear up meandering questions is to ask people for an example of what they mean.

The person who tries to monopolize the discussion or make lengthy observations or comments is another problem. Since the facilitator has stated some ground rules at the beginning of the discussion, they can now be invoked in response to any excesses. If someone persists, you may need to break in on a lengthy comment. Split second timing is important to do this effectively. Briefly summarize the statement and encourage someone else in the audience to respond to that point or express another opinion or idea in order to keep the discussion moving.

SIDETRACKS

Your group's goals, the general interests of the audience, and common sense will determine what is or is not relevant for any specific discussion. Totally irrelevant questions and comments will usually receive a polite silence or nominal response from the other participants. Some typical red herrings and how to identify them are below.

"Why didn't they or they should have done this or that." While this kind of statement is sometimes an honest attempt to analyze the film's position on an issue, it is not the most effective approach.

More often, it is a frustrating and futile although unconscious exercise on the part of the perpetrator, who really wants to talk about the film he or she would have made. It can also be a way of avoiding or dismissing the ideas actually raised by the film. You can deal with this by reminding your audience that no film is meant to be an encyclopedia or the last word on a subject, that filmmakers have to set a focus and time limit for every film, and return the discussion to what was in the film or an exploration of the subject at hand. The discussion, however, is not limited by what was or was not in the film — you can and will talk about the real world.

"Why did they show that horrible scene of this or that?" In a similar state of confusion between films and reality, you will sometimes find people who are upset about seeing something they didn't like in the film and who want to blame the filmmaker for their discomfort. The film may show conditions, events or situations which are indeed upsetting. The filmmaker's exact intention may be to show us that reality in a very direct way. By pointing this out, you may help people to identify exactly what it is they are upset about — the film or the view of reality it shows them. This is a different situation than when the filmmaker, as in the case of exploitation movies, has deliberately **created** a shocking, violent, or upsetting scene simply to manipulate or thrill the audience. It is at moments like these that you'll be glad you previewed the film and are prepared for any possible discomfort.

A variation on this kind of confusion can come when people don't watch a film carefully and critically. In a discussion following the film CAMPAMENTO, a person kept interpreting what they had seen as terribly and unnecessarily violent, when in fact the film is a series of interviews and documents of daily life in a Chilean community. Through discussion it became clear that the interpretation was based on an emotional response to the color red which appeared in banners and posters rather than any actual violent scenes. The opportunity to hear the reactions of others in the group who asked specific questions, and shared their ideas, helped identify the source of the person's feelings and correct a highly subjective response.

"What this film shows is all wrong." Sometimes people want to argue about what is essentially factual information, instead of exchanging ideas. If this goes on for too long, end the frustration and polarization either by going on to another topic or by making a list of the facts in dispute. People can check them on their own or you can organize a committee to report back at a later meeting.

"Everyone who thinks this or that is wrong." A similar polarized situation involves two people who dominate the discussion with their dialogue over irreconcilable positions. The facilitator could summarize each side objectively, point out that further dispute on this particular point is counterproductive, and suggest that people should move on to a new topic. If the two differing points of view are indeed the root of the overall discussion, asking the rest of the audience to speak to one side or another of the issue in a more organized way allows for participation by a greater number of people. In any controversy, the facilitator's objective is to defuse rather than feed inflamed feelings. Naturally, any personal attacks are inappropriate, and the discussion should be one of issues rather than personalities.

Another kind of disruption in any discussion are people who arrive or return after the discussion has started. The facilitator or another audience member will want to give them a brief description of the subject under consideration. A sentence or two should be enough to bring the person into the group.

Occasionally, no matter what you do, the audience seems listless or becomes overly dependent on the facilitator. This may occur if you have not allowed enough free interplay. You might back off from being in a position of control and ask people to respond to each other's comments.

ADDITIONAL SUGGESTIONS FOR FACILITATORS
- Clarify as much as possible any conflicting points of view.
- Help to distinguish between fact and opinion.
- Avoid asking questions that have obviously "right" or "wrong" answers.
- Point out situations where participants are in agreement without realizing it.
- Try to be aware of audience members who have something to contribute, but may be too timid to speak up without encouragement.
- Don't allow discussion to focus so long in any one area that other important aspects are ignored.
- Don't try to plan a discussion too closely, everyone will get frustrated.
- Tune into the group and be responsive to the concerns of your specific audience.

CLOSURE

The majority of discussions will stay strong right up to their natural end. Other times, the facilitator will notice that people are getting quiet, looking at their watches and nudging each other to leave. Whether or not it is the projected time for the end, before this stage has been reached, the discussion will have begun to flag. Either the group has become fatigued or the discussion has covered all the essential points to the participants' satisfaction. It is time then to close, no matter what the clock says. You should never place people in the position where they are embarrassed to admit they are tired and wish to go home.

A formal closing is the logical completion of your program. You should anticipate the closing by a statement like, "One more comment then we will wrap it up." The closing should be done as briefly as possible. If your goal has been to debate, educate, or raise consciousness, you will want to touch on the major points which have emerged. To do this sensitive task, the facilitator must stick to the facts and not evaluate or offer subjective interpretations. If you have agreed on some action, summarize the specifics and implementation plans. If there has been agreement to sign or circulate petitions, set up committees, sign mailing lists, or any other important details, responsibilities should have been clarified at the time of agreement. Simply remind people of them in the closure. If a resolution has been passed, read it. If there are issues or points which the group wants to develop further, identify those people who will carry out this research. If there is another meeting, announce the date, time and place.

As a representative of your group, formally express your interest in hearing opinions and evaluations about the film and the program as a whole, and ask for suggestions for future events. You should be sure to thank any resource people and the audience for attending and sharing their ideas.

Very often the filmmaker or distributor has provided an evaluation sheet regarding the film. You should have passed it out at the beginning of the discussion, asking people to fill it out afterwards, and collect it as people are leaving. Not only will it be useful to the filmmaker or distributor, but it will also help your group in determining what issues were of primary concern to members of your audience, and help you evaluate the success of your own program, both in terms of your film choice and in meeting your goals. You may want to develop a program evaluation form for your own organization. You might indicate other people in the group who could be contacted later with additional feedback.

It is not unusual, if things have gone well, to close on a high level of excitement and energy. Although any number of people may want to leave, others may prefer to stay a bit longer and carry on the discussion in a more informal or social manner. Many groups offer their refreshments after the formal program has ended. This allows people to chat with each other and with special guests, as well as creating an informal atmosphere for people to comment about the program and give suggestions for future events. If you decide upon this kind of format, announce it in your introduction and closure. Naturally, you will have taken care that the area is available for this socializing and that your refreshments committee has everything arranged.

RESOURCE PEOPLE

While a well-prepared facilitator and interested audience will usually have a productive and interesting discussion session, there are instances when the incorporation of one or more resource people will be appropriate. They may be members of your group who have relevant information about the subject of the film. They could include local, regional or nationally known people who have expertise on the subject. Informed speakers are available from unions, churches, government institutions, museums, libraries, universities, and from other community groups. Sometimes the filmmaker will be a good resource person for your program. There are several specific ways in which a guest can contribute to your film program.

SUPPLEMENT

No matter how excellent the film, you may want a resource person to provide additional information, or perhaps an update on some events. Other information might be necessary if the film is on a general topic or about a situation parallel to yours and you need someone to provide a frame of reference. Thus a film on credit unions may deal with the subject in general or show a group in Minnesota setting one up in their town, but if you live in Texas, you may want a local attorney or banker to advise you.

VALIDATE

An outside expert can provide credibility for your group's claim that a particular issue or activity is worthy of public attention. If you hope to gain media attention or the respect of professionals in the field, you may want to bring in an outside validator. Having an expert or celebrity associated with your group or event may help in getting press coverage and in bringing people out to the event. Local standards vary as to who is a celebrity.

A person who helps convince your group of the benefits of a project or the group's ability to carry it out is another kind of expert. This resource person can be someone from your own community with whom your audience can identify. They help people imagine themselves doing what the film shows or advocates. If your group has seen a film about retired people taking courses in college, an octogenarian who has just earned a degree may be a far better choice as speaker than a national educational authority or the president of the local community college. The senior graduate can individualize that experience, discuss different procedures involved, and will know firsthand the fears and capabilities of your audience.

LINK UP

No matter how effective your group is, there are always times when you feel isolated, overwhelmed by day-to-day details, and skeptical that anyone else shares your concerns. Perhaps you are the only group in town trying to provide quality children's film programs, or your food cooperative is considering joining other regional groups to find ways to coordinate their efforts. Some programs cry out for speakers who can provide a general overview and link up what you are doing with other efforts. This linkage can provide your group with a renewed sense of importance, help you evaluate the next step and help clarify the impact of what you are doing. The apparently small measures being taken locally now become part of a much larger construct.

ADVOCATE

An advocate is someone who argues for a specific course of action or a certain perspective on an issue — a ballet teacher trying to persuade the PTA to fund an after school dance class, a politician explaining their position on a particular piece of legislation, or a neighbor who wants a stop sign installed at an intersection. They may be invited to speak following a film which is simply informational or which opposes or supports their own viewpoint. The sponsors may not have made up their collective mind yet, or they may agree or disagree with the speaker. Any number of combinations may produce a good discussion. If your group is undecided, a straight pro and con debate with two resource people may be useful. You can have one lively program with both advocates present, but more information may come out if the advocates are invited on separate evenings when they can concentrate on the issues instead of scoring debating points. If your group already has a position, you may want to invite an advocate who can motivate some activity, or who has the kind of reputation that will help attract new people to your group.

THE FILMMAKER

The filmmaker is a potential resource person who can fill many of the above functions. There is no other individual who knows as much about the film or its particular content. Independent filmmakers generally make films about issues or personalities that are very important to them, that they care passionately about, and that they think should matter to other people. They accumulate much more information than can be put into any one film in the months or years they have spent researching and producing it. Your audience may also appreciate anecdotes they have to tell about the making of the film and its reception in other places.

Especially if you are presenting a premiere or a benefit screening, having the filmmaker present will help with your publicity. Filmmakers do have exploitable glamor value which can work for you in getting press coverage and radio interviews, and people will be thrilled to meet one. Certainly you should feature their participation in your publicity. Another effect of having a filmmaker as a resource person is the demystification of the filmmaking process.

In a discussion, a predictable minority in the audience may want to turn the screening into a celebration of the life of the artist, but most will be interested in an in-depth discussion of the particular film just viewed. The facilitator can keep the discussion directed at the film's subject matter rather than the personality of the filmmaker. Some people concerned with film as an art form or film production will want to know about theory, technical problems, production details, and funding. The better you prepare the filmmaker regarding your audience and your goals for the program, the easier it will be to keep the discussion relevant and focused. Neither you nor the filmmaker want to have a long discussion about the techniques of tracking shots if you are showing a film to alert a community to the dangers of asbestos in the workplace or in public schools.

The fact that more and more independent filmmakers are distributing their films, individually, in cooperatives, or small companies, has increased their accessibility. When a new film is released, filmmakers will often travel with it to provide additional publicity, to have direct contact with film users, and to get valuable feedback from diverse audiences.

The best way to contact a filmmaker is through the distributor of their film. You will discover that many independents self-distribute or have a close relationship with their distributor. They will often agree to appear if they live in the immediate vicinity or are travelling in your area. Filmmakers earn part of their living through personal appearances, and you should pay them an honorarium. Travel time and the film program can easily take three days from their work schedule. If you are not able to pay an honorarium, you may be able to arrange for more than one appearance in your area. One big college or three small community fees can make it worthwhile. Likewise, if you see that someone is sponsoring the appearance of a filmmaker you admire, you may try to get them to spend some time with you as well.

Several resources make it easier to have a filmmaker as your guest. The Film and Video Makers Travel Sheet is published monthly "to encourage and facilitate wider use of exhibition and lecture tours by film and video makers." It lists the film or video maker, speaking dates, locations, films or tapes and an address. This is one way to find out if a particular filmmaker will be in your area in the next few months. Another section contains brief listings of new films and video works.*

Another valuable resource for groups interested in sponsoring film showings are the regional organizations which coordinate touring programs. Such organizations offer financial and technical support to other non-profits. For example, non-profit groups can apply to the Film Bureau coordinated by Young Filmmakers/Video Arts in New York for financial assistance for film rental and speakers fees.** Priority is given to groups showing works by independent filmmakers. The Western States Arts Association has toured innovative feature films to cities with local sponsors. The wide variety of programs offered to a ten state area by the Visual Arts Program of the Southern Arts Federation are received by a broad base of sponsors.*** Most similar programs receive regional or national support and can be located through arts information agencies.

SUMMARY

The resource person needs to be chosen with the same care you put into selecting your film. You need someone whose information and approach to the subject will be appropriate to your group's program and who can relate to your anticipated audience. If possible, talk with someone you respect who has seen the person you are considering with an audience. Being told that someone is a "good" speaker is not sufficient. Ask what kind of audience, what place and what topic the speaker was "good" at. Someone may be terrific in a classroom setting and totally uninspiring in a community center.

WORKING WITH THE RESOURCE PERSON

Once you have made a selection, contact your prospective guest to see if they are interested. Explain what your organization has in mind, and the size and composition of the anticipated audience. The resource person should be briefed on your goals, format and time limits. Describe your group, community, city, other activities

---

* Film and Video Makers Travel Sheet, Film Section — Museum of Art, Carnegie Institute, 4400 Forbes Avenue, Pittsburgh, PA 15213. Also publishes the **Film and Videomakers Directory.**

** Young Filmmakers/Video Arts, 4 Rivington Street, New York, NY 10002.

*** Visual Arts Program, Southern Arts Federation, Suite 712, 225 Peachtree Street NE, Atlanta, GA 30303.

related to the topic, other films in the series or other presentations. Describe the level of knowledge your audience brings to the screening, and explain as precisely as you can why you are inviting your guest to participate. This will help both of you decide how the presentation can be accommodated to your program. Explain your focus carefully, but keep in mind that this doesn't mean you want to rig the conclusion your audience will reach. Focus means that if you want to zero in on the hiring policies of local companies, you do not want a speech about 400 years of American racism. The discussion you have with your guest is important in guaranteeing that they will be a good resource and can provide appropriate information. Some resource people and a lot of filmmakers are very actively involved in networking with other groups interested in the issues presented in a film. Perhaps they have been involved in similar programs elsewhere and have experiences and suggestions to share with your group.

If you are bringing a guest in from out of town, you may find they are planning a national or regional tour, and your invitation will fit nicely into those plans. Whether or not you offer to pay a fee, you should pay for expenses like food, travel, and lodging. If the guest is using public transportation, you should provide transportation to and from the train depot or airport. Once the invitation has been accepted, find out if they need the privacy of a hotel or are willing to stay at someone's house.

An important consideration for both of you is to find out if there are any specific people who should be invited to the screening— for example, personal friends, professionals in the field, or media representatives. As you make your usual publicity contacts, try to arrange an interview on a local talk show or encourage the newspaper to cover the screening as a news story rather than as a listing in the public events section. If your resource person is the filmmaker, they will be interested in giving the film the widest possible exposure. This is an instance where what is a good boost for your group is also going to be good publicity for them. Most people who make films want public feedback and enjoy discussing their film with diverse audiences. Many other invited guests will be equally concerned with gaining attention for the topic of your program.

Finally, there is the matter of etiquette. Be sure to inform your guest in advance what arrangements you have made for transportation, sleeping, eating, payment, publicity, and the like. Ask if there is something special they need. Some may want to chat and others may want a quiet place to relax before the screening. Don't insist on unnecessary or unannounced public appearances. In short, show them the kind of courtesy you would expect.

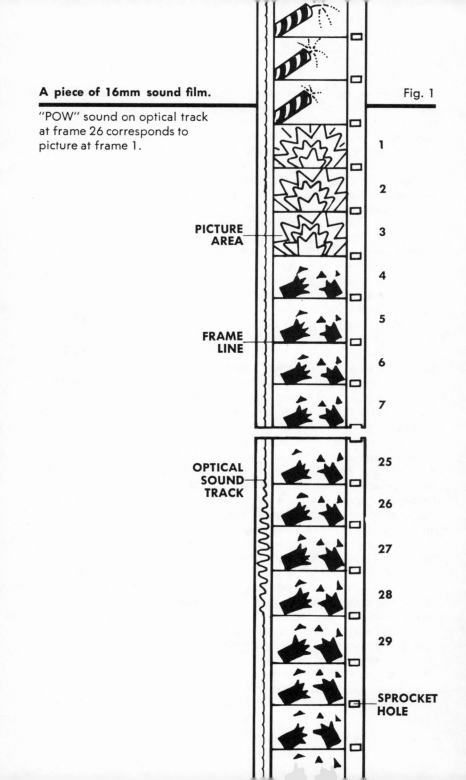

A piece of 16mm sound film.

"POW" sound on optical track at frame 26 corresponds to picture at frame 1.

Fig. 1

PICTURE AREA

FRAME LINE

1
2
3
4
5
6
7

OPTICAL SOUND TRACK

25
26
27
28
29

SPROCKET HOLE

8 | ON PROJECTION

What happens technically in a movie theater is like magic for most people. A single beam of light mysteriously shoots out from a remote window to illuminate a screen with gigantic images. In professional screenings we don't expect any technical problems to interfere with our concentration. The film is never interrupted for a reel change, the sound isn't garbled, the brilliant image is in focus, and the lamps don't burn out in the middle of a scene.

Looking at films, we assume these kinds of optimal conditions. The filmmakers have worked as hard on the technical quality of their film as they have on the content, and hope that it will be well presented. But when most of us think of screening a film ourselves, we worry that we won't do the kind of job a professional theater does. Yet, by working with available resources, using some common sense, and paying attention to details, it is possible to create a situation where the audience can see and hear the film perfectly well. In case you have never done it, you should know that, once you have learned how, operating a 16mm projector is no more complicated than threading a sewing machine or driving a car. With just a little preparation and care on your part, you can reproduce the good sound and image the filmmakers have made possible, while treating the print in a way that will insure it a reasonable life span.

This chapter includes technical principles, procedures and details to help you during your screening. Even if you are experienced you will want to read through this section to pick up new ideas. If you are a newcomer, or have run into difficulties in the past, you may want to give this section several readings. This chapter is intended as a reference and you can take it along during screenings.

THE PHYSICAL PROPERTIES OF FILM

Motion picture film is a strip of flexible material (the base) over which a coating of chemicals have been applied (emulsion). It is made in various widths and measured in millimeters:

- 35mm is the standard for commercial features shown in theaters.
- 70mm is used for theatrical wide screen productions.
- 16mm is the standard for nontheatrical use in classrooms, libraries, etc.

Many feature films available through nontheatrical distributors have been reduced from 35mm to 16mm and many independent and other professional productions are originally shot in this gauge. We will be talking throughout this section about 16mm film. 8mm and Super 8mm are increasing their potential for professional use, but are usually used for amateur productions. Some feature films are available on Super 8mm.

Films are sent to you mounted on reels, inside protective cartons. The beginning of each reel is called the "head", and will usually have up to 10 feet of colored (usually green), black, clear and/or numbered ("Academy") leader on it before the picture starts. Generally, the film title and reel number (e.g., Reel 1 of 3) are identified on this head leader, which is easily replaced and is used to protect the film during shipment, threading and screening. Academy leader is a countdown (from 8 to 2) to the picture start and is intended to help you focus the picture. The end of the film on a reel is called the "tail". It also is protected by leader, usually red.

When you receive a film, open the case and make sure that you have all the reels of the film you ordered. Standard reel sizes are 1,200 ft. (33 min.), 1,600 ft. (44 min.) and 2,000 ft. (56 min.). You are well advised to check the film as soon as it arrives. Occasionally you will get the wrong film and a distributor will need at least 48 hours to send you the proper one. Also, on occasion a film will come to you "tails out" and will need to be rewound.

A motion picture is made up of a series of separate still photographs printed one after another on a long strip of acetate. Each single, distinct frame contains an image, slightly different from the preceding one, a sound track on one side, and one sprocket hole on the other. As the reflected projection lamp shines through condenser lenses onto the film, into the projection lens and out to the screen, the projector pulls the film along in a series of very rapid jerks. The gate in the projector holds one frame at a time in front of the aperture until the claw enters the sprocket holes to pull the film down to the next frame. A shutter intercepts the light from the lamp during the split second one frame is moved out of the aperture and another is moved in. The shutter and the intermittent claw movement are in perfect synchronization, moving the film through the projector at a uniform rate of 24 frames per second (sound speed) or 16 —18 frames per second (silent speed). This movement is perceived by the viewer as an uninterrupted flow. Loops before and after the projector gate aid the free movement of the film.

SIGHT

The quality of your projected image will depend a lot on the quality of the print: how it was printed by the lab, how well it has been treated by previous users (scratches, breaks, dirt), and its age (old color prints may fade and become brittle). Most reputable distributors should send you a good, clean print with few splices.

You have control over the image size and brightness, which are important to your audience. Size and brightness are a function of how close the projector is to the screen. The closer it is, the smaller and brighter the image will be. The size of the image is also a function of the size of the lens on your projector. For example, the standard two inch lens will fill a seven by nine foot screen at a distance of about fifty feet. Figure 2 gives image size for various projector-to-screen distances in relation to lens size. Be sure to ask about the lens size when you borrow or rent a projector (2" is standard). You may want to rent a different size lens that is more suited to your conditions. A "zoom lens" attaches to the prime lens and with it you can avoid moving the projector back and forth to get the proper image size. The adjustment is in the lens itself. A zoom lens is useful for increasing picture size in small rooms.

The brilliance of the projection lamp is also a determining factor. The farther from the screen you move your projector, the dimmer the image will get. Adding a zoom lens to increase the picture size will also cut down on brilliance. If you happen to have a space and screen which approach auditorium or movie house proportions, you may have to rent an arc lamp projector which throws a beam of light 3 to 4 times brighter than most portable 16mm projectors, but which requires a special power pack to moderate the voltage.

There may already be a screen in many of the places you use to show a film. If not, you will have to provide one of your own. Size is crucial, and you will find that most home screens are too small for a group situation (see Figure 3). There are several types of screens you can use.

Beaded screens reflect light best in a narrow angle and are good for long, narrow rooms.

Matte screens are not as reflective, but are good for wide viewing areas since they reflect light so evenly.

Lenticular screens are fairly reflective for a fairly wide angle. They are generally the most adaptable.

Super bright screens are coated with aluminum and can be used in semilight locations if the audience is sitting directly in front.

If a screen is not available, you can project on a white wall, on a pasteboard of the type sold in art supply stores, on seamless white paper taped to a wall, on a well stretched, clean white sheet or a piece of white or gessoed canvas. Whatever option, you must end up with a white, flat surface with invisible seams and no wrinkles (they will show up in the image). Of course, nothing works as well

Projector to screen distances in relation to lens size.

Fig. 2

The use of this chart depends upon what equipment and space you have available.

16mm Motion Pictures—Aperture 380″W x 286H.

SCREEN WIDTH

PROJECTION DISTANCE IN FEET

LENS FOCAL LENGTH	40″	50″	60″	70″	84″	96″	9′	10′	12′	14′	16′	18′	20′	22′	24′	26′	28′	30′
12.7mm — ½″	4.5	5.7	6.7	7.8	9.3	10.6	11.9	13.2	15.9	18.5	21.1	23.8	26.4	29.0	31.7	34.3	36.9	39.6
19 mm — ¾″	6.7	8.3	10.0	11.6	13.9	15.9	17.9	19.9	23.8	27.8	31.7	35.7	39.6	43.5	47.5	51.4	55.4	59.3
25.4mm — 1″	8.9	11.1	13.3	15.5	18.6	21.2	23.9	26.5	31.7	37.0	42.3	47.5	52.8	58.1	63.3	68.6	73.9	79.1
38.1mm — 1½″	13.4	16.7	20.0	23.3	27.9	31.8	35.8	39.7	47.6	55.5	63.4	71.3	79.2	87.1	95.0	102.9	110.8	118.7
50.8mm — 2″	17.9	22.3	26.7	31.0	37.2	42.4	47.7	53.0	63.5	74.0	84.5	95.1	105.6	116.1	126.6	137.2	147.7	158.2
63.5mm — 2½″	22.3	27.8	33.3	38.8	46.5	53.0	59.6	66.2	79.4	92.5	105.7	118.8	132.0	145.2	158.3	171.5	184.6	197.8
76.2mm — 3″	26.8	33.4	40.0	46.6	55.8	63.7	71.6	79.4	95.2	111.0	126.8	142.6	158.4	174.2	190.0	205.8	221.6	237.3
88.9mm — 3½″	31.3	39.0	46.6	54.3	65.1	74.3	83.5	92.7	111.1	129.5	148.0	166.4	184.8	203.2	221.6	240.1	258.5	276.9
101.6mm — 4″	35.8	44.5	53.3	62.1	74.4	84.9	95.4	105.9	127.0	148.0	169.1	190.1	211.2	232.2	253.3	274.4	295.4	316.5

Example A:

Your projector has a 2″ lens, and in your space the projection distance is 48′. Thus you will have an image which is about 9′ wide and will need a screen that size.

Example B:

Your room is only 20′ wide. To get a decent size image you will need a projector with a 1½″ lens and a screen which is 60″ wide.

Room size and seating capacity.   Fig. 3

Room Ratio/Length:Width

Minimum Screen Size	1:1		4:3		3:2	
	Room Size	Seating Capacity	Room Size	Seating Capacity	Room Size	Seating Capacity
40"	20×20'	21	20×15'	16	20×13'	10
50"	24×24'	33	24×18'	26	24×16'	23
60"	30×30'	57	30×22'	47	30×20'	41
70"	35×35'	82	35×26'	69	35×23'	58
84"	42×42'	124	42×33'	118	42×28'	90
6×8'	48×48'	167	48×36'	141	48×32'	128
7×9'	56×56'	234	56×42'	200	56×37'	182
8×10'	60×60'	272	60×45'	223	60×40'	208
9×12'	72×72'	402	72×54'	347	72×48'	318

Screen size and seating guide.   Fig. 4

Width of Viewing Area:
30° each side of center (60°)

Seating:
Theater style, six square feet per chair

Aisles:
Two 3-foot side aisles, 3½-foot aisle after each 14 rows of chairs, 4-foot rear aisle.

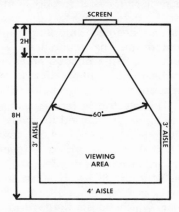

For legibility, members of the audience should be seated within the specified screen angle and should not be seated closer to the screen than two times, nor farther than eight times, the **height** of the projected image. Minimum image height, for legibility, can be determined by dividing by eight the distance from the screen to the rear of the back row of seats. To avoid obstruction of the screen by the seated audience, the bottom of the screen should be a minimum of four feet above the floor.

as a regular projection screen to reflect light and reproduce the image.

Usually you are limited to available projectors, screens, and room size. If you have to project in a large auditorium with a classroom projector, the only way to get enough light on the screen is to place the projector on a table in the center aisle. A different lens might allow you to move it back behind the audience.

Whatever your equipment, arrange the seats, screen and projector so that everyone in the audience has an unobstructed view. If you can get your projector and screen high enough, you can arrange the seats with side aisles, rather than a center aisle which runs right through the central viewing area. This also avoids the problem of latecomers walking through the projection beam. Make sure the image itself is high enough so the heads of the audience do not intrude into view, even for people in the back row. Stagger the seats so that they are not directly behind one another.

SOUND

THE OPTICAL SOUND SYSTEM

The optical **sound track** that goes along with the image is also printed on the film. It looks like a squiggle running along one side. The projector has a second light source, the **exciter lamp**, located after the gate. Light from the exciter lamp is focused by the **sound lens** and beamed onto the film as it goes smoothly around the **sound drum.** The sound track printed on the film will pass light through, but the opaque areas next to it will not. This modulated light beam hits a **photo electric cell** which generates electric current in response to the light hitting it.

The electric current is sent to a **preamplifier** where, first, this weak signal is boosted to levels that are less susceptible to degradation and, secondly, where any signal modification that has been applied during recording is reversed. It is also in the preamplifier that further modifications to the signal are made at your discretion— tone controls, filters, balance and volume, for example. Once the signal has been shaped by the preamp, it is sent to the **power amplifier**, which boosts the level many times. The signal then goes to the loudspeaker.

Most of your sound problems will originate with the optical sound system built into your projector, and will be more noticeable the larger your room and audience. While there is no practical way to improve or modify the existing system, there are some adjustments you can make in speaker placement and room acoustics, and fairly simple ways to supplement the projector's own system. These are described in Chapter 13.

Image synchronized with sound.   Fig. 5

See figures 6, 7, 8, 11 and 12 which identify projector parts.

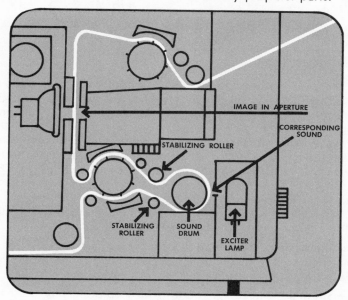

Figure 5 shows the path of the film through the optical sound system. The point at which light passes through the sound track is 26 frames ahead of the gate, so that the sound being reproduced at the sound drum corresponds to the picture in the aperture at the same instant. The 26 frames mechanically and spacially isolate the jerking motion of the film through the gate from the smooth, continuous motion of the film past the sound lens necessary for proper sound reproduction. The claw pulls the film through the gate frame-by-frame, holding it there for a split second.

This mechanical isolation is accomplished in two ways. First, much of the physical vibration imparted to the film by its frame-by-frame movement is dissipated in the loop right after the gate. Second, the film passes over one or two stabilizing rollers which are free-floating and absorb further vibrations. It is important that the film fits snugly over the sound drum or the sound will be garbled.

MAGNETIC SOUND TRACK

A less common method for recording sound on film employs an iron oxide mixture instead of an optical track. This is a magnetic system which works like a tape recorder and generally has better quality than the optical system. Since theatre owners did not convert to this system, however, and since the coating is very prone to wear and tear and is easily distorted by other magnetic sources, it is seldom used in circulating prints. Some projectors are equipped with optical and magnetic sound systems, which both thread in the same path, and the operator has only to change a switch.

16mm PROJECTORS

There are many excellent brands of 16mm film projectors, new and old, which are used by schools, libraries, businesses, churches, nontheatrical (and sometimes commercial) exhibitors, and community groups. Different makes and models have been developed for almost every screening situation, from the auditorium or movie theater professional projector with a bright xenon lamp to the small, portable projector with a built-in speaker. Most machines have the same basic kinds of parts which do the same basic things, although their construction and arrangement varies from machine to machine.

In terms of threading, or putting the film into the machine, there are three kinds of projectors you may encounter.

Manual threading. You thread this machine by hand. All of the film path is visible, and the film is always accessible to the projectionist. While you must do the work, you also have control.

Automatic or self-threading. You trim the head of the film, put a lever in the "thread" position, start the machine, insert the film into a path, and mechanical claws guide the film by its sprocket holes along the threading path. Most of the parts are enclosed by a case. Should something go wrong (a bad splice, a series of torn sprockets) it is difficult to unthread the machine. Self-threading projectors were developed because some film users felt learning to thread manually was too much trouble. Nevertheless, we must warn you that self-threading machines can cause a lot of trouble and damage the film if they are out of alignment, if dirt or some other obstruction gets into the film path, or if the head leader or any part of the film is in bad shape. They can accordion pleat or chew up film at the standard rate of 24 frames a second. A poorly maintained machine, a bad print, or a nervous projectionist can produce disastrous results with an automatic machine.

Channel or slot-loading. With slot-loading machines you do half of the work. A lever is moved to the "thread" position, you put the film around the first sprocket wheel, through the gate, pull the film through a channel in the machine (which sets the bottom loop and puts the film around the sound drum), then put it around the last sprocket wheel. On both this and the automatic machine, the lever has to be put into the "operate" position for proper projection.

We are going to use manual projectors as models in this section. They are easier to operate than most people think, are actually preferred by projectionists, are encountered by most film users, and their parts also appear on other kinds of projectors. If you learn how to thread and operate a manual projector, the basic principles will stand you in good stead with other machines as well.

Basic projector parts:

Feed and take-up arms on which to mount the feed and take-up reels. Almost all machines feed from the top or front and take up on the bottom or rear.

Sprocket wheels guide and move the film and are synchronized with the claw. One is always right after the feed reel, before the first loop and the gate. There may be one between the bottom loop and the sound drum. Another is always between the sound drum and the take-up reel. The sprocket holes of the film fit on to the pins of the sprocket wheels. A shoe or clamp holds the film tight.

The gate is where the lens housing meets the body of the projector. It is exposed by either swinging the lens housing out towards you (away from the projector) or sliding it forward with a lever. The film should make loops before and after the gate, and there are usually lines to guide you. Inside the gate is the **claw** which pulls the film along by its sprocket holes, the **aperture** through which the projection lamp shines into the lens, and a **pressure plate** mounted on springs to hold the film flat.

The sound drum is accompanied by floating rollers. The sound drum is always close to where the exciter lamp is housed, and is always accompanied by two or three guide rollers or stabilizers before and after it. These rollers help change the jerky motion of the film as it comes out of the gate into a smooth motion as it goes around the sound drum.

Other parts of the projector include:

The framer, usually located at the top or bottom of the gate, controls the top and bottom of the frame line.

Frame line adjustments. Fig. 9

A and B incorrectly framed, C correctly framed.

A   B   C

Three typical 16mm sound projectors: threading diagrams and parts.

1. Feed reel
2. Sprocket wheel
3. Sprocket shoe
4. Guide, snubbing or stabilizing roller
5. Film gate
6. Projection lens
7. Projection lamp
8. Aperture
9. Focus knob
10. Framer
11. Inching knob
12. Tilt control knob (to raise or or lower machine)
13. Sound drum
14. Exciter lamp
15. Power switch
16. Motor switch
17. Lamp switch
18. Amplifier or volume control switch
19. Tone control switch
20. Take up reel
21. External speaker jack
22. Loop restorer
23. Rewind button

Eiki   Fig. 6

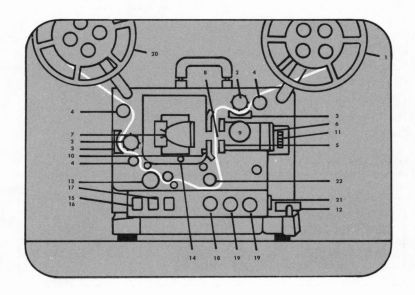

Kodak Pageant

Fig. 7

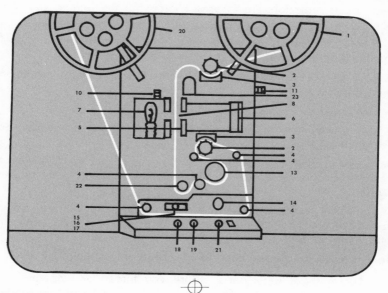

Bell and Howell

Fig. 8

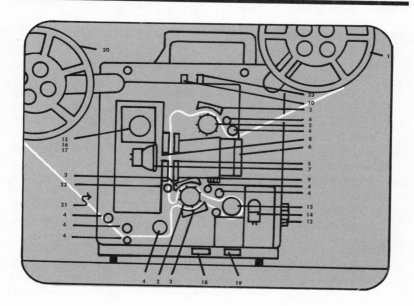

Output jack for external speaker plug.

The focus knob usually extends out from the lens housing, although some older projectors are focused by moving the lens in and out.

The inching knob (or hand test knob), usually located on the front of the machine body, can be used to manually test the proper movement of the film through the machine or to extend the claw.

A knob or lever to raise or lower the machine is usually located in the front.

A power switch to turn on the machine.

A motor switch to run the machine forward or reverse and turn on the cooling fan.

A lamp switch to turn on the projection lamp (power/motor/lamp controls will be in different combinations according to make and model).

An amplifier or volume switch to turn on the amplifier and adjust sound volume. In some machines this turns on the exciter lamp, on others this lamp comes on with the motor.

Tone controls (treble and bass) to adjust the sound fidelity.

Locate these basic parts before you thread and operate the machine. Trace the threading path. Does the film go over or under snubbing rollers, stabilizers, sound drum? How does the gate open? Where are the sprocket wheels?

CHECKING OUT THE PROJECTOR

You should always check out your projector well before the screening. If you are borrowing or renting a machine, arrange to have a knowledgeable person show you how to operate it when you pick it up. You want to be sure everything is in good working order and that you know how to run it. Take five minutes to plug it in and have them demonstrate how to thread the machine, how to turn on the motor, lamp, and sound, how to adjust the tone controls, the focus knob, and the framer. Make sure you know how the machine rewinds, and how to plug in the external speaker. If you are renting a machine, extra projection and exciter lamps should be included; if you are borrowing one you should ask for them. Ask how to remove and insert each lamp. Finally, ask if the machine has any peculiarities which you should know about. Taking the time now will save both you and your audience possible frustration later.

If a projector and sound system are installed in the hall you are using, you should either use the regular projectionist, or ask them to lead you through the operation of the system. Don't just look. That shiny projector in the auditorium might be broken, missing

The pencil test, how the film comes off a reel.   Fig. 10
Movement of claw to engage sprocket holes.   Fig. 11

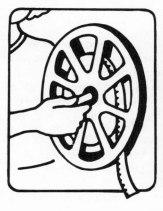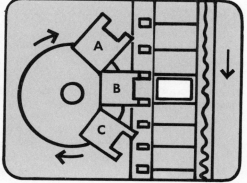

Claw moves from A to C; B is the
engaged position.

Threading through the gate.   Fig. 12

Set top and bottom loops as indicated on your particular machine.

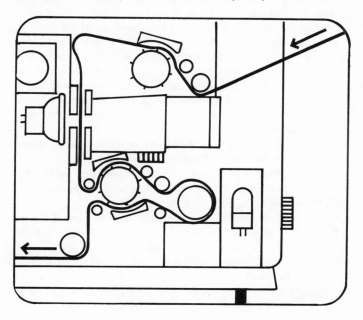

a lamp, aimed off the screen, or disconnected from an idiosyncratic sound system. In any case, ask an experienced person to check you out as you thread the machine, run it, or actually try changing the bulbs.

THREADING A MANUAL PROJECTOR

Threading a projector manually consists of making a series of loops and fitting the film's sprocket holes onto the claw and sprocket wheels. Most machines have an abstracted threading diagram on the body or inside the case which you should always examine. We have reproduced three typical threading diagrams on pp. 98-99. The most troublesome threading area is the gate, Figures 11 and 12.

- Set the projector securely on the table and plug it in.
- Open up the arms. Usually there is a button to push and they lock into position. Some have both an "operate" and a "rewind" position.
- Aim the projector squarely at the screen, turn on motor and lamp, and center the light on the screen. Make sure the projector is level. It should never be placed at an angle to the screen, as this results in a Keystone Effect (trapezoid shape). To adjust image size, move projector nearer to or further from the screen.
- Place the feed reel (with film) on feed spindle and take-up reel on take-up spindle. Secure them. Both reels should be the same size (take-up reel must be able to hold all the film on the feed reel). Almost always the full reel will go on the front and the empty reel on the rear arm. They will turn in a clockwise direction. To check proper film loading, as you face the screen, the image on the film should be upside down with the sprocket holes on the right side (side away from projector) as in Figure 10.
- Open all of the sprocket shoes and open the gate. Never try to force any mechanism on the projector.
- Unwind about three feet of film. Place film under the first sprocket wheel, fitting sprocket holes onto the pins. Close the shoe to hold film in place.
- Make the first loop before the gate: follow loop diagram for proper size. If this loop is too large, it will chatter; if too small, the claw will tear the sprocket holes.
- Place film in the gate, in the path between the runners. Slide it up and down slightly until sprocket holes are engaged by the claw. If the film slides freely in the gate, use the inching knob to extend the claw so that it en-

gages the sprocket holes. Check top loop. Close the gate, being sure the film fits flat so you do not crease it.

- Leave a second, properly spaced loop below the film gate. This is the loop which determines whether the sound is synchronized with the picture. If it is too short, the sound will be heard ahead of the image; if it is too long, the sound will be heard after the image. Hold the loop in place as you secure the film around the second sprocket wheel or through the stabilizing rollers and around the sound drum. If your projector has three sprocket wheels, the second one will be here; other projectors (those with two sprocket wheels) will take you directly from the bottom loop to the sound drum.

- Negotiate the rollers and stabilizers and make sure the film fits securely and smoothly around the sound drum; if it doesn't the sound will be mushy, faint or garbled.

- Place film around last sprocket wheel and close shoe.

- Bring film around the final snubbing roller before it goes up on take-up reel, and attach film to take-up reel.

- Check your threading calmly before turning on the machine. Trace the path again with your finger and move the inching knob, if there is one, forward one cycle to check the proper movement of the film. Make sure the claw is engaged. Check your loops one more time.

- Most prints come with at least three feet of colored or numbered leader before the picture starts. This is so you can thread and test the focus before getting into the picture, since leader is easily replaced. Now you can turn on the motor and lamp and check your focus. If you run into the picture while focusing, you will have to unthread and rethread the machine. You may want to run into the picture so you can also test the sound. When you rethread, try to leave about two feet of leader before the image to allow the machine to be up to speed when the image comes into the gate. Running the machine in reverse is usually not a good idea. You greatly increase your chances of losing your loops and damaging the film.

SELF-THREADING MACHINES

Read the instructions. You will have to clip or trim the head of the film (a trimmer is usually on the front of the machine) so it will travel smoothly through the film path. There will be a lever to put in the thread position. The machine is turned to "run", the film end inserted at the beginning of the threading path, and the

Causes and prevention of film damage.   Fig. 13

1. Scratches

a. Dirty rollers, gate, film channel.
b. Cinching film on reel.
c. Letting loose film fall on floor.

a, b, c. Clean projector, handle film carefully.

2. Creases

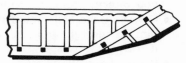

a. Stepping on film.
b. Pinching film in closing film can.

a, b. Handle film carefully.

3. Enlarged sprocket holes

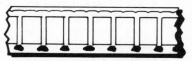

a. Too much tension on gate or take-up reel.
b. Jerking movement of take-up reel.
c. Pull-down claw worn or out of adjustment.
d. Worn sprockets.
e. Loss of loops.

a, b, c, d. Have projector checked by approved repairperson.

e. Rethread.

4. Torn sprocket holes

a. Too much tension on gate or take-up reel.
b. Jerking movement of take-up reel.
c. Worn pull-down claw or sprockets.
d. Dry film; loss of loops.

a, b, c. Have projector checked by approved repairperson.

d. Humidify; rethread film.

5. Breaks

a. Faulty film splice.
b. Sudden jerk on take-up reel.
c. Film improperly placed in film channel.
d. Failure to allow loops.

a, b, c, d. Make correct splice; rethread machine.

6. Sprocket holes on sound track or on film

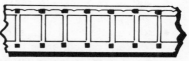

a. Running a sound film on silent type projector.
b. Incorrect threading (sound track and sprocket track reversed).
c. Film failing to engage sprocket teeth.

a. Use appropriate equipment for type of film.
b. Make sure film is on reel properly, coming off the top.
c. Rethread and check.

7. Burned spots

a. Faulty or sticking protective shutter.
b. Projector running too slow without protective shutter in place.

a, b. Have projector checked by approved repairperson.

8. Dirt on film

a. Improper or careless storage (out of can).
b. Dirty projector.
c. Improper handling of film.

a, b. Clean projector. Clean film.

c. Handle film carefully.

machine pulls the film through. Some machines even wrap the film around the take-up reel. You may have to give the film a slight tug to get the loops and levers into the "operate" position.

THE PROJECTIONIST'S KIT

Below is a list of materials to have or to bring with you in your kit to any screening. Even if you don't use a particular item, you will find it wiser to have it handy if you need it, than to be unhappy that you didn't bring it. Some of these items may not be necessary with given machines or specific locations but, when in doubt, take everything. You won't be sorry.

- One or two projectors and a screen.
- The film.
- One or two take-up reels equal to or larger than the reels your film comes on.
- Extra projector lamp and extra exciter (sound) lamp. You can't get either on the spot. Check to see what model your projector takes. Know how to change them.
- The external speaker and connecting cords. Your projector will usually have an external speaker and a cord. Sometimes the cord will not be long enough for your situation and you will want to bring a longer one. Make sure the jacks are all compatible. Sometimes you will want to bring a hi-fi speaker to use instead of the one supplied with the projector.
- Extension cords.
- A three prong adapter. Projectors have three pronged plugs. Many walls have two pronged outlets. This 39¢ item has been known to save entire screenings.
- Cotton swabs and alcohol to use in cleaning the gate. Never touch the lens with these. A soft camel hair brush or a soft, lintless cloth could also be used.
- Lens tissue to clean the lens.
- Flashlight or tensor lamp.
- Masking tape to put up flyers, tape down cord, tape broken films, secure film ends. Never use transparent tape on film. Gaffer's tape or duct tape are the best for taping down wires and cords so that people don't trip on them, but masking tape will do.
- A handkerchief or other soft cloth to handle hot bulbs if you have to change them.
- A small Phillips and a regular screwdriver.
- A solid table to set the projector on. Generally such a

table is available at the screening location, but you should know for sure. Some A-V suppliers rent portable projection tables which are just large enough for one projector. The legs screw on and are adjustable to heights from three to six feet.

SETTING UP TO PROJECT

The projectionist and assistant should arrive at the screening location early enough to be completely set up half an hour in advance of your announced starting time. Most people allow one hour for setting up, but if you lack experience, you might want to schedule more time. You do not want the pressure of people arriving while you are still preparing. You should have checked out the space in advance of the screening so that you have brought all the necessary equipment.

- Put up your screen.
- Position your projector on a sturdy table.
- Put your speaker on a chair under the screen. Getting it up off the ground will greatly improve the sound.
- Run the sound cable from the speaker to the projector and plug it in.
- Plug in the projector.
- Clean the film gate and path with cotton swabs and alcohol. Clean the lens with lens tissue. Make sure the projector controls are on "sound speed" and "optical sound" if there is a choice, or unless you are showing a silent (16 fps) film.
- The rewind mechanism should be disengaged. Turn on the projector (forward, operate) and lamp and center the light on the screen. Test, by having people sit in chairs, that the image area is visible from different locations. You can get a rough focus by sharpening the sides of the image area. Make any adjustments in projector placement or height. If you are using two projectors to show a two or three reel film, line both of them up on the screen. The image area should be of uniform size and brightness. Make sure you have enough room to operate both.
- Make sure your sound connections are good and that your exciter lamp is working by turning on the amplifier, turning up the volume and listening for hiss from the speaker. You can also test it by moving a thin

paper card between the sound lens and the sound drum—you will hear a thumping noise on the speaker.

- Secure and tape down all of your cords and wires so that people do not trip over them and the projector doesn't get disconnected during the screening.

- Open the film case and stack the reels in the order you will show them.

- Put on the take-up reel, and feed reel, and thread the projector according to its diagram and procedures on pp. 102-103.

- Turn on the amplifier and volume control to a moderate setting. Set the tone controls in the neutral or flat position.

- Turn on the motor, then the lamp, and check the position of the image on the screen, the focus, and the framing. Focus on the grain of the image. (Use binoculars if you are a long distance from the screen.) Keep the projector running while someone else checks the sound for volume and tone quality from various locations in the room. Try to set for the dialogue sections. Raising the treble or lowering the bass can often make a lot of difference in the way the film sounds. Since bodies tend to muffle and absorb sound, making it more bassy, you may want to make slight adjustments when the screening really starts, but you can do this easily after you've started the film if you work carefully now.

- Unthread the projector and rewind whatever film has been used. Do not run the machine in reverse. This can easily tear up the film, lose the loops, and isn't great for most projectors.

- Rethread the projector. Check the focus using the Academy leader if possible. Make sure the claw is engaged, and that you have about two feet of film before the picture starts.

- Straighten up your area and store your things out of the way but within easy reach.

You may want to make sure that all of the shades are down and that the room will be as dark as possible. Are there any lights falling on the screen? Speak with the house manager to check the agenda for the evening. Who is going to turn off the lights? Make sure they know where to steer latecomers so their heads don't get in the way of the projection light.

RUNNING THE SHOW

When the introduction to the film and the program have been made, the show is all yours.

- Turn on the amplifier a few minutes before you will start (with the volume low). Some amplifiers require a little time to warm up, others have transistors and will go on instantaneously.

- When the lights go down, turn on the motor, wait a couple of seconds for the picture to get into the gate, and turn on the lamp. Ease the volume up to the level you selected during the test. Check your focus. Check the sound volume and tone or have the house manager do it for you.

- The projectionist should stay with the machine throughout the entire film, and be alert to sound and focus problems. You should also be ready to turn the machine off at once if the picture starts jumping, if the machine loses a loop, or if the film breaks.

- If the film breaks, do not attempt to resplice it. Simply unthread, overlap the loose ends on the take-up reel (or fasten them with masking tape), rethread and continue the showing. Never try to repair the film yourself. Just put a note to the distributor in the film case when you send the film back. Most films are professionally inspected and repaired by the distributor, and you will not be charged for this. Your note indicating any repairs which are necessary will avoid further damage to the print as it is rewound.

IF YOUR FILM HAS MORE THAN ONE REEL

Professional theaters which regularly show feature length films are equipped with either one projector which can handle all of that film on one reel, or two projectors to show alternate reels without interruption. The motors, projection lamps and sound systems of the two projectors are controlled electronically through a "change-over box", so that as one reel reaches its last images, the second projector is started (in the leader without lamp and sound). When the first reel is into the last ten frames, the second projector cuts in with image and sound, the first machine continues running, but without image and sound. This change happens instantaneously and is not perceived by the audience. Most feature films have cue marks in the upper right hand corner to alert the projectionist. On the first cue, the projectionist starts the second machine. On the second cue, they push the button for the changeover.

If you have two or three reels and one projector, you can still show them with a minimum of interruption. At the end of the first reel, simply remove the now full take-up reel from the back arm, put the now empty feed reel on the back arm to use as take-up. Mount and thread the second reel of your film and continue. You do not need to rewind between reels, but can rewind everything at the end of the show.

You can change over two projectors manually without a change-over box. It will not be as smooth as the electronic changeover, but is much smoother than stopping at the end of each reel to thread up the next. Each projector should be connected to its own speaker. Set up, thread, and test both projectors; "A" with reel 1 and "B" with reel 2. Thread projector B in the leader with the picture start of reel 2 about a foot from the gate. As reel 1 ends (cue marks or end leader), turn off the lamp and sound on projector A. At the same time, turn on projector B's motor, wait for the picture start to enter the gate, turn on the lamp, and ease up the volume to your pre-set level. Check the focus. Turn off projector A, rethread it with reel 3, and continue alternating projectors. Good timing, and familiarity with the projector's controls can result in a manual changeover which will not distract the audience. If you have a three reel film and two projectors (sitting side by side), mount reels 1 and 3 on the most accessible projector. This makes threading reel 3 (in the dark) much easier.

TROUBLESHOOTING

If you follow the procedures outlined above, thread the projector properly according to the diagram, and have a print which is in good condition, you should not have any problems during the screening. The most common problems are the result of 1) an improperly maintained machine, 2) an inexperienced or unskilled operator and 3) previous unrepaired damage to the print. There is no set formula for success. Your screening will go smoothly if you take the time before hand to learn how to operate the projector, and set it up carefully. Always clean the film path before threading the machine so that small particles of dirt do not scratch the print. Always start the machine with the claw engaged. Always stay with the machine while it is running so that you can turn it off immediately if anything goes wrong. Keep an eye on the screen, and listen to the sound of the film and of the projector. Never let the film fall onto the floor (and if it does, don't step on it), and make sure your take-up reels are large enough.

FIVE COMMON PROBLEMS

1. Chattering noise and jumping picture. Either you did not thread the projector properly (your loops may be too short) or you have run into a length of damaged sprocket holes. Sometimes a bad splice going through the gate also will cause this.

Stop the machine and rethread properly. Check your loops to be sure that they are still the proper size. Check ahead on the print to see if there is sprocket damage and whether or not it continues. If it does, wind forward until you reach a clear section and rethread. Most sprocket damage is concentrated at the head of reels.

2. No sound or no picture caused by a blown bulb. When a projection or exciter lamp burns out, it most commonly does so when you turn it on. Projection lamps have lives of 12 to 50 hours (depending on the kind), and exciter lamps much longer. But you may have set up, focused and tested everything in advance, turned the machine off, and, when you start the film, one of the lamps goes out.

This can be handled easily if you have a spare and know how to change the lamp. When replacing a projection lamp, unplug the machine, and do not touch the reflector or filament of a new lamp with your fingers.

3. The film breaks and starts spilling out of the machine. The film can break at an old splice or from excessive tension.

Do not attempt to repair the film. Simply stop and rethread beyond the break, and either lap the end over the take-up reel or attach the two broken ends with masking tape and continue your screening.

4. The film starts to pile up on the floor.

If the take-up reel is not turning check the visible belts which drive the take-up arm, and make sure the reel is not hitting a wall or something else which obstructs its movement. If a belt is broken, you may turn the take-up reel by hand, but it is difficult to keep proper tension on the film. Also check to make sure that the take-up arm is in the "operate" (not "rewind") position and check the position of the rewind lever.

5. A hair or clump of dirt appears in the picture. This is some piece of material which either was in the film path or came off the print.

The best way to avoid this is to clean the gate carefully before threading. A blast into the gate from a small can of compressed air (available at photo stores) will dislodge most materials. Manual blow brushes ("foofers"), or just blowing into the gate are the next best solutions.

OTHER PROBLEMS

No Picture
- See if the lamp switch is turned on.
- Check and replace the projection lamp if it is burned out.

No Sound
- Check sound/silent or optical/magnetic settings on the projector. They should be on sound/optical.
- Check to make sure the exciter lamp is on and replace if defective.
- Check amplifier and volume switches.
- Check the threading around the sound drum.
- Check to see if the film indeed has a soundtrack.
- Check the connections between the projector and the speaker. Do this at a low volume setting so that you don't blow out the speaker with a loud rush of sound when you make the connection. If your projector has an internal speaker, and you are using an external speaker, disconnect the external speaker to pin down the problem. If you get sound from the internal speaker, then your problem is in the connection to the external speaker rather than in the machine itself.

Distorted Picture
- Adjust focus.
- Close the film gate, and make sure the film is flush (between the runners) in the gate.
- If the picture is too small for the screen, move the projector back. If it is too large, move the projector closer.
- If the frame is split (some of the top at the bottom or vice versa) adjust the framer.
- If there is fluttering with a lot of noise, stop and rethread. You have lost your loops, the sprockets and claw are not engaging the sprocket holes properly, and you are tearing the film.
- If one side or another is out of focus, realign the projector squarely in relationship to the screen, or realign the screen. Check the position of the film in the gate.
- Flickering picture can be caused by running the projector at silent speed.
- If the picture is jumping around (unsteady frame line) try rethreading. If this problem is severe, it could mean the projector needs maintenance.

- A dim or unevenly illuminated picture indicates either a bulb at the end of its life, or a very dirty lens.
- If the image looks stretched (tall and thin), you may be showing a cinemascope (wide screen) film without the correct (anamorphic) lens. Always check the catalog to see if the film is in cinemascope. Sometimes, a cinemascope film will be stretched through its titles, and then the rest of the print will have been flattened.

Distorted Sound

- Warbling or gargling (the voices sound as though they are underwater) is caused by improper threading around the sound drum. The film must fit snugly over the sound drum, and be held there securely by the stabilizing rollers.
- If the sound is not audible, try adjusting the tone controls (treble and bass) until you get understandable sound. A slight adjustment can make a lot of difference.
- If the picture is out of sync with the sound track, your bottom loop is either too short or too long. The distance between the gate and the sound lens should be 26 frames for proper synchronization.
- Ticks and pops in the sound can be caused by splices in the film or dirt on the film. If a tick, pop or thud is regular, there could be dirt on the sound drum. Remove the film from around the sound drum and clean the drum with a soft cloth or alcohol and q-tip.
- Hums and buzzes in the sound can sometimes be caused by a loose wire in your connectors or a grounding problem. If your projector has a three prong plug, the third prong (the grounding contact) should be connected to an earth ground. If the wall outlet is of the three hole variety, it is probably grounded. If you are using a three prong adapter, the green wire coming from the adapter must be connected to a ground. If you are not sure, attach a long piece of wire (any kind of insulated wire will do) to the adapter's green wire; connect the other end of this wire to an earth ground such as a radiator pipe, or copper cold water pipes.
- For more suggestions about improving sound and solving acoustical problems, see Chapter 13.

The above are the most common problems which occur during screenings. The operator's or owner's manual for your projector will also have a troubleshooting guide for that particular machine.

If anything does go wrong, stay calm, take your time, and let the audience know that you are working on the problem.

References

Filmmaker's Notebook: Buying A Used Projector by Andrew C. Bobrow

Filmmakers Newsletter, Volume 6, Number 1, November 1972, Filmmakers Newsletter Company, 41 Union Square West, New York, NY 10003.

   Article describing a number of considerations when buying a used 16mm projector.

9 | EVALUATIONS AND FOLLOW-UP

The day after your screening you should deposit any money made, return the film and equipment, pay the final bills and think about thank you letters. The screening committee should have a meeting about a week after the event to evaluate the program and the budget, plan any necessary follow-up, and make recommendations for the future.

THE EVALUATION MEETING

You will have gathered audience response to the film and your entire program through the evaluation sheets, the post film discussion session, informal conversations at the event, and conversations in the following days. The more information and the less speculation the better. A major New York exhibitor/distributor often stood in his theater lobby surveying the audience as they left about their reactions to a new film and asking how they heard of it. The group presenting their own film selection should be just as concerned as the professional in knowing how effective their programming and publicity has been. You may even want to call a few people whose opinions you respect to get reactions to your program. Don't seem to be fishing for compliments, but make clear that you are interested in frank feedback about the program. If they raise criticisms, don't be defensive but try to learn from them. What do their comments tell you about the kinds of films your audience likes? What do their responses suggest about limitations in your program you should overcome the next time? Gathering information of this kind should be part of your ongoing evaluation process. The more data, the more solid the foundation for planning successful film programs in the future.

Every sponsor will want to evaluate their screening and how their organization functioned, whether it was better than expected, a disaster, or turned out pretty much as anticipated. The evaluation process should be a forward-looking enterprise designed to improve future efforts by reflecting on concrete experience. Look at the screening, the preparations and go over your campaign step by step, giving special consideration to your goals, whether or not they were met, and why or why not. Even the most effective process can be improved, and most mistakes can be avoided in the future if the participants reevaluate their resources, reconsider their approaches and plans, or restructure their objectives. On the following pages are some topics for your consideration.

TOPICS FOR EVALUATION

The Film

- How appropriate was your selection (length, subject, content, issues raised, type and style, quality)?
- What do the audience evaluation sheets indicate about their response to the film?
- Did it generate the response you anticipated?
- Was it an effective choice in terms of your goals? What can you learn about your previewing and selection procedures?
- What do answers to these questions imply for future film choices?

The Program Format

- Was your choice of date and time a good one?
- Was the location good in terms of access, appropriateness, capacity, comfort, screening facilities, etc?
- Did you plan and implement each part of your program agenda effectively?
- How did the discussion and the film work together?
- Did your discussion format produce the kind of response and participation you wished? Why or why not?
- What alternatives are there for future programs?

The Audience

- What was the composition of the audience?
- How many people came? How does this relate to the number you expected? How many came from your target audience? Look at this carefully, not only at the total number of people.
- What did you learn about why the people attended? A "How did you hear about the screening" question on the evaluation sheet is often useful in evaluating the effectiveness of your publicity efforts.
- How did the audience response compare with what you had expected and wanted?
- Were there any surprises in terms of who came, reaction to the program, etc? If they were positive, how can you make it happen again; if negative, how can they be avoided? What suggestions have come up that would make good future projects?

The Group's Effectiveness

- How effective were you in planning and organizing the event? Refer to your schedule, and analyze the following: Was the timing good? Is the schedule realistic for your group? Should you modify it in some way?
- Did people accept and carry out responsibilities? Did they have the right skills and enough time to do so?
- Did you utilize your resources well?
- How effective was your publicity and outreach?
- How were decisions made and what were the consequences?
- Were your expenses and income what you had projected? If there were differences, discuss the reasons why and how those decisions were made.
- Was the energy expended justified by the results?
- What mistakes were made, why, and how can you learn from them?

Conclusions

- What does your group learn from this evaluation about its planned goals, organizational ability, effectiveness in accomplishing its aims? What unexpected things happened?
- What do you learn about the community's response to your publicity and program?
- What are the implications of this evaluation for future projects and ongoing work?

Each time you screen a film, you will acquire additional expertise. An evaluation session is one place where anything learned about specific tasks can be shared with others so that your overall competency as a group is enhanced. Identifying limitations, mistakes or problems in an even-handed, rational way can help you make your programs more effective. In any organization you must be able to deal with individual personalities. Yet your evaluation should be directed towards finding concrete suggestions related to time and process, rather than laying blame (having a "spilt milk" session), or catering to subjective interpretations.

BASIC FOLLOW-UP

After the evaluation you should have a list of people who should be thanked, either by thank you notes or calls, for helping you in some way. The resource people and the filmmaker or distributor would also probably appreciate receiving your evaluations. If there were any major problems which your group is responding to, you should decide how to deal with them in the evaluation session. For example, at a very successful program presented by a Free Women's School about 200 people were turned away from a sold out house. The organizing committee, while pleased with their success, received complaints from people who could not get in. They decided to send out a letter explaining to the community how the response exceeded their expectations and giving the date of their next film program, to be held in a much larger space.

Other kinds of follow-up activities include implementing decisions made during the group discussion, whether it was a call for information or the formation of a committee. If the audience expressed interest in another film or some specific activity, it should be organized soon before enthusiasm gets diverted. Perhaps there are specific skills which it is now apparent your group needs to develop and you should find ways of doing so.

An important follow-up to any event involving outreach and publicity is the incorporation of new contacts into your mailing and phone lists. All those little scraps of paper which you worked with in the heat of preparing for the event, and the names of new people who expressed interest in your organization, should be put into some legible and organized file or list so that they are accessible for future activities. Many of these contacts—key individuals in your community, press people or foundation representatives—may not want to become active members of your group, but will be interested in getting your newsletter or announcements of future activities.

10 | FILM SOURCES

If your group decides to continue using films, you will need to broaden your methods for selecting and locating them. If you belong to a large organization, films may be available through national or regional networks, like a church or union audio-visual or educational center.

There are a number of sources, however, from which films can be purchased, rented or borrowed: film distributors of various kinds, public or state university film libraries, and other non-profit organizations which are discussed in this chapter. Places which can advise you about film resources include media arts organizations, arts councils or associations, and other information services. They may also publish books and periodicals, or maintain libraries of reference books, periodicals, journals, catalogs and filmographies. These are discussed in Chapter 11.

DISTRIBUTORS

At some point, most film users will want a film that is available for rental, lease or purchase from a company whose primary business is the distribution of films. Some deal exclusively with the commercial first- or second-run theaters which show films in 35mm, others with the semitheatrical market for 16mm and 35mm, and some concentrate. on 16mm films for educational and nontheatrical use. Some distributors are involved in all three markets. There are several hundred film distributors, from huge companies with several thousand films to small companies which distribute the work of one filmmaker.

The commercial distributor may have several to several thousand films in its collection. Whenever a particular title is rented or sold, a negotiated percentage is usually returned to the producer/filmmaker in the same way that royalties are earned by authors. A company may offer films about every conceivable subject, or may specialize in a particular kind of film, or films about a specific topic. Some distributors are concerned only with high quality films of whatever type, and others have arrangements to take all films from particular producers. Some are a combination of both. The only way to know what a distributor has available is to examine their catalog and educate yourself about their films.

The semi-commercial distributor may also have educational, cultural and artistic (in addition to profit) motivations. These include the smaller, independent distributors who operate on lower profit margins, and filmmakers who have set up distribution structures to handle their own films — individually, as a cooperative or as a small business. Descriptive materials available from small or self-distributors naturally describe fewer films, but usually treat those few in greater detail. Many special interest groups will find these film sources useful. Self-distribution is a growing practice among independent filmmakers who choose to promote their own films rather than sell the distribution rights to another party. Although the distribution effort cuts into the time available for filmmaking, the self-distributor has control over how the film is promoted, and can give it special attention rather than considering it as just one item in a voluminous catalog. Many self-distributors are filmmakers interested in developing direct contact with film users and are receptive to working out arrangements for benefits or special programs.

Two key reference books list films available for nontheatrical screenings alphabetically by title, give director, release date, running time and other credits, and the name of the distributor. In both books, abbreviations for the distributor of each film are keyed to distributor lists in the back. If you know the title of the film, you can find the distributor's name, address and phone and arrange for the rental. Other sources for locating films and distributors are listed in our bibliography.

Feature Films on 8mm, 16mm, and Videotape compiled and edited by James L. Limbacher
Sixth Edition, R. R. Bowker Company, New York and London, 1979.
    Appears on a more or less biennial basis and supplements are published quarterly in **Sightlines** (available by subscription from the Educational Film Library Association, 43 West 61st Street, New York, NY 10023).

Film Programmer's Guide to 16mm Rentals compiled and edited by Kathleen Weaver
Third Edition, Reel Research, P.O. Box 6037, Albany, CA 94706, 1980.
    Revised periodically, it not only lists Hollywood and foreign feature films but also silents, classics, independent releases, animations, shorts, documentaries, experimental and underground films. Also outlines each distributor's rental policy.

Most groups (as opposed to a commercial movie theater or television station) usually deal with distributors like the ones listed in the above books. They describe their films in catalogs which they mail upon request or for a nominal fee to interested organizations, institutions and individuals. The first time you receive catalogs, especially from the big distributors, it is exciting to be confronted with hundreds of new films. The kind of information each distributor provides about its films varies with their target audience. You can get a sense of the relationship between catalog descriptions and how useful a particular film would be for you by seeing what is printed about films you are familiar with. Be critical of a catalog description consisting simply of superlative adjectives or quotations. Some catalogs are actually very informative and contain interesting material such as interviews with directors, lists of resources, and bibliographies for the films. Also remember that descriptions may have been written with a particular audience, which may not include you, in mind. You will usually want to get other information about a film to help you evaluate its appropriateness for your program, since booking a film solely from a description in a distributor's catalog can be an expensive adventure.

DEALING WITH DISTRIBUTORS: STANDARD PROCEDURES

Procedures for dealing with distributors are fairly standard, and the policies of each company are usually included in their printed materials.

Payment

Most distributors require payment in advance (at the time of your written order) if you are a small group, renting from them for the first time, or do not have a credit reference. You will want to consider this factor when determining how much cash you will need for the screening, since the distributor will not ship the film to you until they have received your check or money order. Exceptions include: institutions which send out purchase orders (such as universities), institutions which send a formal letter on official letterhead (such as film exhibition programs), and organizations which have previously established credit with that company.

Rental Rates

Most rental rates listed in film catalogs are for one showing only. Additional showings are generally charged at one-half times the daily rate, and the price per showing usually decreases as the number of showings increase. The base rental (or minimum guarantee) established for a film is a function of a number of considerations including:

- The film: its popularity, box office performance and potential, supply and demand, age, factors affecting how much each print cost to make (length, black and white or color stock, the distributor's expenses for rights and customs charges).

- The context in which it will be used: public or private (often classroom) showings, audience size, whether admission will be charged or not, one time or multiple use. When admission is charged for screenings, the quoted rental rate will usually be a minimum guarantee versus a percentage (50-65%) of the gross receipts. You pay whichever is greater.

Some ball park figures for one showing based on 1979 prices (film rental rates change almost yearly):

- Features can rent for $35 or less for older films to over $750 for the latest block-buster. The average rental or minimum guarantee for newer films when admission is charged is $125-250. Many fine and interesting feature films are still available for $125 or less.
- Documentaries and other short films generally rent from $25-125, in a rough proportion to the length of the film, whether it is color or black and white, and how new it is. Many small and self-distribution companies have established sliding scales for rentals.
- Short experimental or animated films rent for roughly $2.00 per minute, although a five minute color film may cost up to $15 and most films rent for at least $7.50-10.00.

Some distributors provide discounts to small community groups, and others give discounts for ordering several films at one time. Terms are in the catalog and you can inquire about discounts when you call to book the film. Film users are advised to be honest when describing their group and how the film will be used. If not, you could find yourself unable to rent films in the future, or incurring additional charges.

A difficult issue for independent/self-distributors and film users are the frequent requests for free screenings from potential users who share the viewpoint of a particular film but have little or no money for the rental. Each time a print is used, the distributor has fixed shipping, cleaning, warehousing and administrative costs, and the print suffers unavoidable wear and tear. The self-distributor is usually still paying the film's production costs and the salaries of the people who worked on it from the film rentals and sales. Free screenings, therefore, cost someone money. A group that is short of funds should consider cutting costs by co-sponsoring the screening with another organization, finding someone willing to donate space or equipment, or somehow reducing other program expenses. If they are not planning to charge admission to their screening, they could also check to see if the film is in the collection of their public library and borrow it without charge (see public library section in this chapter).

Booking the Film

When you have chosen and located the film, telephone or write the distributor to book it. Many of the larger distributors have toll-free (800-) numbers for their clients to call. Telephoning has several advantages: you can find out immediately if the film is available for the date of your choice (always have alternatives in mind); you can discuss the rental rate; and you can request any promotional, informational or graphic materials and have them sent out that day. There is also the possibility of negotiating the rental price. Many of the small distributors, however, have put a lot of thought into their rates, operate on a low profit margin, and simply cannot afford to let the film out for less than their announced price. Don't be offended if these groups cannot barter with you. If you telephone, your conversation will go something like this:

- Tell whoever answers that you want to book a film; you may be put through to a regional agent.

- Identify yourself and the film you want to rent: "I am (your name) from the (your group) in (city). I am calling to see if (name of film) is available for (#) of showing(s) in (city)." Make sure that your first date choice is at least three to five weeks from the date you make the call. Alternate dates would be later. Ask the name of the person with whom you are speaking, and write it down.

- The booker will check the availability of the film, tell you your date is ok or ask for an alternate date.

- They will ask you for an address to which the film should be shipped and will assume this is also the address for correspondence (confirmations and bills). Tell them if there is any difference. Usually distributors will not ship to an individual's home, and you should use an address where someone will be in during regular business hours to accept delivery of the film. They will also ask for a telephone number.

- While you have the booker on the telephone, you should discuss the rental rate and the billing arrangements. Tell them if you have never booked a film from them before and a little about your organization and showing if they ask about it. Standard questions from bookers include: "What is the seating capacity of your hall?" "What admission will you be charging?" "How many people will be seeing the film?" These questions are for their records and to establish the rental rate.

- If you want publicity material (stills, reviews) about the

    film, ask them to send it to you or find out where it
would be available.

- When you have arrived at an agreement, ask them to
  reserve the film for you on that date.
- If the film you want is booked up for the following year,
  you might ask if the distributor has it "exclusively", or
  if it is available from another company. Some bookers
  may try to sell you another film. If the other suggestions
  sound interesting, ask for more (written) information.
  Say you will check on them and call back. You probably
  want to discuss any changes with the other people on
  the planning committee. If you are interested in showing
  films on a regular basis, ask the distributor to send
  you their current catalog.

You will have to follow up your telephone conversation with
a letter confirming your request. Use your organizational letterhead,
business letter format, and keep a copy. Telephoned reservations
are usually honored for about a week, so you should send your
letter (and check if required) right away. Basically, the letter should
repeat all of the details discussed on the telephone, and would
read something like this:

Address of distributor   Date

Dear _____:

    I am writing to confirm my telephone reservation
of (name of film) for (# and kind of) showing on (day, date,
year). The film will be shown in (name of hall), and should
be shipped to (address). We expect an audience of about
(#) people and will (will not) be charging an admission
fee (of $). Our check for the minimum guarantee of ($)
plus the ($) shipping charge is enclosed. We will appreciate
very much receiving the publicity materials and reviews
which you offered to send to help with our publicity efforts. Please address any correspondence to me at
(address). I can be reached by telephone at (#).

Sincerely,

If you choose not to telephone first, the letter should:

- Identify the film, the showdate and an alternate date.
- Give a billing and shipping address.
- Describe the kind of showing you plan (how many
  people, public or classroom, admission charge or not,
  how many times the film will be shown).

- Give the name and telephone number of the person responsible.

If you place your initial order by mail, do not send payment until the distributor sends an invoice. Check the back of the catalog for forms to use when ordering a film and include all of the requested information.

Don't put your schedule into effect until you have actually booked the film for a specific date. Within a week to ten days you should receive a written confirmation of your order from the distributor. Check this to be certain there are no mistakes (or unwanted substitutions) of title, date or price. Call or write immediately if you discover any errors. If you do not receive the written confirmation, call or write to find out what is wrong. Most often, you will not receive the film if you have not gotten the confirmation.

If you decide **not** to show the film for some reason, you must cancel your order well before the film is shipped to you (4 to 14 days, depending on the company). If you do not cancel in time and the film is shipped, you will be responsible for the rental fee whether or not you actually show the film.

Shipping of Prints

The distributor's responsibility is to send you a good print in time for your playdate. Ninety-nine times out of a hundred, there will be no problems regarding film delivery. If it is two days before your screening and the film has still not arrived, call the distributor to find out what is wrong. At that stage there is still time to rush another print to you; but if you wait until the day of your show to call, you could find yourself without a film. You pay the cost of having the film sent to you in addition to the rental fee. It is usually indicated on your confirmation order as a shipping/handling charge. You are also responsible for the costs of returning the film promptly the day after your scheduled playdate. Failure to send the film back can result in additional rental charges for each day you are late and, if you do not return the film on time, some other user may not have it for their showdate. Instructions for the return shipment are usually on your confirmation and restated in a form in the shipping case. Your contract will specify that you must insure any film when you send it through the mail or by a private carrier and usually will indicate the minimum amount of insurance.

Standard film shipping:
- U.S. Mail from a Post Office: Special 4th class or library rate, special delivery, insured. Also consider Express Mail service.

- United Parcel Service (UPS): Will usually pick up with 24-36 hours advance notice. You must call them with the following information — where to pick up the package, the dimensions, weight, and contents (educational materials) of the case, amount of insurance, and addressee (has to be a street rather than P.O. Box number). You can also take the film directly to the UPS depot.
- Bus: For short distances only (Next Bus Out Service, insured). This is also an emergency method. If you have to ship a film this way, call the distributor and arrange it beforehand. They will need to know the bus company; the name it is being sent to (bus companies file records alphabetically under the name of the addressee); the date and time the bus left your city; and when it will arrive in theirs.
- Air freight: very expensive but guaranteed overnight delivery.

No matter how you send the film back, get a receipt. Hold on to that receipt for six months or so. If anything happens to the film during the return shipment, you are responsible and will need the receipt to file a claim with the carrier.

Film Care and Liability

When the film arrives, open the carton, check the packing slip, the number of the reels, and the head leader of each reel to make sure that what you have is indeed the film you ordered. Make sure it is all there, and that it is "heads out" on the reels (usually the first three feet of film will be green leader marked with this information: film title, "heads" or "start", and Reel # of 1, 2, or 3). If there are reels missing, or any other problems, call the distributor immediately. If the film is "tails out" (usually red leader), you will have to rewind it before your showing. Do so immediately to confirm the title and reels. Don't believe anything written on the metal or plastic reels since they often get exchanged. More often than not what you receive is exactly what you ordered, but it is better to check and be sure.

From the time the film arrives to the time the distributor receives it, you are responsible for any damages or loss, so it is crucial that you use the film only as you have agreed, and keep it in a safe place. All prints are inspected on their return to the distributor's shipping house. You should report any damage to the print by placing a note in the case describing where and what the damage is. Most minimal damage will be considered by the distributor as normal wear and tear, for which there will not be any charge. You will be asked to pay for damages of a more serious nature, however, like a ten foot long section with broken sprockets, or a deep scratch throughout a new print—clearly not normal usage. You will be charged for the replacement cost for that section of the film. Your best protection is to use an experienced projectionist and a projector in good working order.

Remember that you have contracted to show the film a certain number of times at a particular time and place. Any unauthorized variations on your agreement with the distributor is a violation of the U.S. Copyright Law and carries extreme penalties. There have been prosecutions. Users should be aware that they are required to file an attendance report where admission is charged or rental is on a head count basis. These and other records can be audited by groups like the Non-Theatrical Film Distributors Association. As a renter, you are legally responsible for any loss, serious damage, or illegal use of the film on lease to you. You have a contractual obligation to the distributor which you assume when you order the film and receive your written confirmation. All these are compelling reasons not to loan the film to others. If you want to do an extra screening on your own, it is better to tell the distributor, since additional screenings during the same booking are charged at low rates.

PUBLIC LIBRARIES

George Rehrauer, in **The Film User's Handbook,*** presents a detailed chronology of the use of motion pictures in educational situations. We've excerpted some moments in the long history of film services in public libraries since they were among the first to recognize the importance of film in public education.

1914   Orrin G. Cocks argues for the acquisition, circulation, and presentation of motion pictures by libraries in his article, "Libraries and Motion Pictures — An Ignored Educational Agency."

1925   At the American Library Association Conference the recommendation is made that urban libraries contain information on sources of film, a selected group of libraries be encouraged to collect and distribute films in their areas, and an office be established to develop and implement a program of cooperation between public libraries and motion pictures.

---

* George Rehrauer, **The Film User's Handbook: A Basic Manual for Managing Library Film Services** (New York: R. R. Bowker Co., 1975).

1929   The Cleveland Public Library cooperates with a local movie theater to publicize the film SCARAMOUCHE by furnishing a bibliography, books, etc., designed to supplement or enrich viewing.

1939-45   About a dozen large urban public libraries organize their holdings of film and begin film services.

1946-49   Approximately 70 larger libraries establish collections and services.

1951   About 100 larger public libraries in the country circulate more than 36,000 films.

1953   The U.S. Office of Education reports that 2,600 institutions, companies and organizations, including about 166 public libraries, rent or lend films.

1972   Tom Brandon, former president of Brandon Films, estimates there are more than 1,000 public library film collections in the U.S.

The film departments of our public libraries are an enormous reservoir of free or inexpensive films, equipment and services. They are also one of the most important and accessible sources of information on all these areas (see Chapter 11). These services are available throughout much of the country, whether you live in a city, small town or rural area. Many groups are able to organize several screenings or an entire film series by using films from the library. Some libraries regularly program public exhibition series from their collections. People who are not accustomed to using the library should realize that libraries are public institutions, supported in part by tax dollars and designed to serve the public.

While policies and procedures will vary from library to library, individual users will be pleased at the spirit of cooperation that is typical of librarians. Mary Bullard, the young adult coordinator in a New York county library, described the services they offer in **Film Library Quarterly** (Vol. 10, #3 & #4, 1977):

The circulation of films to individuals, particularly teens, is probably not known to most county residents. Films may be both booked through branch libraries and picked up and returned to branch libraries. Popular films, though, must be booked well in advance. The length of use varies with the availability of the film and is two to five days.

She says that the Monroe County branches have audiovisual equipment for patrons to use and some have separate areas for film previewers. Her system has an active outreach program to church, school and community groups. Some film programs have been planned jointly for a branch library or at the group's meeting place. She concludes by stating that her staff is pleased to respond to genuine needs and welcomes community impact upon the library.

Mary Bullard's attitudes are characteristic of most librarians. Any group, regardless of size or specific interest, will find staff and services available. Familiarity with library routines will help you make effective use of its resources. The League of Women Voters, for example, has been using library films and materials for years in programs which they plan months and even years in advance.

Within each state, public libraries are organized into systems with a variety of resources and services. In addition to books, journals, periodicals and catalogs about films, libraries have collections of films, tapes, records, and, sometimes, film projectors which can be checked out. (If you borrow a projector, ask for a quick lesson on how it works). The only restrictions, in most cases, are that you have a library card, make a reservation in advance, and do not charge admission for a program using library materials. The library may also have an auditorium or room which groups can use for their programs.

Your local neighborhood library may be part of a city, regional, county and state system. Your neighborhood branch may not have all these resources available on the spot. Access is through your branch's connection with the larger systems. Many times a film will not be stored at the local library but at a central library which makes regular deliveries to the branches. You may have to wait a week or a month to obtain the title you want, but if the film is within the system (listed in the catalog or card file) you can usually have it delivered to a library close to you.

New York State, for example, is divided into 22 Public Library Systems. From one to five counties participate in each of these systems with as many as 55 member libraries within those counties. Member libraries have some resources of their own, depending on their size and organization, or, if not, they can utilize the resources available to all member libraries within the system. If you live in Pleasant Valley, New York, and want to show a program of animated films to children on Saturday morning, you can choose from the films available to member libraries in the Mid-Hudson Library System. You order the films from the system catalog and pick them up at the Pleasant Valley Library. In large cities, you may get quicker service by going directly to the main or central library.

THE COLLECTION AND CATALOG

You can get an overview of available films by looking through your library's film catalog. Some libraries acquire new films each month, but publish catalogs only once a year or every two years, so you might also check printed supplements or the card file for new purchases. The catalog contains an annotated alphabetical listing of system-owned 16mm films, often followed by a subject index, a name index, and listings of producers or directors. Libraries own films of every kind, from short experimental works to major motion pictures or television productions. Unlike a commercial catalog, no hard sells or testimonials will be used to describe the films. The listing will be straightforward and factual. The catalog will also indicate the films' appropriateness for use with different age groups, and often the librarian can answer other questions you may have about the film or tell you where to find the information.

RESTRICTIONS ON FILM USE

It is the policy of most library systems not to make films available for classroom use, school clubs or auditorium programs. Instructors are urged to use the film resources of their school instructional materials centers or approach distributors directly. You cannot charge admission to a film which you borrow from the library.

SCHEDULING AND BOOKING

An organization or individual can generally borrow a film if they have a library card and another form of identification. In some library systems a special audiovisual card is needed. The borrower will be asked to sign a registration form for the film and accept full responsibility for the safekeeping and prompt return of the film on the due date. Film requests should be made as far in advance as possible, usually through the member libraries of the system. Be clear about the booking procedures since confirmation methods vary. Some systems don't consider the film booked until it is confirmed by the system. Normally, you will be asked to fill out a media loan request form with the title, show date and other information. Some libraries have restrictions on how many films you may borrow at one time. If you need to cancel your reservation, do so as soon as possible to allow someone else to use the film. The film will be delivered to the library where you can pick it up the day before or the day of your showing and return it the day after. Overdue charges may be set by the library. In addition, if you don't return the film on time you may be keeping it from another user and this can result in the loss of your borrowing privileges. The library may ask you to fill out an attendance report which helps them evaluate the value and usefulness of the films, and allows you some input into the selection of films to be added to the collection.

DAMAGES

One important aspect of your relationship with the library is a basic respect for the material borrowed. All films are inspected after each screening and should be in good condition when loaned. If the film you have taken out breaks, you should report it to the librarian when you return it. The same holds true for any difficulties with a borrowed projector. If you follow the directions in Chapter 8, you are not likely to seriously damage equipment. But if something goes wrong, tell the library about it. Whereas film distributors have many prints of any particular film, libraries rarely have more than one. If you seriously damage a library film, you might be taking it out of circulation for everyone. The earlier problems are spotted, the less serious the repair is likely to be. The reference books, catalogs and other materials should also be handled scrupulously. It would cost you hundreds of dollars to purchase them on your own. If a library has to dole out funds to replace marked up, cut up, or torn materials, that leaves so much less in the budget for expanding the film and book collection.

WORKING WITH THE LIBRARY

Once you've looked through the film catalog and reference materials, you may want to set up an appointment to speak with the librarian about how the system works and to find out what other resources are available. Libraries review their film collections periodically, and some well-used prints go out of service while new films and replacement prints are purchased. Responsiveness to public needs is a library policy. If a community group or a consortium of groups is interested in a particular film they would use often were it available, they should recommend it to the librarian for purchase. Any title will have to go through the library's usual review, evaluation and selection process, which can be somewhat lengthy and complex. Nonetheless, films in which there is a demonstrated public interest, if suitable for the collection, may often be purchased.

An example of library and community cooperation comes from Toledo, Ohio, where in the seventies there was an increase in the Mexican-American population. The Farm Labor Organizing Committee (FLOC) came into existence to relate to all aspects of Chicano life, but specialized in the problems of the farm workers. They established a working relationship with several other community groups and together asked the local library to purchase a print of YO SOY CHICANO, a film used frequently in their educational work. The library benefited by adding a film to its collection which had a broad appeal to a large ethnic group previously not served. The community, in turn, had easy access to a film which was valuable and useful for its work. The library found that YO SOY CHICANO was also being used by church, civic and neighborhood groups which did not have predominantly Chicano memberships. The cooperation between FLOC and the library led to further discussion and the purchase of other films.

You can explore other ways of working with the library. For example, if your group owns a film, but has no way to inspect or clean it, you might donate it to the library where it will be adequately maintained, available for your use and for other groups as well. If a group is interested in purchasing a particular film, but doesn't have adequate funds, they could propose that the library review it for purchase and perhaps contribute a part of the print cost.

UNIVERSITY FILM LIBRARIES

Another film source is the state university film library or audio-visual center, which will have media produced at the university and often a large selection of all kinds of other films. While the primary purpose of most university film libraries is to make films available for their classroom use, many also serve the general public's need for continuing education. They usually operate on a self-supporting basis. A large university with several campuses may have one library service center for all of the campuses as well as the general public.

As sub-distributors of educational materials, university library systems have various restrictions on the circulation of their often quite substantial collections. Geographic limitations to the campus, region, or state may be imposed, but some universities will send their films anywhere in the United States. In some systems, films may be free only to campus faculty or organizations. Other universities charge fees for use, delivery, late return, loss and/or damage to prints, and catalog purchase. Methods of payment vary.

Catalogs of films in a university's collection, as well as bulletins that update acquisitions, are available directly from the university audiovisual library. These centers sometimes offer media-related services like equipment rental, equipment delivery and pickup, operator's services and film preview services (by reservation) within the local area. Film users should note any restrictions or special conditions governing the use of films as set forth in the catalogs. Observance of these conditions is the client's responsibility. Films may not be used as part of any profit-making or fund-raising program since permission to charge admission to the exhibition of these films usually cannot be granted by the university library. The primary national distributors retain this right, and only they can grant such permission. The university catalog will provide a distributor directory for the films, so if your group is planning a fund-raising event, it is easy to use the catalog to locate the national distributor.

OTHER FILM SOURCES

Churches, labor unions, professional organizations and interest groups all buy films and maintain them for use by their membership. If you are a member of such an organization or part of the constituency they serve, you can usually use films in their collections. Many public service organizations, ethnic federations, corporations and other institutions also have films for public use. There are a considerable number of sources for free films. The American Cancer Society may have a film on the effects of smoking. The Amalgamated Clothing and Textile Workers Union has a film called THE INHERITANCE, which is a stirring tribute to working class immigrants, and another called TESTIMONY which is about textile workers. Naturally, if someone has sponsored a film production or is providing it free of charge, they are likely to have a specific interest in doing so. That interest may coincide with yours or be opposed to it, but either can result in an interesting program.

LABOR UNIONS

Both national and local trade unions often have libraries of films dealing with economic, social and political issues of interest to the union and compatible with a trade union perspective. Some were produced by the unions and others were bought from outside producers, including independent filmmakers. Contact local affiliates first. They may have prints of their own or will be able to get prints from the parent organization. Each union's policy regarding access to the films and any costs involved will vary. In almost all cases, rental fees are nominal. While films have been produced or purchased for the educational use of the union membership, other groups involved in educational activities may also be allowed to use them. The Education Department of the union can generally provide you with a catalog of their films.

CHURCHES

Many church denominations have national audiovisual service centers for their members. Local churches may also buy prints of films, especially when they touch on issues of concern to local residents. Films may be used in regular presentations to the general church membership, for programs of smaller church groups or committees, and for special training or educational programs. These programs might be limited to church members or be open to the general public.

A catalog describing materials, procedures and policies is available from either a national service center or the local church. It will include films which have been produced specifically for the church and acquisitions on topics of interest to the church constituency. Many of these films deal with both national and international social issues, as well as concerns of various ethnic, age and interest groups. Churches make their film resources available to members and sometimes to other groups with similar concerns.

NON-PROFIT ORGANIZATIONS AND INTEREST GROUPS

There are many non-profit national and local organizations which will have useful films for special interest groups. You will want to investigate what films are available from organizations and associations involved in education programs or activities related to your own interests. If an organization uses a film regularly they probably know resource people who can speak on the subject. A women's health clinic may get useful films from a local women's organization or from groups involved in health related activities — a community health center, a local hospital, outpatient clinic, or consumer or public interest group providing information about health issues. As you investigate the resources in your local area, you should compile lists of films, equipment, spaces and resource people which are available for your on-going programs. As you develop this list, you may discover other local groups who will want to consult your resource lists and can add to them from their own experience. You may eventually develop a centralized information center and begin to build a network of people with similar concerns.

BUYING PRINTS

As indicated earlier, the commercial or self-distributor usually both rents and sells prints. If there is a particular film you plan to use more than three times, then it is usually cheaper in the long run for you to purchase the print rather than renting it each time. You may also have heard of a film which you believe would be particularly appropriate in your work. You should rent the film once before you purchase it to be sure it is actually useful for your group. Most distributors will send free preview prints to a group only if they are bona-fide film buyers like libraries. Many distributors have a policy, however, which discounts the film rental costs from the purchase price if you buy the film within a certain time after your rental. This policy in essence allows even non-institutional buyers to have a free preview prior to purchasing a film.

You will also discover that if you own a print of a film, you are likely to use it more often and in more innovative ways. Besides the intragroup screenings which may be part of your regular film program, you may develop ideas for public screenings with a variety of goals in mind: public education and information; consciousness raising; outreach; developing action programs; supplementing a speaker; or for entertainment. When you are low on

immediate cash but plan on using a title many times, you might consider working out a joint purchase arrangement with other groups,
or with a local library.

You must note the terms on the sales contract which the distributor will send you. A fairly standard contract used by many self-
distributors is an agreement between the distributor (who may be
the filmmaker) and the purchaser (your organization). The purchaser
agrees that purchase of the film is made subject to these conditions:

> . . . the film will not be altered or copied in any manner
> whatsoever, televised (either broadcast or closed circuit),
> shown commercially or theatrically, shown for profit, or
> advertised by paid public advertising without specific
> written authorization from the distributor. The film is sold
> only for showing and educational use by the purchaser
> (by 16mm optical projection only) and may not be re-
> rented, loaned for a fee, leased or sub-leased to others.

In essence, purchase of 16mm prints by an individual organization
or group is only for the use of that group within its own structure,
for its own programs. Purchase of the film does **not** make the
buyer a distributor.

PRINT MAINTENANCE

When you purchase a print for your group's use, make arrangements to keep it in good condition. All distributors inspect, clean,
and repair any damage to prints after each screening. This systematic
maintenance insures long print life and more pleasant film screenings. You will want to do the same. If you are part of an organization
with an audiovisual service center, these services may be available
to you directly. Both public libraries and university libraries with
film departments have similar services. If you are a group with
none of these resources, and have bought a single print or a few
films for your own work, you may want to make an arrangement
with an audiovisual center in a larger organization to periodically
inspect and repair the print for you.

Another arrangement might be to have a library maintain the
print for your group, making the film available to you as well as
to other interested organizations. You might also find a local filmmaker or film department who would be willing to inspect the print
for you periodically for a reasonable fee.

If you do buy a number of prints, you should consider buying
an inexpensive set of rewinds and do the work yourself. A print
should be checked for damage every time it is screened, and cleaned
with a dry, lintfree cloth to get off surface dirt which has accumu-
lated. This will prevent the dirt from getting ground into the film

and creating scratches and other damage (see Figure 13). Periodically, perhaps every five screenings, you should clean the film with professional film cleaner. Instructions are generally on the bottle. To prevent streaking, be sure to note that you should dampen the cloth and wind slowly through the film, making sure the cleaner dries as you go.

Other kinds of film maintenance — repairing broken sprockets, torn frames, creased sections, etc.— should be taken care of by a film professional. The most important thing to remember is that what you don't take care of initially will certainly worsen to create greater problems for you later — either by causing more serious, perhaps irreparable damage to your print, or by damaging a projector. Both can require more time and expense in repairs. If you should seriously damage a section of your print, you can contact the distributor who sold you the film and ask them to order a replacement section. The expense is minimal and keeping the print in top condition can make a great difference when you are showing one of your favorite films.

References

Educational Film Locator of the Consortium of University Film Centers
R. R. Bowker Company, 1180 Avenue of the Americas, New York, NY 10036, First Edition, 1978.

A unified list of titles held by the 50 member libraries and a standardization of their separate catalogs. The **Locator** provides a selective compilation of approximately 37,000 film titles listed alphabetically, annotated by CUFU librarians with an indication of each CUFU library holding the particular film. Other features include access by major subject groupings; subject heading and cross index to subject; subject, title and audience level index; series index; foreign titles index; and a producer/distributor directory. It also describes the policies and procedures of each library.

Handling, Repair, and Storage of 16mm Motion Picture Films
Research Technology Incorporated, 4700 Chase, Lincolnwood, IL 60646, 1977.

Pamphlet describing causes of damage to 16mm film, suggestions for the promotion of long film life, cleaning and lubrication, splicing, storage and inspection.

11 | INFORMATION SOURCES

National information services are listed in Chapter 14. In the chapter on film sources there are descriptions of public and university libraries which are also sources of information for those interested in researching and locating films to use. Libraries have a variety of reference materials as well as experienced people to help you. A quick look in the card catalog will locate books in the reference collection. The librarian will be able to direct you to other resources: film books and periodicals; catalogs of library owned films; files containing distributors' catalogs; and sometimes brochures from film exhibition programs.

Our bibliography provides a list of basic reference books, periodicals and filmographies that may be available in your library. Like films, printed materials may be available through an inter-branch or inter-library loan system. University libraries have similar reference materials and experienced staffs. You will want to find out what services they offer to the general public in addition to those for the university community. Some are members of the Consortium of University Film Centers mentioned earlier, are state or land-grant colleges, or have policies permitting them to serve people outside the university structure. If the university has a film studies or communications department, you may find that the library has developed an especially good section on film.

MEDIA ARTS ORGANIZATIONS

Across the country there are over 100 Media Arts Organizations or Media Arts Centers which generate a wide variety of film activities, programs, and services. For example, the exhibition, film archive, and distribution programs of the Museum of Modern Art in New York City, have, for 50 years, been an important source of education about the art of film. Many Media Arts Organizations emerged in the 1960's and now offer a broad range of film and video programs and services, including:

- The presentation of public exhibitions.
- Personal appearances, lectures, workshops and residencies by film and videomakers.
- The provision of production and post-production equipment and facilities.
- A wide range of courses in film and video studies, history, criticism, theory and production.

- Private screenings for study.
- Archives and collections of national and regional films and tapes.
- The maintenance of specialized book and periodical libraries.
- The publication of scholarly periodicals and newsletters.
- Workshops, seminars and training programs.
- Broadcast or assistance in broadcasting programs seen on public and cable television.
- Sponsorship of touring programs.
- Provision of public information services.
- Services for the independent film and videomaking community.

Not every organization offers all of the services listed above; many have specific focuses such as exhibition or equipment access, and some specialize in particular aspects of the field. They are major centers for film/video activity in a region, and will have highly developed resources and experienced staff people. When they can, Media Arts Organizations will make their resources and expertise available to members of the public.

SMALLER ORGANIZATIONS

Some cities will have small organizations working locally as facilitators of film use. They may serve as a centralized information center or may even have a small collection of films available for use by community groups. For example, the Star Film Library in Boston provides information on films, programming, promotion and other skills for putting on a film program. They help groups find out about distributors, local filmmakers, equipment, spaces for local film programs and have recently started offering workshops on film use. Other small groups are involved in similar activities throughout the country.

You will find that other local organizations with similar interests are good sources of information about specific films. When considering their suggestions, keep in mind how similar or dissimilar your expected situation and constituency might be. Your final evaluation will ultimately be in terms of your own goals, not those of another group. Perhaps an organization receives or publishes a newsletter or other materials where films are described. Regular film programmers and exhibitors such as a university film society, a film showcase, an art theater, a person who teaches film at a college or high school, a local filmmaker, or even a commercial theater may also be good information sources. While they are not necessarily service organizations, they are constantly on the lookout for films to show and may be able to give you the information you need. Public broadcasting stations can help you find the distributor for programs they have aired.

STATE, REGIONAL OR LOCAL ARTS AGENCIES

A resource that many groups may be unfamiliar with is the arts council which exists in every state. They range from a state council on the arts to various local councils, agencies, and commissions. The amount of help and information such agencies can provide varies considerably from one state to another and even from year to year depending on budgets. For example, New York State has no less than 78 community arts councils which serve virtually every city, town, and county.

Councils are often perceived primarily as sources for grants, but they may also have personnel who can direct groups to unknown resources. Arts council people will know, for example, the location of film collections in the state and what funding sources are interested in film programs. Some organize touring programs of films and filmmakers in cooperation with local sponsors. While some arts councils are trying to serve a general information function, basically they will know about their grantees or do liaison work. Listed below are the types of services offered by councils around the country.

- Publish newsletters or cultural calendars about artistic events in their area. They can often be used as a clearinghouse to avoid conflicts of scheduling.
- Provide directories of cultural resources within their state or community.
- Maintain specialized libraries of interest to the artist and art organizations.
- Sponsor workshops and seminars in subjects of interest to arts organizations such as fundraising, accounting, and public relations. A few offer bookkeeping services, health plans for independent artists, and group purchase plans.
- Give scholarships, grants, and awards or serve as intermediaries for those who do. They are able to advise on deadlines and procedures for the National Endowment for the Arts grants and other sources of financial support.
- Provide funds for low cost printing for arts groups.
- Publish directories of space for exhibitions, performances, or meetings.

There may also be an organization in your city or region which acts as a clearinghouse for information about the arts. The institution may provide local, regional or statewide information which you can receive by writing or calling a central office. There may also be local initiatives by groups responding to specific community needs, as well as government funded programs.

References

Report on the 1979 National Conference of Media Arts Centers at Lake Minnewaska, N.Y.
From Pittsburgh Filmmakers, Inc., P.O. Box 7467, Pittsburgh, PA 15213 or from the Foundation for Independent Video and Film, Inc., 99 Prince St., New York, NY 10012.

Film and Video Makers Directory
Film Section, Museum of Art, Carnegie Institute, 4400 Forbes Ave., Pittsburgh, PA 15213.

A listing of individuals and institutions in the USA and abroad "intended to encourage and facilitate a wider use of exhibition and lecture tours by film and video makers" includes many of the Media Arts Organizations.

12 | EXPANDED FILM PROGRAMS

If you found that screening films — whether for your own group or for the general public — was a productive experience, and one you would like to repeat, it is time to consider long-range planning. Chapters 10 and 11 discuss the resources and information which can help you. Long-range planning is dependent upon realistic goals and clearly defined purposes, so your evaluation process should guide you. This chapter offers suggestions about planning film series or festivals, using films for fundraising, and special events. These activities require planning, commitment, and the organizational, public relations and technical skills discussed previously.

It is not necessarily desirable or advantageous for all groups to move from simple film events to series, festivals or premieres. Many groups limit their film activities to small audiences or situations which require minimal efforts. Others may find themselves creating a small film library for long-range educational work. There is nothing wrong with showing one film at a time and discovering what is most effective, or using the same film many times. Other groups have found that a series, a yearly film festival, or an annual premiere works well for them. There are groups which show films once or twice a year, and those which present screenings regularly. Your concern is to develop the program which is most advantageous to you.

FILM SERIES

You may want to consider presenting a series or another film program when:

- More people attend than you expected.
- After the show, people suggest films relating to your group's concerns.
- People express their enthusiasm about your program and their interest in opportunities for similar experiences, to see more films about that issue, or "like that one."
- Weeks afterwards, the film and ideas raised by the film or discussion, are still topics of conversation.
- The conclusions of your evaluation session indicate that a logical next step is to present more films.

If you did have a successful screening, beware of dangerous complacency. Let's say that many people came, you achieved your group's goals, and everyone had a good time. Obviously you had the right film at the right moment for that audience. You have something positive and concrete to build on, but it does not necessarily follow that more of the same will be equally well received.

If you do not evaluate conscientiously, you may find yourself working under false assumptions. If the group decides to screen another film, do you want to show a film "like that one," something different, or a less well-known film that is considered important? Do you want to show a film at all? Will as large an audience be attracted? Does that matter? Could you compensate for a lesser known film through special publicity, word of mouth, or networking with groups you have now contacted? Should the group consider a film series?

The advantages to presenting films in a series:

- People look forward to and save time for regularly scheduled events. Running a program over a period of time allows word of mouth about it to build. You have the advantages of long-range planning.
- There are educational benefits since you can balance areas of interest. Each film in the series provides a new dimension to a given topic. Another approach is to move from a simple overview type of film to more detailed examinations of the same subject. Programming like this develops a common body of shared knowledge and your discussions at the fourth and fifth program will be much more exciting.
- Your time is more efficiently used when you plan to show six or ten films as a series than when you show films on six or ten separate occasions. Less time is needed to organize, arrange space, choose films, and plan publicity, since these tasks can be done once for six events rather than starting from scratch each time.
- As in any volume business, there are financial advantages. You will need only to print one poster and flyer for the series. While they may have to be larger to include the necessary information, and you will have to print more of them for staggered distribution, over all it will still be much cheaper than printing six individually. A hidden financial advantage is that you are able to budget for the entire series, and can book some expensive films and some that are cheaper. Profits from the better-known films can subsidize possible losses from those which aren't surefire draws.
- Good programming will give you room for experimentation. The attraction for coming to one film in a series

is partially to see how it relates to the others. Even if people are not familiar with the film's reputation, they are more likely to take a chance if they have confidence in the series as a whole.

- A series may become a service to the public, a forum offering cultural, artistic or informative programs which would otherwise be unavailable in that community.

The disadvantages to presenting films in a series:

- The commitment of your time and energy to one activity is greater and longer. If you let people know that you are going to show six particular films within a given time frame, you must follow through on that commitment, even if you get tired of setting up chairs or something else important comes up.
- You will incur a greater total amount of film rentals unless you are borrowing the films from a library. This prospect may not be wise for some groups, and all groups should, of course, prepare a complete budget for the entire series before committing themselves. Even if the films are free, you might incur other expenses.
- A series is not a good idea if you don't like the idea of long-range planning, since you will have to book all of the films in advance, work out a publicity strategy, and keep telling people about the program. If this is not your style, if your group is not stable, or there is a high turnover and you can't count on people consistently, the screening committee might dissolve after the second film with four more to go.
- Don't plan a series if there are not that many films you really think should be shown. Sometimes the idea of a series can push you into renting films just to fill a slot rather than because they fulfill your goals or relate to your programs. This would be a big waste of effort. Single screenings of those really important and worthwhile films which meet your needs, or screenings of essential films as they come to your attention would be more effective.

PLANNING A SERIES

All of the considerations at the beginning of the book about planning, organizing, budgeting, and publicity, apply to film series or festivals. A series is around six or more films presented as some kind of "package," but a series can include as many films and events as it makes sense to you to present. In planning a series, you evaluate not only each individual film, but the whole thing. There should be an overall theme or direction so that the whole is more than the sum of the parts. Think of an overall name for the set of programs and a rationale to help people understand why this is a series. Film series have been organized around every conceivable topic, issue, country, ethnic group, film genre, director, performer, ideology, or chronology, but, as with single programs, you will want to design something that makes sense for your group.

The order in which the films are shown is important to a series making sense as a whole. You might pay attention to historical developments, move from general to specific films, from films which report on the facts to films which raise questions, or to films which offer various analyses. If the films explore aspects of a subject, determine an order to that exploration. Don't leave it up to chance, but try to structure a series that moves along logically. The process is not unlike planning or taking a course if you are a teacher or a student. You probably will not want to start with the most difficult film, but with those films which prepare the audience to get the most from the later, more challenging ones. One strategy is to show the best known film first to get the attention of your potential audience, and then explain to them how the other films relate to it.

Each film series will have its own dynamics. Consider which film is the most dramatic, comic, heavy or lightweight; which one leaves people feeling energetic, which one demands concentration and reflection. Is there a film which moves in a stately manner and one which has a rapid-fire pace? Try to balance the rhythms and energy levels of the films so the series provides a variety of experiences. Pragmatic factors such as the availability of particular films will also enter the picture, so plan different films and alternative sequences. Make up an events calendar and check with other groups to see how the films fit into the rhythm of other events in your area. As with single programs, you should plan for resource people, visiting filmmakers, discussions, program notes, refreshments, and other program variations.

The timing and duration of the series is another decision to be made with care. Generally it is better to spread the films over a longer period of time than to concentrate them. A film festival or a series of films for a particular celebration would be a possible exception to this. Five films in a series on successive Mondays would generally be better than showing all the films in one week. The hardcore public you can count on is much more likely to give you one night a week for five weeks than every night of a given week. The longer time also gives you a chance to build up momentum and for people to hear about the films through word of mouth. Another choice would be to show the films every other Monday, or the first

Center Screen's 8th Annual Winter Animation Series

THE LARGEST ANNUAL PRESENTATION OF INDEPENDENT ANIMATION IN THE U.S.

CENTER SCREEN
information: 253-7620.

A project of the University Film Study Center, Inc., presented in collaboration with the Carpenter Center.

Independent Film
Winter Series

**Carpenter Center
for the Visual Arts
19 Prescott St.
Harvard University
Cambridge, Ma.**

1) Fri., Sat., Sun., Feb. 9, 10, 11.
7:30 and 9:30 p.m.

13th INTERNATIONAL TOURNEE OF ANIMATION.
New England Premiere.

James M. Shook s TITLES John Boster s MANDARIN ORANGES Otto Foky s BABYFILM Scenes with Beans Co Hoedeman s SAND CASTLE Le Chateau du Sable Hovt Yeatman s CANNED PERFORMANCE Marcel Janovics THE FIGHT HUZOOK Benvis Dovnikovic s N N Vincent Collins FANTASY Istu Patel s DEAD GAME Sara Petty s FURIES C Henry Selick s PHASES Aleksandar Marks and Vladimir Jutrisa s NIGHTMARE Moa Steve Lisberger s EVENING AT THE POPS Guido Manuli s FANTABIBLICAL and Derek Phillips Stan Hayward and Ted Rockley s WHEN I M RICH

The New England Premiere of the most recent Tournee an annual selection of some of the finest animation from around the world sponsored by the international animation organization ASIFA. Although a few of these films have been shown by CENTER SCREEN and others this is the first showing of the 13th Tournee itself in this region including John Boster s MANDARIN ORANGES a parody of a Busby Berkeley theme using costumed and choreographed oranges Sara Petty s FURIES a study in pastels and charcoal of the dynamic movement of two cats with music by Ned Bovern and Marcel Janovics THE FIGHT on the give and take between a sculptor and his creation

2) Fri., Sat., Sun., Feb. 16, 17, 18.
7:30 and 9:30 p.m.

NEW PERSONAL ANIMATION — Part I.
Boston-area Premieres.

Suzan Pitt s ASPARAGUS Susan Rubin s NOVEMBER '47 JANUARY 1978 and SCISSORS and THE PARK BENCH Kathleen Laughlin s A ROUND FEELING Michael Leaf and Gwen Stores s ECCH DIRTY John Weldon and Eunice Macaulev s SPECIAL DELIVERY Al Sens A HARD DAY AT THE OFFICE POETS ON FILM Part I Margaret Baxin Doogan s SCREW Derek Lamb and Janet Perlman s WHY ME Ishu Patel s AFTERLIFE and Veronika Soul s TALES FROM THE VIENNA WOODS

New works by film artists who use animation as personal expression including Suzan Pitt s ASPARAGUS a visual poem that is an erotic allegory of the creative process in which a woman views and performs the passages of sensual and artistic discovery John Weldon and Eunice Macaulev s SPECIAL DELIVERY a tale of the rigors of mail service Al Sens A HARD DAY AT THE OFFICE on the strains of office work and Margaret Baxin Doogan s SCREW a rendition of the poem by Diane Wakowski

3) Fri., Sat., Sun., Feb. 23, 24, 25.
7:30 and 9:30 p.m.

NEW PERSONAL ANIMATION — Part II.
Boston-area Premieres.

Kathy Rose s PENCIL BOOKLINGS Larry Bevder s LOOTS Jeffrey Hale s BLIND MAN S BLUFF John Canemaker s CONFESSIONS OF A STARDREAMER Sara Petty s SHADOW Al Sens INTERVIEW with the MAN JOHI SO/ILI S PUXETSUN HELP Patri s Veronika Soul s INTERVIEW HELL ARE YOU Steven Weatherly s THE WALKER Maureen Selwood s SEMPRE LIBERA and others

More new works of personally expressive animation including Kathy Rose s PENCIL BOOKLINGS an encounter between the artist and her independently minded creations Veronika Soul s INTERVIEW HELL ARE YOU a spirited collage animation exchange of letters and Jeffrey Hale s BLIND MAN S BLUFF in which a sightless character dependent on other senses to its demise is seduced by its own ego

4) Fri., Sat., Sun., March 2, 3, 4.
7:30 and 9:30 p.m.

CUT-OUT ANIMATION.

Stan Vanderbeek s SCIENCE FRICTION Jean Francois Laguionie s A DEMOISELLE ET LA VIOLONCELLE Lotte Reiniger s MARGEEN1 George Dunning s UPRIGHT AND WRONG Bernhard Barisen s L IDEE THE IDEA Emanuele Luzzati and Giulio Gianini s PULCINELLA THE CIRCUS directed by Jo Tinka and others

A rare public showing of works which highlight the possibilities of cut-outs one of the oldest animation techniques including George Dunning s UPRIGHT AND WRONG in which cut out shapes are released from their obligations to gravity THE HUMAN CIRCUS a series of circus acts designed and animated by Tinka and three other Czech artists that demonstrate the limitations and potential of cut out movement and Bernhard Barisen s L IDEE THE IDEA 1932 an Expressionist masterpiece on the revolutionary struggle between the artist s idea represented by a woman and the forces of oppression Programming consultation by Len Berter of the Art Gallery of Ontario

5) Fri., Sat., Sun., March 9, 10, 11.
7:30 and 9:30 p.m.

POLISH ANIMATION.

Boston-area Premieres of Marek Kurosa s VIEW FILM THE TRIP Marian Cisarns s NIGHT LIFE Zbioniew Kudla s SQUARE ASU Piotr Szpakowicz s THE RUINS and Jerzy Kucia s THE CIRCLE Jan Nienicjek Nizinski s AUDILOGUE Zofia Oraczewska s THE CASTLE Dariusz Zawilski s SCREW and others

Recent premieres of modern animation from the Polish studios often represented with united poetic statements and a true ethnic humor in Marek Kurosa s VIEW FILM THE TRIP an adventurous character discovers the ultimate future s SOLVABLE ASU a parable while fumbling to find a way to rise to the highest levels to reveal an absurd worldview Zbioniew Kudla s SQUARE ASU then another early works from six other animating units

6) Fri., Sat., Sun., March. 16, 17, 18.
7:30 and 9:30 p.m.

ANIMATION FROM HOLLAND.
Boston-area Premieres.

In cooperation with The Ministry of Culture, The Hague, The Netherlands

Paul Driessen s DAVID and THE KILLING OF AN EGG Tsvia Oran s THREADY GAMES Peter Brouwer and Gerrit van Dijk s BUTTERFLY Rene Reus CARTOON TEKENFILM and SELF PORTRAIT Gerrit van Dijk s "Janeat" tube and SPLINTFLESH Bas Berna and Dennis van Boven s LATEX AMATE k Ronald Bonima s BRAINWASH and others

Recent works from Holland which in the past few years has been producing a wide range of imaginative animation including the two new films by Paul Driessen AN OLD BOX CAT S CRADLE DAVID and THE KILLING OF AN EGG both of which will demonstrate how easily big creatures spoil the lives of the small Gerrit van Dijk s cube MENcube in which two cubes—a man and a woman move through their life-cycle telling the story of the games people play and in Rene Reus SELF PORTRAIT the component parts of a portrait become individual beings

7) Fri., Sat., Sun., March 23, 24, 25.
7:30 and 9:30 p.m.

ABSOLUTE ANIMATION.

Hy Hirsh s SCRATCH PAD Robert Russell s NEURON Walter Rutmann s OPUS II, III and IV Roger Anderson s TABLADONS Barry Spinello s 6 LOOP PAINTINGS Jules Engle s TRAIN LANDSCAPE Robert Breer s LMNO Larry Cuba s 378 Mary Ellen Bute s MOOD CONTRASTS Oskar Fischinger s CIRCLES Paul Glabicki s DIAGRAM FILM and Franos Lee s SUMI-E

A program of works made frame by frame many presented in their Boston-area Premieres which continue the tradition of the absolute film of Walter Rutmann Hans Richter and others Absolute film has nothing to do with narrative tends toward the abstract and purely graphic and emphasizes those properties which are available only in film including 378 a new computer animation by Larry Cuba best known for his special effects work on STAR WARS Barry Spinello s 6 LOOP PAINTINGS produced by scratching and painting directly on the film stock and Robert Breer s most recent film LMNO

8) Fri., Sat., Sun., March 30, 31, April 1.
7:30 and 9:30 p.m.

ANIMATION BY CAROLINE LEAF.

Caroline Leaf in person will discuss her films at both shows on Friday, March 30 only. Presented under the auspices of the Canadian Consulate General, Boston.

The World Premiere of a new film by Caroline Leaf and Veronika Soul plus Caroline Leaf s PETER AND THE WOLF or SAND 1969 ORFEO 1971 HOW BEAVER STOLE FIRE 1972 THE OWL WHO MARRIED A GOOSE LE MARIAGE DU HIBOU 1974 THE STREET 1976 and THE METAMORPHOSIS OF MR SAMSA 1977

A retrospective of the work and personal appearance by Caroline Leaf whose exceptional use of sand, ink on glass and other techniques to tell stories and animate began in her class-work at the Carpenter Center. We expect to present the World Premiere of a new as yet untitled film by Ms. Leaf and Veronika Soul. The program also includes THE OWL WHO MARRIED A GOOSE a sand animation based on an Eskimo story, THE STREET in which ink on glass is used to tell the Mordecai Richler story of the meaning of death to small modern and SANDs or PETER AND THE WOLF her first film. This program is part of the Canadian Consulate General, Boston s celebration of the National Film Board s 40th Anniversary.

(or second or last) Monday for five months. Whether you choose a weekly, biweekly or monthly schedule, try to make it regular so that people can plan on it easily. If possible, show all the films at the same location. This makes your set-up easier and people get used to one location; alternatively, several groups cooperating on a series may want to rotate sites in various communities. If you are planning a series with more than six films, consider a short break into two parts rather than one long series. The audience for a series will probably consist of some regulars who come to every film, and other people who attend the particular films which interest them.

If you are charging admission and hope to attract the general public as well as a core of regulars, a series ticket (in addition to single admission) encourages people to attend. A series ticket can be sold in advance, which helps your cash flow, while psychologically committing the buyer to seeing most of the films. If the admission to each of the five films in your series is $2.00, you can discount the series ticket so that five admissions cost only $7.50. Decide whether or not you want it to be transferable and if the ticket can be used for more than one person at a time. Larger series — for example, one which shows twenty films in six months — should offer series tickets which are still reasonably priced and don't commit the buyer to all of the films. In this case, if a single admission is $1.50, then a series ticket of ten admissions for $10.00 would be quite attractive, and with two series tickets a dedicated regular could see all 20 films for only $20.00 instead of $30.00.

A publicity campaign like the one outlined in Chapter 5 contains the basic elements for publicizing a series. Book all of the films at one time so that your schedule is secure and you receive publicity materials from each of the distributors. For flyer and poster design, follow the principles outlined previously, although a larger size may be necessary to accommodate the necessary information about all of the films. Additional information will include:

- The series title and some copy about the organizing theme or focus.
- The place, day, and time for all the films. If this is the same for each film, you only have to put it on once. Make sure it is clear that all films will be at this place, on this day, at this time. If this data varies for each film, make it readily apparent.
- The date for each film.
- Information about series tickets.

Your media work should take advantage of the "packaging" of the films in the series, and can emphasize the theme, subject, or issues covered. The long-range planning for the series will also include the timing of press releases and public service announce-ments. Initial releases can go out announcing the opening of the series, concentrating on the theme, the special nature of the whole event, and the schedule. A newspaper article about the series can be beneficial as you are about to begin. Additional releases featuring information about each program in the series can be prepared at the same time, and sent out on a staggered schedule to assure regular listings. You will usually get greater media response for a series than for a single screening, and if you bring in a resource person or filmmaker, you should get attention for that as well.

It's a good idea to test the waters first before going to all the work of planning a complete series. Try out some single films, per-haps free ones from the library, and evaluate the results. If you plan a few single film showings, save all the suggestions for films which come up during selection or after the screening. Get catalogs from distributors and review the information sources available to you locally. Send letters of inquiry to national organizations, compile film lists from relevant filmographies, and generally familiarize your-self with what films are available. By the time you want to do a film series, you will already have a lot of resources.

The distinction between a film series and a film festival is not at all a clear one. Film festivals of international importance have rules about entries and are competitive, with juries which give prizes. Others are essentially marketplaces. In the United States, the major film festivals are often responsible for introducing new films to the public, film critics and distributors, and the reception a film gets at a festival can influence whether or not it is released and dis-tributed. Festivals are usually annual events, and often show films from early morning to late at night, sometimes in several locations at once. They may take place in a time span of two to three days or two to three weeks. Some festivals present all kinds of films, while others focus on a particular kind such as shorts, independent films, experimental, or documentary films.

You can call a series of films a film festival if you like. This may be appropriate if the series is really special, is a celebration, a competition, if you are soliciting entries from filmmakers, if it features some new films, films not yet shown in your area, or the participation of filmmakers, speakers, and celebrities. A "festival" may have a less academic sound for publicity purposes than "series" does, and if your primary intent is entertainment, fundraising, and publicity, you should think more along these lines.

PREMIERES

A premiere is simply the first time a film is shown publicly in a given area. A film festival may include older films or some premieres, and single premieres of new films are great fundraising events. A premiere has a certain "first on your block" appeal. It is truly surprising how many excellent films, some internationally and nationally acclaimed, often do not play even in the commercial theaters of major urban areas. Simply because a film has not yet been shown publicly in your area doesn't mean that it will not draw people, and many groups use premieres not only to raise funds, but also as an effective way of calling attention to themselves and the issues in the film. If the film relates to your concerns, and you mount a good publicity campaign, you should do quite well with a premiere. Of course, if the distributor or filmmaker is holding out for an opening of the film in a commercial theater, they will usually not let your group have the film first. If this is the case, later on in this chapter we discuss working with your local movie theater in a variety of ways including premieres.

Your best chance for success with a premiere or film festival is if you have access to a large mailing list and are satisfied that you have the outreach capabilities to really attract people. The screening committee for a premiere or festival might include some people who are prestigious within the community as well as people doing the organizational work. As with any program, a film which you premiere should have special relevance to your group. The finances and arrangements would be similar to any program. If you want to keep informed of new films, you should follow **Variety***, a weekly trade publication, the Sunday edition of **The New York Times**, and film journals.

A good candidate for a local premiere was HARLAN COUNTY, USA, which won an Academy Award as best documentary before it had been screened in many of the nation's rural areas or smaller cities. The film had many publicity "hooks" for groups to work with. It could be billed as a film about Appalachia, about mining and energy, about union struggles, as the work of a woman director, or as an example of documentary technique. Commercial Hollywood features that deal with specific ethnic groups, important events, or notable people are other possibilities. International films are also worthy of consideration by some groups. They have often attracted national media attention despite limited distribution and exhibition. There are also probably many independent features, documentaries and short films which have not played in your community.

The exposure for a group doing a premiere can be very high, and the public service and glamor aspect is an asset when appealing to the media. Consider treating any out of town visitor as a personality for the media. For example, in a small town you could hold an

---

* **Variety**, 154 West 46th Street, New York, NY 10036. Reports on film popularity across the country and internationally. Available by subscription or in the library.

PHILADELPHIA PREMIERE

HARLAN COUNTY, USA

HARLAN COUNTY, USA is about a Kentucky miners' strike. Director Barbara Kopple evokes affection and admiration for the men — and even more, the women - of Harlan County. This is a warm and incisive film which documents the traditions of mining families, their attempts to unionize and to reform a corrupt union.

"A REMARKABLE PASSIONATE WORK. A REMINDER THAT THERE CANNOT BE NEUTRALS—ANYWHERE."
– Judith Crist

"A GREAT SUBJECT, AND THE TASTE AND SENSITIVITY NOT TO BETRAY IT."
Pauline Kael

Produced and Directed by Barbara Kopple/Principle Cinematography Hart Perry/Director of Editing Nancy Baker   From Cinema 5 PG

live music
HAZEL DICKENS

playing with WINNIE WINSTON, JULIA GOLDENSOHN, and the FICTION BROTHERS
—mining and union songs—

NEW WORLD THEATRE 19th & MARKET
WEDNESDAY   MAY 25   8 PM

RECEPTION TO FOLLOW
with
Refreshments $3.50 ADMISSION

BENEFIT SCREENING

A Benefit for THE INDEPENDENT PUBLISHING FUND OF THE AMERICAS and THE PEOPLE'S FUND in support of THE PHILADELPHIA RANK AND FILE LABOR LAW PROJECT -- NLG.   Done in cooperation with the NEIGHBORHOOD FILM PROJECT.

airport press conference for an arriving filmmaker. Asking other groups to co-sponsor the premiere can help expand your media contacts. A distributor may be able to arrange for a guest appearance by the director or another of the film's principals. Premieres can be especially big affairs outside of the major metropolitan areas, and a distributor will be pleased if one of their films gets a boost in an area where they cannot usually afford extensive promotional efforts. If you are premiering a film, sometimes distributors will negotiate with you regarding publicity costs, letting you deduct some percentage of them from the film rental.

While premieres tend to be thought of primarily as fundraisers and ways of creating a lot of publicity, there are other considerations. An experience on the east coast illustrates this. A group had just formed around the issue of rights of mental patients. They were aware of a new documentary, HURRY TOMORROW, which presented that issue in a compelling fashion. Although this film was usually shown in educational settings, the group decided that a film premiere would be its first public activity. Despite their limited resources, the group prepared a mailing of flyers, presented a press screening, and got excellent reviews and media coverage. The issue was a difficult one, however, and the attendance for the week-long run of the film barely paid expenses. By all apparent criteria, the effort could be evaluated only as a partial success. The next six months proved that judgment inaccurate.

Each night, members of the group had been at the theater, introduced the film, had literature in the lobby, and talked individually with members of the audience. A significant number of people who either came to the film or were aware of it became interested in the group and its work, and some were deeply affected by what they had seen or read. These people got in touch with the sponsors. The first noticeable effect was an increased demand for the group's literature. This was followed by invitations to speak to school classes, church groups, and at various organizational forums. Membership began to rise. People who had seen the film and were impressed with it and the representatives of the group, began to refer people to them or to call upon their assistance. In that six month period, of course, the group had also been quite active, but they concluded the film premiere had been a good introduction to their group, given them media contacts, and provided them with more visibility and concrete outreach than they might have gained through years of conventional approaches.

PRESS SCREENINGS

If the films are special, consider a "press screening" or preview for the media in your area in addition to your regular publicity. Try to interest the media people enough so that they will write reviews or feature articles (about the film and the festival) or interview the filmmaker. Films that open commercially in major cities usually have advance press screenings, sponsored by the distributor or exhibitor.

You will have to make arrangements with the distributor to get the film(s) in advance. In some cases, this means receiving the print for a press screening, returning it to the distributor, and having it sent again for the actual program. Your press screening must be far enough in advance for journalists to be able to write their reviews and get them into the respective media before your opening night.

Call the press to see if it is within their policy to preview films from your festival. Some media have policies, for example, which prohibit their reviewers from covering films not opening for extended runs in commercial theaters. This rule may be overlooked if your film has never been shown before, if a reviewer is very interested, or if it is an important film which simply has not been picked up by a theater. Other media may review anything they think will be of interest to the public.

The press screening should be held at a convenient place during regular business hours. About ten days to two weeks before the screening send out a professional-looking press release to your media list, inviting them to the screening and telling them about the film. Mount a major effort, beginning with the most important press and media outlets, and contacting not only film critics, but also entertainment and feature editors, columnists, political writers, or any writer who covers an area relevant to the film. In a large metropolitan area, this means sending releases to several different people at the same paper and all major radio and television stations. In addition, contact campus newspapers, community newspapers, local magazines, appropriate newsletters, FM radio stations, public television, and any other media voice in your area. You may also want to invite people who can help you with the word of mouth campaign, as well as resource people and the members of your group who will be working on the event. Four or five days before the screening start your follow-up calls to the list, beginning with the most important contacts first. If you get regrets, offer to send them some information about the film.

It is standard practice to prepare a "press kit" for the media to be given out at the screening. The more information you provide the potential reviewer, the less effort it will require for them to write an interesting review or article. At the minimum, you should have materials that describe each film and the purpose of your program. Be sure to include:

- Production data, credits and cast.
- A synopsis of the film.

- Background information about the film.
- Awards, major festival screenings, and other information that lends importance or credibility.
- A brief biography of the filmmaker.
- Reprints of interviews with the filmmaker or other background material.
- Black and white still photographs from the film (5" × 7" minimum).
- Reviews of the film from other cities.
- Information about when, where, and why the film will be shown publicly.
- Information about the availability of someone from your group or the filmmaker for interviews.
- Background on your group and a contact person.

Press kits do not need to be expensively produced; they can be mimeographed or xeroxed. If during your calls interested media people say they cannot attend, ask if they would like you to mail or drop off a press kit. Many smaller newspapers are hungry for copy, have limited staffs, and may end up running your press kit materials as an article. If you will be having the filmmaker as a guest, contact all the talk shows at local radio and TV stations.

Many distributors will furnish you with materials appropriate for a press kit. In fact, you may find yourself working closely with a distributor to get readymade newspaper ads, background on the film, graphics, and the use of films for press screenings. In some cases, distributors may help to put a festival or premiere together and work actively with local sponsors. If you are showing films by independent filmmakers, they also will care about the coverage of their film by the press, and can help out a lot.

FUNDRAISING WITH FILMS

If your primary purpose is fundraising, here are some standard methods which have worked for groups to increase the fundraising potential of film events. Of course, they all depend on good publicity, organizing, and volunteer efforts.

ADVANCE TICKET SALES

If you can get your publicity material out at least a month in advance, preselling tickets by mail and personal contact can help increase your attendance. A form for advance tickets can be included on the flyers; be sure to include the price of the tickets, the mailing address, a cutoff date for mail order, and space for name, address and zip code. Ask people to send a check or money order, payable to your group, and a self-addressed, stamped envelope (SASE) for returning the tickets. You can offer a discount for advance orders, and add all those names and addresses to your mailing list. Print up advance tickets with the name of the event, the date, day, time, place, price, name of your group and an information phone number on them. They should also be numbered. Make up a ledger to record all orders, how payment was made, and when the tickets were sent out. All mail orders received after the cutoff date should be held at the box-office for pick up at the screening.

Advance tickets can also be given to members of your group and other cooperating groups to sell. People who are supporters of your group might be persuaded to buy a number of these tickets for their own use or to be given away as gifts. Always give the sellers copies of your flyers. All advance tickets and money from sales should be called in the day before the event so you know how many have been sold, and the number of seats left for people who show up that night. People who have advance tickets need not wait in line and should be guaranteed seating.

SPONSORSHIPS

In addition to advance tickets, you can list sponsors of the event on the flyer. Sponsors or patrons can be individuals, other organizations and businesses or other sources who can make contributions to insure that the event is successful in meeting its fundraising goal. Some groups pay all of their expenses out of sponsorships, and keep the admissions as profit. Depending on the level of income, nature of the event, amount of commitment to your group, and your other fundraising strategies, you can ask sponsors for $5 to $100 or more. Sponsors might receive two tickets to the event, even though they won't necessarily attend. This gives people who support your work an opportunity to contribute. It is thoughtful, as long as the sponsor does not want to remain anonymous, to thank all sponsors in print on your program or program notes.

A variation on sponsorship is to sell advertising space in your program for the evening, either to sympathetic businesses or other well-wishers. While such support can't compare with the results of ads in a newspaper, it is good public relations for local merchants and many groups cover printing costs of a particularly nice program in this way.

OTHER FUNDRAISING TECHNIQUES

A film can be combined with many other standard fundraising techniques. Having a dinner or a wine and cheese reception, selling refreshments or literature at the screening, holding a raffle, an auction, a concert or dance in conjunction with a film are just a few suggestions. Use your imagination about what will draw people, make a nice program, and raise extra money.

At a town meeting in a medium-sized town in the Midwest, the high school athletic budget was completely cut. Over a period of eight months, a local group of citizens organized themselves as a fundraising committee to pay for the sports program. They decided to present a day long (morning and afternoon) Saturday program of cartoons at the high school. They planned the event so that it could be a true family affair, where people could come and go, and where kids could bring their parents or come alone. They used the high school auditorium which had a projector and screen, and plenty of parking space nearby. All these factors contributed to a pleasant, well attended and financially successful community event.

WORKING WITH LOCAL MOVIE THEATERS

Local movie theaters can help you in numerous ways besides providing information about films. If the films you want to show are available only in 35mm, or you are planning for a big audience or want a larger screen, consider renting a local movie theater rather than renting the 35mm equipment. A theater is also a good option if your other location choices are not desirable. Most theaters have 35mm equipment (some also have 16mm equipment) and professional projectionists. Your best bet will be the independent theater that is managed locally, because it is difficult for local theaters that belong to large national chains to make their own decisions, and you may encounter lots of red tape. Consider the location and ambience of the theater as critically as you would any other space. While a weekend night is obviously best for a large audience, that is also when theaters make most of their money on admissions and concessions. If they give you their prime weekend slot, they have to charge you for the money they are not making in addition to the rent and other costs for the theater facility. The best times for them to rent you the theater will be on weekend afternoons when they are not open or do only moderate business. Other theaters are open only on weekends, and perhaps you can rent them for one of the nights they normally are closed.

Do some legwork and phoning to see which local theater manager is amenable to your festival, series, or premiere idea. There are no fixed terms, so be ready to negotiate. Most managers will ask that you pay a part of what is called their "house nut" — the fixed weekly costs of running the theater. These expenses include overhead, utilities, staff (including a union projectionist) and publicity. They may or may not ask for part of the box-office proceeds. In one small town a theater owner agreed to give a group a Wednesday night for free if he could keep all the money from the food concessions. Consider the audience you are trying to reach before agreeing to any particular night or afternoon. If you are appealing to a younger audience or are located in a college town, you might consider a midnight screening. Theaters in some large cities have found this to be a great time for "cult" or "fad" films. Get a firm commitment in writing from the theater owner, specifying the price, the hours during which you are renting the theater, what staff and equipment he will provide, and other details.

If you are using a commercial theater, members of your group should handle ticket sales and collections. If this is not possible, and the theater staff works the box office, you should be able to check on them, count the ticket stubs, and get the opening and closing ticket numbers.

The theater owner/manager may also help you order the films. The same film in 35mm will generally cost him less to rent for a theatrical showing than it would cost you for a nontheatrical showing. Shipping costs, however, are much higher. Work out a budget and see what will be best. If you are booking the film in 16mm, make absolutely sure that the theater has 16mm equipment. If you have to rent high-powered 16mm equipment for the theater, on top of paying rent, this might make using the theater financially unwise.

If you know that a new film that interests your group has just opened nationally and you don't want to wait until it is available nontheatrically in 16mm, you can try to find out what theater is going to play it locally. If the theater will work with you, you can negotiate for your group to hold a premiere screening at the theater. The rationale goes like this: Especially with art, special interest, or limited audience films, it is to the theater's advantage to have the opening night (or a special preview night) sold out to an enthusiastic audience, who will generate good word of mouth for the rest of the commercial run. It also may bring new customers into the theater who will return for other films. Films often open on "off" nights such as Wednesday, so the theater has a chance to make more profit than normal for that night. Your best selling points are that this film interests your group, that they and their friends will fill the theater and be enthusiastic, and that you can work with the theater in a business-like way.

You could also contract to rent the theater for the opening night and negotiate a ticket price. Your group, with its enthusiastic volunteers, should get all or a good percentage of the box-office for doing all of the legwork. You can charge more for tickets to this special premiere because the money is going to a good cause.

A variation on working with the theater for a premiere is to simply plan a theater party for your group. Sometimes the theater will let you have blocks of tickets at a discount which you can resell at the regular price. If you have twenty people in your group who will each commit themselves to selling 15 tickets, you can reserve 300 seats. Your group can earn $600.00 by reselling at the usual $4.00 price a ticket you bought for $2.00 at a discount. If the theater is showing this film anyway, you don't have to worry about booking or doing much publicity out of your own funds.

Generally, you should select a film most people would be planning to see whether as a benefit for your group or not. You are simply adding spice to the premiere or theater/movie party by getting everyone together on the same night and making it a major social affair. You might consider having a party or reception before or after the film at another location, or adding a dance, dinner, or something else to make the evening really special.

FILMS WITH OTHER PROGRAMS

Films can be an effective part of a larger program. Neighborhood groups, schools, college clubs, and churches often hold special events which feature food, music, and entertainment of various kinds. Films may be able to provide some dimension not otherwise possible. A Greek community, for instance, may be having an ethnic festival or one of its churches may be trying to add to the building fund. A film performance of one of the Greek tragedies, a film about Greek immigration, or a travel film featuring the Greek islands, would be an exciting extra in such an event.

In a conference context, a few years ago, a weekend program dealing with the problems of immigrant workers was held in Detroit for trade unionists. The program was capped by showing the German made ALI — FEAR EATS THE SOUL. This film deals with a young Moroccan man who works in a German industrial center. The audience was fascinated to see the parallels with the problems of Arab workers who had come to work in the local automobile factories. What would normally have been a film for an art house audience accustomed to unusual formats and subtitles was a big hit with a group of rank and file trade unionists. It was the right film at the right time both because of its content and because it was a film and not one more lecture. Both conferences and educational programs can benefit in similar ways.

GOING OUTDOORS

There is probably no more dramatic way of doing community outreach with film, whatever the specific purpose, than showing a film outdoors on a nice night. A group of organic farmers presented films outdoors in their rural area to acquaint their neighbors with why and how they farmed organically. An urban community group that was concerned with frequent fires, arson, and false alarms did an outdoor screening aimed primarily at raising consciousness among young people in the area. In New York City, a special Downtown Drive-In was sponsored by the Whitney Museum of American Art. A donated parking lot was transformed into Manhattan's first drive-in theater when a two evening marathon screening of 25 films by independent filmmakers was presented in late July. The drive-in provided an informal setting for viewing the films — bleachers were set up for about 150 people — and the two-and-one-half hour program was free. The films all documented New York City and its inhabitants in some way. As the event's publicity suggested, it was appropriate that these films be shown outdoors, back in the streets where they were filmed.

An outdoor screening will require a vacant lot, a parking lot, or a grassy area such as a park, where people can sit comfortably and will not disturb others. Backyards, bandstands, parks, plazas, malls, sculpture gardens, ampitheaters — there are many visually exciting and comfortable places where people can watch films outdoors. In Philadelphia, the parking lot for a foreign car service station was turned into an outside theater for five Friday nights. To maximize the sound, the speaker was placed in a corner where two brick walls met, and the films were shown on a gessoed canvas which was hung on the wall and removed each night after the screening. An art gallery across the street donated a sculpture pedestal for the projector, projection supplies were set up in the back of a station wagon, and a loft backing on the lot sent down an extension cord. People sat in chairs from the gallery (which they carried over and back) or pulled their cars up in the huge space. Use your imagination in selecting an outdoor location and encourage people to bring chairs and blankets if you don't have bleachers.

When scouting for locations, check them out during the day and also at night, since there can be a lot of elements which could affect your screening. These include:

- Street or traffic lights that will wash out the image.
- Noise from traffic, bars, restaurants, or machinery operating at night.
- Wind or dust that can make a location uncomfortable.
- Other activities nearby or in the same space that you hadn't counted on.
- Safety and accessibility for walking around in the dark.

An outdoor screening is not a situation where admissions can easily be charged, although passing around a hat or asking for donations is always possible. You may need to get a permit from the local police. You may attract an audience that will include curiosity-seekers, younger people, passersby, and others who may only be marginally interested in the films. Any problems such a crowd might create are greatly minimized by having people from your own organization in the area. Members of your group should give directions, make explanations and help with the equipment.

For an outdoor screening you will have to provide your own power source and bring in all of the equipment, so a trial run is suggested. You should be concerned with the following:

Power. If you can't plug a long extension cord into someone's house, try planning the screening close to some other power source. Park buildings, for example, might have power. Some malls have outlets which are accessible. This will be a primary consideration in choosing a location if you don't want to rent or borrow a noisy generator.

Sound. Since sound dissipates when not enclosed in a room, consider the sound system you need for an outside screening. How can speaker placement, using walls or baffles, or boosting the power through additional amplification augment your sound?

Image. Screens on legs or frames are very susceptible to being blown over by relatively small gusts of wind. If you can't stabilize and protect a screen from the wind, don't use it outside, since most screens are expensive to replace and almost impossible to clean or mend. Putting something up on a wall or against another flat, stable surface (a van or truck) is the easiest solution. You can use a sheet, a white wall, paper from a huge roll, a canvas, anything that will be flat, white, somewhat reflective, and large enough for your image. Sheets of paper can be stretched on a frame or weighted with a dowel at the bottom.

Rain. Either plan and announce a rain date or locate your outdoor screening close to a space where you can move for an indoor screening. Be prepared to protect your equipment and film immediately should it start to rain.

The major advantage of an outdoor show is that it provides immediate and high visibility for very little money. By its very nature, the event is informal and fun. Interest is sure to run high. Your promotion might establish a playful atmosphere. Certainly everyone will want to know who is showing the film and why. By their actions, the sponsors will have demonstrated their imagination and their ability to do something new. The media may cover the event as a news story rather than as a screening of a film. More important than outside coverage, however, is the impact an outdoor screening has on a neighborhood. The sponsors will have added a bit of excitement to everyday life in the community.

13 | SOUND IMPROVEMENTS

In many ways it's easier to properly reproduce the visual part of a film than it is to reproduce the sound. An adequately bright, in-focus image located on a screen that everyone can see will satisfy your audience visually and, barring mechanical problems with the projector or a bad print, there is little that can compromise the quality of the projected image. But the sound is a different story.

When audiences complain about the technical quality of a screening, it's often because of a problem with the sound. It may be too loud or not loud enough; the dialog may be unintelligible, or the music distorted. The mechanical sound from the projector may interfere with the film sound. Even if there is nothing specific to complain about, audiences are often vaguely dissatisfied — and may not come to subsequent screenings — because the sound quality really is not satisfactory.

There are a lot of ways to improve sound quality, many that don't require much expense. This section provides a little theory about sound reproduction, and some methods for improving sound quality. It will be particularly useful for groups who are planning a screening in a large space, for groups who find that they are running films regularly, and for anybody who wants to make the sound better.

THE NATURE OF SOUND

Sounds are essentially vibrations in the air, which can be represented as **waveforms**, like waves in water. The air doesn't actually move, but a system of pressures, shaped like waves, moves through the air.

The information contained in a waveform consists of two things: **amplitude** and **frequency**. Amplitude is the measure of the depth of the wave, from the top of a "peak" to the bottom of a "valley" — actually a measure of the amount of pressure being exerted by the wave. We hear amplitude as **loudness**. The unit of measurement is the Decibel (**dB**) which is the difference in loudness between one sound and another that can be perceived by the human ear.

At a given air pressure all sounds move through the air at the same speed, but the length of a waveform can vary. Frequency is the measure of the number of waveforms moving past a stationary point per second. The unit of measurement is Hertz (Hz) or, less commonly, Cycles per Second (cps). We hear frequency as **pitch;**

the musical scale, for instance, consists of sounds that increase in frequency from the lowest to the highest.

Pure waveforms — consisting of only a single frequency at an unvarying amplitude — do not exist in nature. The sounds we hear are much more complex. A note played on a musical instrument, or a word spoken by a human being, is a waveform consisting of its basic pitch (its **fundamental**) plus a number of other frequencies present in various lesser proportions to the fundamental (called harmonics, or overtones — always higher in frequency than the fundamental). This whole complex waveform is also being **modulated** — varied in amplitude — from second to second. It is the unique mixture of fundamentals with overtones and modulation patterns (together with **rise time** — how long it takes a sound to get from silence to full loudness — and **decay time** — the time it takes a sound to die out) that give various instruments and voices their own tonal qualities, or timbre.

Every sound, then, consists of an extremely complex waveform passing through the air from its source to our ear. Contained in this waveform is all the information our brain needs to properly identify and interpret the sound.

SOUND RECORDING

In order to "capture" and store a sound intact and then "release" it to be heard, the sound must be put into a storable, static form. This is done by creating an **analogue** of the original sonic waveform. An analogue is something that contains one piece of information which corresponds exactly to another piece of information in the thing being duplicated, but in a different form. For instance, the figure 6, 9, 12, 13 is an analogue, in numerical form, of the word "film". Analogues of sound waves can exist in a number of dynamic or static forms. Dynamic analogues — ones that move — correspond to the original sound in frequency, amplitude and time. Electricity is a dynamic medium, and sound analogues can easily be transmitted as electronic impulses.

Static analogues of sound waves — ones which contain all the information about amplitude and frequency, but which have been "frozen" in time — can be created in physical form, such as the modulated grooves of a phonograph record, graphic representations on paper or film, or as magnetic patterns on recording tape.

PLAYBACK

To reproduce the sound, the storage medium — film, tape, or record — is moved at the same speed used for recording, thus restoring the element of time. The proper mechanism reads the analogue and converts it into electrical impulses. Chapter 8 contains a brief description of the optical sound system of most 16mm projectors. Every sound system is composed of the same basic components of source, preamplifier, power amplifier and loudspeaker. The system can be as simple as a portable radio or as complicated as a $100,000 auditorium sound reinforcement system. Each of these elements has its own job, and each can perform its job well or badly. This chapter examines those elements which can be changed and adapted to improve the quality of sound for an audience.

LOUDSPEAKER IMPROVEMENTS

With audiences larger than five to ten people, the speaker built into many projectors will be inadequate — and even five people may not be happy with the sound. For one thing, the speaker is right next to a noisy projector. Also, the sound comes from **behind** the viewer, which doesn't help the illusion of reality. Thirdly, the sound itself may be understandable, but poor. Improving the speaker element of your sound system is easy, and not expensive.

EXTENSION SPEAKERS

Some projectors have detachable speakers in the projector cover. Most manufacturers of all-in-one projectors also make matching extension speakers to work with their projectors. These speakers plug into a jack on the projector marked "speaker," or "ext (-ension or -ernal) speaker". Putting a plug into this jack cuts off the built-in speaker (if there is one), but all the sound controls on the projector still work. Using an extension speaker designed for your projector means you don't have to worry about matching one to the other; the plug will fit the jack, the impedance will match, etc. Getting the speaker away from the projector and up **off the floor** will do wonders for the sound.

USING HIGH-FIDELITY SPEAKERS AS EXTENSIONS

This is an easy way to improve sound quality by many orders of magnitude. You, or someone you know, probably have a pretty good stereo system at home. A speaker that is designed for high-quality reproduction of music will work as well for film soundtracks. To match a projector with a hi-fi speaker, you must consider:

Speaker efficiency. For a given volume level coming out of the speaker, some speakers have to be fed more power from the amplifier than others. There is no simple measurement of speaker efficiency, but speaker manufacturers suggest the amplifier power that their units will work with, usually a range like "10 watts rms minimum 60 watts rms maximum." This tells you the amplifier you need to drive that speaker to room-filling sound levels without distortion.

The projector's power output. In the list of technical specifications for your projector you should find amplifier power output, which will be stated in watts (like "12 watts rms into 8 ohms at 1% THD", though many projector manufacturers are not that precise). What you need to know is the power output (watts) and the speaker impedance (ohms or Ω) the amp needs to "see" in order to produce those watts.

Speaker impedance. Almost all speakers have an impedance (resistance to electrical flow) of 4, 8 or 16 ohms. This specification can usually be found somewhere on the back of the speaker cabinet. Almost all amplifiers' speaker outputs are designed to work into one or all of those impedances. Look for the **minimum** load specified for the amp's speaker output. If it's 4 ohms, you can run any speaker from that output. If it's 8 ohms, don't use a 4 ohm speaker, etc. But most of the time both speaker and output will be 8 ohms.

Will it work? If you have all the specifications, and they match properly, it should work. **Don't** connect speaker and amplifier if there is an impedance mismatch; it could damage the amplifier. If you are not sure about the power match, you can go ahead and try it. If you hear distortion of the sound when the volume is turned up, most likely the speaker is too inefficient — there is not enough amplifier power. What happens is that the amplifier reaches the maximum power output of which it is capable, but it is still not loud enough, so you turn it up some more. The amplifier is trying to increase the amplitude of the waveform, but it can't, and the tops and bottoms of the waveform get "clipped" off. This is known as **clipping distortion**, and it sounds like harsh, grating noises added to the sound. If you hear this kind of distortion (which is often interpreted as the speaker being overdriven), you will need to try a more efficient speaker or add a booster amplifier (see below).

Making the connection. Most projector speaker output jacks take a standard ¼" **phone plug** (see Figure 14). These plugs are available from any electronic parts store. Some projectors take either nonstandard phone-type plugs, or other kinds of plugs altogether. If this is the case, you can usually obtain the proper plug from an audiovisual dealer that sells your brand of projector — and the dealer can usually make up a cable for you. But making the cable is not hard. All you need is a length of wire, the plug that fits your projector, and the plug (if any — most speaker connnections accept bare wire-ends) that fits your speaker. Use standard lamp cord for speaker wire. This wire comes in various gauges, or thicknesses, and is sold by the foot at hardware stores or electrical supply houses. For lengths up to about 20 feet, you can use No. 18 gauge; for 20-50 feet, use No. 16 which is heavier; for longer lengths use No. 14.

Sound plugs.   Fig. 14

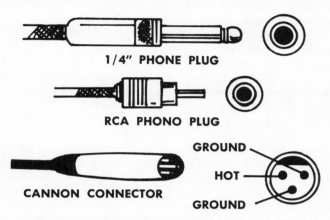

1/4" PHONE PLUG

RCA PHONO PLUG

CANNON CONNECTOR

GROUND
HOT
GROUND

In any case, avoid the lightweight cord sold as "speaker wire" — the kind that usually has clear plastic insulation. Use of this kind of cord can result in dissipation of power in the wire. Lamp cord is marked for polarity, either with grooved or a flat surface molded into the rubber insulation of one conductor of the wire. See Figure 14, and connect one wire to the "ground" or (—) lead of the plug. Remember whether you used the marked or unmarked side of the wire. Connect the other wire to the "hot" or (+) terminal. These connections **must** be soldered. If your speaker requires a plug too (most high-quality speakers take bare wire leads) it is probably an **RCA phono plug** or a ¼" phono plug. Be sure to attach the same wire to the ground terminal of both plugs. If your speaker takes bare wire leads, mark the one you connected to the ground terminal of the plug. Connect this to the (—) or ("0") or black terminal of the speaker, and the other lead to the (+) or red terminal. Insert the plug into the projector. Make the speaker wire as long as necessary to run it under rugs, along baseboards, etc.

AMPLIFICATION AND MULTIPLE SPEAKER ARRAYS

Your projector and one speaker will be quite adequate for a screening, if your room and audience are on the small side. But for large screenings, you may find your amplifier driven into "clipping"; or that single speaker may not cover the room adequately enough so everyone can hear. If you expect a large audience — 100 or more people — and your screening room is large — a church sanctuary, a gym, an auditorium, a lecture hall — then it is probably a good idea to plan a better sound system right from the start. Such a system should include two high-quality speakers and a fairly high-powered amplifier. Such sound systems are not really hard to find, they are easy to interface with projection equipment, and can often be borrowed or rented cheaply.

HOME STEREO SYSTEMS

Lots of people have good quality audio systems in their homes, with components already pre-matched to work well with each other. The characteristics that make them good for listening to music can also work in a screening room.

Most home stereo systems are built around a unit called a **receiver**, which consists of a radio tuner, preamplifier and power amplifier all on one chassis. Others use an **integrated amplifier**, which is the same as a receiver without a tuner. Some have each element—preamplifier and power amplifier — as a separate component. The format matters only in terms of convenience. The considerations are the same as matching projector amps with extension speakers: adequate power output from the power amplifier, matched with speakers that will play loud enough when driven by the available power. Home stereo speakers are often of relatively low efficiency, requiring high-power amplifiers.

You may have to do some experimenting. You can't go wrong using the highest-power amplifier you can get, as long as the speakers are rated to take that much power. The more efficient a speaker is (look for the "minimum power" spec), the less power you need.

Care must be taken in interconnecting the projector's sound output with the preamplifier's input. Most often the projector's only sound output is the extension speaker jack. You can use this output to connect to the amplifier input, but be careful. Keep the volume control on the projector turned down, so as not to overload the amp inputs; use the amp's volume control to set sound levels. A little experimentation will show you the volume setting which will give enough signal to the amp so it can develop its full output without overload.

To check out a system like this, follow these steps:

- Set up projector; thread film; make sure projector's sound system is working properly; then **turn off the projector.**
- Set up the amplifier or receiver where the controls are easily accessible.
- Set up the speakers in front of the room (see "Room Acoustics and Speaker Placement" below).
- Connect the speakers to the amplifier's speaker terminals (find out how from the owner or the instruction manual).
- Connect the projector's audio output to the amplifier's input ("aux[iliary]" or "spare"). There will be one for the

left channel and one for the right; if you are only using one projector, it doesn't matter; if you are using two, plug one projector into each. The amplifier input will usually be an RCA phono jack; on some semi-professional and all professional equipment the input will be ¼" phone jacks. You will need a cable with a plug to match the amp (phone or phono) on one end, and a plug to to match the projector (phone, phono or some special plug) on the other. The cable must be a shielded audio-type cable, and it should be as short as possible. Many of these cables are available ready-made at audio stores; special cables can be made by audiovisual shops.

- Make sure everything is plugged into the wall.
- Turn the volume controls on both projector and amplifier all the way down.
- The amplifier will have a "**mode control**". It can:

    Mix both left and right inputs together and send combined signal to both speakers. Set it to the mono position. If you are using two projectors, keep the volume of the projector you're not using turned all the way down until the changeover.

    Take either left or right input alone and send it to both speakers. Select the position that connects the input from the projector you are using to both speakers. If you have this set up, you can leave the volume on both projectors on, and just change the mode switch on the amp at changeover time.

- Set the volume on the projector about ⅛ up from "off"; start the film.
- Wait for a section of dialog; now slowly turn up the volume control on the amplifier. If you are getting volume with no distortion by the time the control is about halfway up, then everything is fine. If there is no distortion but it's not loud enough, start turning up the projector's volume control; if doing this gives you adequate volume but no distortion, you're ok. If you start getting distortion, and you know that the amp should have enough power, then you need a transformer: the projector is overloading the amp's input, and this system does not work.
- If the sound is loud and clean at this point, you can set tone controls and filters on the amplifier as needed.
- Test your system well before your show date.

PUBLIC ADDRESS EQUIPMENT

There are dozens of different kinds of public address systems available, and some can be used with film equipment. Sometimes the choice of PA equipment is preferable to hi-fi systems, especially if your program includes a guest speaker for whom you'd like to provide a microphone. Many types of PA systems will **not** be suitable for use with film equipment, because of poor sound quality or technical incompatibility — or both. A good rule of thumb is to stay away from any system that can be easily carried in its entirety by one person — things like combination lecturn/microphone/speakers, or cases that unfold to reveal a detachable speaker and a small amplifier/control unit. Systems in this class are designed to amplify only the limited frequencies of the human voice in small rooms.

Look for a system designed to reproduce both music and voice at fairly loud volume levels. Many local musical groups, churches, coffeehouses, etc., have such systems, and you may be able to borrow or rent one cheaply. These systems usually consist of three basic units: two loudspeaker systems (often in columnar form) and a control/amplifier unit (referred to as the "head"). The head includes two main sections built on a single chassis: a microphone mixer and a power amplifier.

The mic mixer will have four to eight separate, identical input channels. Each channel will have one or more input jacks designed to accept signals from microphones, plus possibly other input jacks for signals from high-level sources like tape decks and tuners. Each input channel will also have its own set of volume and tone controls, and possibly controls for special effects like reverberation.

The signal from the mixer is then sent to the built-in power amplifier, which drives the loudspeakers. These PA systems are almost always monophonic — even though there may be more than one speaker, the same signal is sent to each one. Because there are so many variations from system to system, your main guide to using a PA system will come from its owner. The normal function of such a system is to amplify signals from microphones.

In order to use the system with your projector, you'll need to experiment. Sometimes each input channel will have only one input jack, the one labeled "microphone." This will be one or both of two kinds of inputs: a high impedance microphone input will be the standard ¼" phone jack, described previously. A low impedance microphone input will be of the three-pin Cannon jack variety (see Figure 14). If the Cannon is the only input on the head, it won't work. Look for another one.

The cable from one or more of the input channels may also have an input jack labeled "auxiliary," "accessory," or "line." This will be either a ¼" phone jack or an RCA phone jack. This input is designed for high-level sources. If it is present, you should be able to connect a cable to it from the speaker output on your projector; then use that input channel's controls and any master controls to adjust the sound.

If the only input is a high-impedance microphone jack, you will have to experiment. Connect a cable from the projector's speaker output to the mic input. Turn the volume control on the projector up just a little, and start the film. Now slowly raise the volume control on the head input channel. If you get adequate volume before you turn the volume all the way up, and there is no distortion, you're ok. If there is not enough volume, turn the input channel control down to half, and start raising the volume on the projector. If you get to a good loud level without distortion, again you're ok. But if you get distortion no matter how you adjust the controls, that means the output of the projector is overloading the microphone preamp in the input channel. In order to use that PA head, you will have to get a mic line transformer.

If your program combines a film screening with a speaker or live music, there are several ways you can integrate sound systems for both functions. The key is the necessity for having the sound controls for the film located near the projector.

One system for all functions. If you have a PA head that has both 1) low impedance microphone inputs and 2) high impedance auxiliary inputs, then you can use the one system for everything. This is because low impedance mic cables can be run for 100-foot or longer distances. Assuming you have enough mic cable, you can locate the mics at the front of the room, the head at the back near the projector, and run all the cable from front to back.

Combining two systems. Cables from high-impedance mics can only be run about 20 feet; using longer cable causes loss of signal and hum pickup. If you only have a high impedance PA system, the head must be located near the front of the room. That means you will need a separate sound control/amp system — like the high fidelity equipment previously described. You can still use the speaker systems from the PA for both purposes. Usually the connection terminals on PA speakers consist of a single ¼" phone jack. You simply have a pair of speaker cables coming from the film amp (terminating in ¼" phone jacks) which are plugged into the speakers during the film. When it's time for the discussion, unplug those cables from the speakers, and plug in the cables from the PA head instead. Not very elegant, but it works. Be sure the speakers are placed closer to the audience than the microphones; this helps minimize feedback "squeal" — caused by sound coming out of a speaker being picked up by a microphone, which sends it back to the speaker, then back to the microphone, and on and on. You'll have to do your best to correct whatever acoustical problems arise.

Single speaker positions.   Fig. 15

A. Speaker raised above screen.   B. Speaker up off the floor.

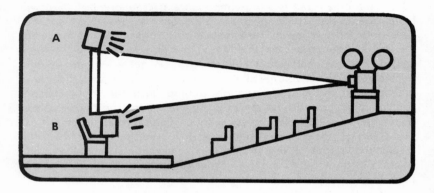

SPEAKER PLACEMENT

The location of your loudspeakers can serve to correct or compound room-acoustics problems. Here are some things to watch out for.

SINGLE SPEAKER SYSTEMS

Your choices are limited. The speaker must be located near the screen, and high enough so the sound is not blocked by the people in the front rows. It helps to know approximately the speaker's angle of dispersion.

Sonic energy increases in directionality as frequency rises. This means that bass notes are essentially omnidirectional. Place a speaker in the middle of the floor, and walk around it as it plays music. The low bass notes will be audible through 360°. But when you listen to the higher frequencies, you'll find them harder and harder to hear as you move away from the front of the speaker. (This refers to conventional "front-firing" speaker cabinets; some hi-fi speakers are designed to be omnidirectional across the entire frequency spectrum, but they are not usually suitable for screenings because they should be placed away from walls.)

Speakers differ in their angle of dispersion of high frequencies. At home, you can get an idea about yours through this test: hook up a radio to the system that feeds your speaker, and tune it to the "hiss" between stations. This is white noise, consisting equally of frequencies. Set the speaker up at ear level. Now walk back and forth in front of the speaker and note at which point the sound starts to get "dull." Do this at various distances from the speaker, and you'll get an idea of how wide the speaker's dispersion is.

Now back to the location of our single speaker. If you're just doing a screening for a few dozen people in a small room, it won't matter too much; just set the speaker up. as high as you can near the screen. In larger rooms for more people, you might see if it's possible to hang the speaker **above** the screen, angling it downward. Your knowledge of the speaker's dispersion characteristics will tell you how much of an angle to use so that people in the front and back will hear the high frequencies; too steep an angle, and the people in back won't hear; too shallow, and the sound will pass over the heads of the people in front. The width of dispersion will also tell you how wide you can make the rows of seats, especially in the front.

Of course, using a single speaker limits the size of your audience; one speaker usually can't deliver sound to everyone in the room. One exception to this is the one huge speaker in commercial theater-style setups, which is behind the screen. But for you to get good sound for screenings in large rooms for large audiences you may need multiple speaker arrays.

TWO-SPEAKER SYSTEMS

If you're using a hi-fi or portable PA system, you'll likely be using two speakers anyway. There are a number of ways they can be set up, depending on room and audience size, speaker type, and the acoustical problems the room gives you to contend with.

First, make sure the speakers are in phase — meaning that as the speaker cones vibrate, they are moving in and out together, rather than one moving out while the other moves in. If your speaker wire is marked for polarity, connecting both speakers the same way ("plus" or "hot" terminal on the amp connected to the "plus," "red" or "hot" terminal on the speaker; "negative" or "common" or "ground" terminal on the amp connected to the "ground," "negative" or "0" terminal on the speaker) will assure that they are in phase — assuming that the speakers are identical. If you're using a PA or other system where the speaker cables terminate in plugs that plug into jacks at the speaker end and at the amp end, then phasing is taken care of there.

If in doubt here's a test: Connect both speakers, and place them right next to each other. If it's a stereo amp, switch it to "mono." Play music through the speakers, and listen for the amount of bass. Now reverse the connections on one of the speakers. If there is less bass, the first connection was correct. If more, leave them the way they are. It's a good idea to mark the ends of the wires so you can reconnect them correctly.

Two-speaker systems.   Fig. 16

A. Centered placement.   B. Crossfire placement.

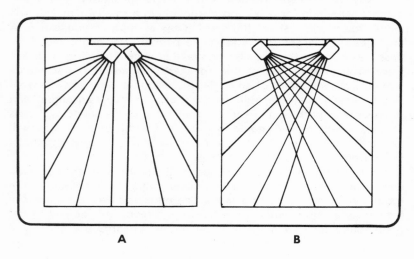

A   B

Centered placement. If there is room, locate them directly under the screen, (assuming they are high enough to shoot over the heads of the people in the front). Angle them **slightly outward**, away from each other, and slightly downward towards the audience. Use your evaluation of their dispersion characteristics to adjust the angles to cover the whole audience. By locating the speakers next to each other, the sound will appear to emanate from the center of the screen no matter where the listener is sitting.

Crossfire placement. If the space beneath the screen is insufficient, raise one speaker as high as you can on each side of the screen. This time, angle them **inwards**, and downwards. When a mono signal is played through two speakers placed apart, the sound will appear to emanate from a point midway between the two speakers — if the listener is also located between and in front of the speakers. Moving to the side causes the source to move. By angling the speakers inward, the difference in perceived volume between the two speakers will cause the apparent sound source to remain near the center of the screen, no matter where the listener is. The location of the speakers will also affect the way room acoustics will respond to them. The closer a speaker is to the junction between two room surfaces — say, a wall and the floor — the more bass frequencies will be accentuated. Maximum bass is perceived when a speaker is located in a corner, on the floor or up against the ceiling, because the extended flat surfaces leading away from the speaker act like a huge horn. This phenomenon can be used to help compensate for problems in room acoustics. In a very "bassy" room — one with standing wave problems — moving speakers away from corners can help reduce booming bass. Least bass accentuation will be encountered with the speakers located halfway up a wall, several feet away from the adjoining walls. Conversely, in very absorptive rooms where all your power is being eaten up by upholstery, rugs, drapes, etc., moving the speakers into corners and turning up the treble on your amp will make the sound perceptibly louder without taxing the amplifier.

COMPENSATING FOR ROOM ACOUSTICS

If you're stuck with a very reverberant room or one with a pronounced echo, you may have to take more energetic measures to improve the sound. Here are some ideas:

DEALING WITH REVERBERATION AND ECHO

If excessive reverberation is ruining the sound — and you can see that the reverberation is caused by too many "hard" reflective surfaces — an obvious solution is to deaden the room. Put carpets on the floors, hang sheets or blankets on the walls, cover large glass windows. Remember that what seems like excessive reverberation during a sound check may be substantially reduced when you fill the room with people.

Since reverb problems are caused by too high a proportion of reflected to direct sound, you might be able to increase the direct sound. There are four ways to do this.

- You can try to move the source of direct sound — the speakers themselves — closer to the audience, or vice-versa.
- You can try to make the room effectively smaller. For instance, if you're working in a partially filled dining hall or gymnasium, you might be able to find some portable blackboards, partitions, or coatracks. Hang some sheets or blankets over these, and locate them around the perimeter of your actual seating area. Then aim the speakers so as little of the sound as possible gets beyond your artificial walls.
- Aim the speakers so that much of the sound is absorbed by the bodies of the audience. Raise them as high as possible, then aim them down towards the audience.
- You can increase the number of sources of direct sound using multiple speakers. If, in addition to the pair in

front, you locate another pair of speakers halfway towards the back of the room, angled towards the rear, the people in back will hear mostly those speakers. The overall volume from each speaker can be reduced, producing less sound to reverberate around the room. This system reduces the illusion that the sound is coming from the screen.

DEALING WITH FREQUENCY ABERRATIONS

The frequency response problems in some rooms are sometimes much more complicated than just too much or too little bass. And sometimes it's a matter of degree — there's so much bass buildup that even moving the speakers to optimum locations leaves a booming, muddy bottom end. Now you have to try to change the sound signal itself, boosting the frequencies that the room tends to cover up, reducing the frequencies that the room accentuates.

Your first recourse is the tone controls on your amplifier and projector. Many projectors have a single control labeled "tone". This is usually a simple treble-cut control, which progressively reduces the amount of high-frequencies in a signal. It may sound like the bass is being increased, but it's only relative to the reduced treble. Such a control probably won't help you correct for a bad sounding room — but go ahead and try.

Of more help are the bass, treble and sometimes midrange controls found on most stereo equipment and some PA equipment. These are capable both of cutting and boosting parts of the frequency spectrum. The bass and treble controls are usually designed to act on broad portions of the sound spectrum. Midrange controls, on the other hand, usually center on a specific frequency — around the frequency of the human voice — and are progressively less effective above or below that frequency.

If the room sounds boomy, sometimes turning the bass down a lot will help. It will also wipe out a lot of the low-frequency content of the soundtrack, since you're reducing all the bass frequencies, not just the one(s) causing the boominess. If the dialog isn't clearly intelligible, sometimes a combination of bass cut and treble boost will help. If you have a midrange (sometimes labeled "presence") control, turn that up to make dialog clearer.

Using these broadband tone controls will often help turn total mush into something at least audible and understandable. If you want to make it sound good, and you can't do it with the tone controls and experiments with speaker placement, you might try a **frequency equalizer.** This is a device that connects to your stereo amp or receiver and consists of a series of **narrow band** tone controls — usually five, seven or ten bands.

If your screening room has some bad resonances, for example, it's likely that one of the bands on a ten band equalizer comes close to matching the frequency of the resonance. By reducing the level at that frequency only, the resonance can be smoothed out without much disturbance to the rest of the frequency spectrum. If you can find one to borrow or rent, it's worth trying; if you contemplate a fair number of screenings in a problematic room, you might even want to buy one; single-channel ten band equalizers designed for musicians cost around $75 (try a musical instrument shop).

CORRECTING DEAD SPOTS

With the system set up and running, walk around the room and listen for places where volume drops off, high frequencies are lost, or other radical changes in the sound occur. Often, complaints are received about the sound at a screening from just one or two individuals who were sitting in a dead spot. Dead spots can usually be eliminated:

- A small adjustment in speaker aiming can solve this problem. Make sure the re-aiming didn't create new dead spots.
- Sometimes an absorptive piece of furniture or an isolated drape can prevent reflections from reaching a particular spot; try to make sure that the room is symmetrically "live" or "dead"; a room with a lot of glass on one side and a lot of drapes on the other will be full of dead spots.
- If all else fails, and there are still a few seats where the sound is really bad, just don't let anyone sit there. The location and severity of dead spots may well change when the audience is in the room.

THE SOUND CHECK

If at all possible, you should do a dry run of your screening with enough time to spare for trouble-shooting afterwards. The procedure given here uses two projectors (manual changeover), a stereo integrated amplifier and a pair of speakers. You can adapt it for whatever system you use. It assumes, of course, that you've tested the system as previously discussed, and know it works.

- Set up the projectors.
- Set up the amp where you can reach the controls easily.
- Mount and aim the speakers.
- Connect the speakers to the amp. When running cable from the speakers to the amp, be sure it's all hidden

and/or taped down so there's absolutely no possibility of someone tripping in the dark.

- Make sure the amp and projector are **turned off** before you connect the cable from the projector speaker output to the amp's auxiliary input; if it's on, the electrical transient caused by making the connection could blow out your speakers or short-circuit the amp. It's a good idea to find out what fuses your amplifier takes — there are usually fuse sockets on the rear panel with the fuse value printed near it ("2 A[mp]" or "3 A Slo-Blo") and have spares handy.
- Now turn on the amplifier power; set its mode selector to mono. Set all the tone controls straight up, make sure the "tape monitor" switch is off (if it's on you'll get no sound), and that the speaker selector matches the speaker terminals you used on the back of the amp. If you have a tuner or tape deck, try it first; it's an easy test that the sound system is working.
- Note the volume level you used (for later reference), then turn it all the way down. (Re)select the auxiliary input (the one the projector's connected to).
- Start the projector, and turn its volume control a quarter of the way up; set its tone control at the halfway point. Wait until the film actually has sound on the track; slowly bring up the volume on the amp until you're happy with it. Wait for some dialog, and adjust the tone controls for pleasing sound and understandable dialog.
- Make note of the settings of all the controls. Repeat this procedure for each reel of film on the projector you'll use for that reel. Two different projectors of the same model may have very different sound quality.

CHANGEOVERS

If your screening involves a changeover between projectors, it's a good idea to rehearse it beforehand. Your two projectors are probably plugged into the left and right auxiliary inputs of the amp. The stereo/mono **mode switch** on the amp may be one of two types.

It can have two positions — a stereo position and a mono position where both channels are added together. At changeover you won't change anything on the amp. Both projector amps should be on, with the volume up on the one that's running (A), all the way down on the one that's waiting (B). When you make the changeover, turn up the volume on projector B to the predetermined setting, and turn down projector A — but don't turn it off, or a "pop" may be transmitted to the speakers.

The other kind of stereo/mono mode switch has two or more mono possibilities — left channel only to both speakers, right channel only to both speakers; both channels to both speakers; and normal stereo. If projector A is in the left channel input, and projector B is in the right, you simply select the "left only — mono" mode while A is running, and switch to "right only" at changeover. You can leave the sound controls on both projectors at their normal settings at all times, since the one that's not running is disconnected from the speakers.

During the dry run, be sure to turn the house lights off as you will during the screening. Make sure you can see and find all the controls in the dark — keep a flashlight handy.

EVALUATING EXISTING SOUND SYSTEMS

Many of the rooms that can be used for screenings already have built in sound systems. You may be tempted to use the built-in system, if it's available. You'll want to consider:

- What is the system ordinarily used for? If it was designed for simple public speaking, it's probably not adequate for film.
- Where are the speakers and amplifier? If the speakers aren't reasonably near the screen, the cinematic illusion won't be maintained. If you can't get a cable from the projector to the amplifier, or if the projectionist can't operate both simultaneously, it's clearly non-suitable.
- How does it sound? Will it be loud enough, and does it reproduce all the frequencies in your film? A system that will reproduce music loudly and clearly is much more expensive than a speech-only system, and one usually isn't installed unless that's its purpose.
- Can you interface your equipment with it? Is there an accessible high-impedance high level input that will take a signal from your projector?

If you're offered the use of a built-in sound system, find out if it's been used before for film screenings, how and with what results. If you still have doubts, and have access to a portable system, don't take chances, use your own.

14 | RESOURCES

NATIONAL INFORMATION SERVICES

American Film Institute (AFI)

J. F. Kennedy Center for the Performing Arts, Washington, D.C. 20566 — (202) 828-4088, Center for Advanced Film Studies, 501 Doheny Road, Beverly Hills, CA 90210 — (213) 278-8777.

The American Film Institute is a non-profit national organization established in 1967 by the National Endowment for the Arts to "preserve and advance the art of film." The AFI operates an advanced conservatory for filmmakers, gives assistance to new American filmmakers through grants and internships, supports basic research, preserves film classics and operates a national film repertory exhibition program. **American Film: Journal of the Film and Television Arts** is published monthly.

The AFI National Education Services provides guidance to film teachers and educators and publishes the **AFI Guide to College Courses in Film and Television** and the bimonthly **AFI Education Newsletter.**

The National Information Services provides clearinghouse information on media organizations and publications; 16mm film distribution; feature, documentary and independent film and video production; grants; and careers in film and television. They publish **Factfile**, a continuing series of reference publications compiled by the Information Services staff to meet needs for basic information about film and television. Write for a complete listing of the **Factfiles** (currently 12), which include Film and Television Periodicals in English; Independent Film and Video; Film/Video Festivals and Awards.

Association of Independent Video and Filmmakers (AIVF)
Foundation for Independent Video and Filmmakers (FIVF)

99 Prince St., New York, NY 10012 — (212) 966-0900.

The Association of Independent Video and Filmmakers, Inc. (AIVF) is a non-profit trade association formed in 1973, and open to independent film and video makers (producers, directors, technicians, etc.) and others interested in the production and distribution of independent video and film. The Foundation for Independent Video and Film, Inc. (FIVF) is the non-profit, tax-exempt "sister" of AIVF, and as such administers programs and projects of interest to the general public as well as the independent community. They publish a monthly newsletter, **The Independent.**

AIVF/FIVF is involved in activities and services in the following areas: monthly meetings, screenings and workshops; information files on festivals and grants, equipment and jobs; advocacy in the areas of institutional and legislative policy decisions; community service; and information. **The Media Awareness Project** studies the relationship of independents to public telecommunications and maintains a resource center on media policy and issues. The **Short Film Showcase** distributes independently made shorts to commercial theaters.

Educational Film Library Association (EFLA)

43 W. 61st St., New York, NY 10023 — (212) 246-4533.

Since 1943 the Educational Film Library Association has served as a national clearinghouse for the distribution, production and dissemination of information on 16mm nontheatrical films and other non-print media. EFLA is a national membership organization, however, a number of services and resources are available to the public. The EFLA office houses a research library (open to the public) containing over 2,100 books, 150 periodicals, distributors' catalogs, subject files, festival files, stills collection, and other reference materials. The staff is prepared to assist film users to locate sources of films, suggest films for particular needs, supply information about film library administration, advise about film distribution and assist researchers with special projects.

EFLA activities include workshops on film related topics, a program of evaluation of new releases, sponsorship of the annual American Film Festival (a major showcase for nontheatrical 16mm films), and publication of **Sightlines**, the annual **American Film Festival Guide**, the quarterly **Independent Film/Video Guide**, and books like **16mm Distribution**, which includes articles on distribution and exhibition of 16mm nontheatrical films. A brochure listing other available titles is available on request from EFLA.

The following six sections are basic reference and resource materials, many of which should be available in your public library or from the publishers.

RESOURCE GUIDES

Audiovisual Equipment and Materials: A Basic Repair and Maintenance Manual by Don Schroeder and Gary Lare

Scarecrow Press Inc., Metuchen, NJ, 1979.

Easy-to-read troubleshooting guide with pictures for those involved with the equipment aspect of any audiovisual program. Suggestions for in-house maintenance and repairs.

Audiovisual Marketplace 1979

R. R. Bowker Co., New York, 1979.

Directory to audiovisual services, including reference lists for public radio and TV programs, equipment manufacturers and dealers, reference books, periodicals, state AV administrators, associations, awards and festivals, as well as funding sources.

Children's Media Marketplace edited by Deirdre Boyle and Stephen Calvert

Gaylord Professional Publishers, P.O. Box 61, Syracuse, NY 13201.

Detailed listings of children's book publishers, AV producers and distributors, periodicals, grants, awards, etc.

1979 Directory of Educational Film Festivals in the USA by K. Bury

Learning Resource Service, Southern Illinois University, Carbondale, IL 62901, 1978.

Information listings of educational film festivals, their sponsors, locations, times. Simple, clear. Valuable information for filmmakers and programmers.

Educational Media Yearbook 1978 edited by James W. Brown
R. R. Bowker Co., New York, 1978.
An annual publication. I. The Year in Review; II. Mediagraphy: Print and Non-Print Resources; III. Guide to Organizations, Training Programs, and Funding Sources.

Educator's Guide to Media Lists by Mary Robinson Sive
Libraries Unlimited, Inc., Littleton, CO, 1975.
An index to the filmographies, articles, books, and lists published on certain subjects. Also arranged by media.

Film Library Administration — Selected Bibliography — 1978 Revised Edition compiled by Maryann Chach and Carol A. Emmens
Educational Film Library Association, 43 W. 61st St., New York, NY 10023.

The Film Users' Handbook: A Basic Manual for Managing Library Film Services by Dr. George Rehrauer
R. R. Bowker Co., New York, 1975.
A librarians' guide for developing, organizing and designing film programs. Includes appendices for selected periodicals, associations, evaluation services, etc.

Gadney's Guide to 1800 International Contests, Festivals and Grants by Alan Gadney
Festival Publications, P.O. Box 10180, Glendale, CA 91209, 1978.
Thorough listings for film, video, TV, photography, journalism, and other media. For amateurs, professionals, students. Easy-to-use.

Getting into Film by Mel London
Ballantine Books, New York, 1977.
An overview of the film production industry including sections on jobs in writing, cinematography, sound, film vs. videotape, women, grants, schools, festivals, unions, animation and job-hunting.

Guidebook to Film: An Eleven-In-One Reference by Ronald Gottesman and Harry Geduld
Holt, Rinehart, and Winston, New York, 1972.
Contains short annotated bibliography of books and periodicals. Lists theses, museums, schools, equipment sources, distributors, bookstores, publishers, organizations, festivals and awards.

International Film Guide 1980 edited by Peter Cowie
A. S. Barnes and Co., Cranbury, NJ, 1980.
Annual guide to motion picture industries in 40 countries. Pieces on "Director of the Year." Chapters on film festivals, film music, awards, television, film publications, etc.

Museums with Film Programs compiled by Hollis Melton
Educational Film Library Association, New York, 1974.
Over 500 U.S. and Canadian museums that show films.

North American Film and Video Directory: A Guide to Media Collections and Services compiled by Olga S. Weber

R. R. Bowker Co., New York, 1976.

Lists some 200 college, public, special library and media centers (including museums), with collections of film and/or videotapes available for loan, rental, or on-site viewing and auxiliary services. Detailed information for each entry. Appendix of film circuits and cooperatives.

The Reel Revolution by Neil P. Hurley

Orbis Books, Maryknoll, NY 10545, 1978.

An essay-style book on consciousness-raising through educational films.

Report on State Library Film Service by Robyn I. Foreman

Educational Film Library Association, New York, 1977.

Based on a questionnaire sent to 50 state libraries. Summary, charts, description of programs by library. Includes addresses, phone numbers, directors.

TV Movies, Second Edition, 1979-1980 by Leonard Maltin

New American Library, New York, 1979.

Ratings, credits and descriptions of 10,000 movies and made-for-TV movies.

University and College Film Collections, compiled by Indiana University AV Center

Educational Film Library Association, New York, 1974.

Lists over 400 libraries, including personnel, budgets, size of collection.

Women and Film: A Bibliography by Rosemary Ribich Kowalski

Scarecrow Press, Metuchen, NJ, 1976.

Four sections: Women as Performers, Women as Filmmakers, Images of Women, Women Columnists and Critics. Includes books, periodicals, and newspaper articles.

FILM LITERATURE INDICES

The Film Book Bibliography 1940-1975 by Jack C. Ellis

Scarecrow Press, Metuchen, NJ, 1979.

Indexes all books, monographs, and dissertations about films in English made during 1940-1975. Film Reference Materials, Techniques and Technology, Film Industry, Film History, Film Classifications, Biographies, Film Analysis, Interviews, Individual Films, Theory and Criticism, Film and Society, Film and Education. 5400 entries.

Film Literature Index 1973, 1974, 1975 edited by Vincent J. Aceto, Jane Graves, and Fred Silva

R. R. Bowker Co., New York, 1977.

Annual cumulations of the quarterly **Film Literature Index**. Contains entries from 140 U.S. and foreign periodicals, with access by subject, author and title and cross-references.

International Index to Film Periodicals 1976
St. Martin's Press, New York, 1978.

Guide to the articles that appeared during the year in the world's 80 most important film magazines. Three main categories: General Subjects, (includes film distribution and exhibition, sociology of film, film history, criticism, etc.); Films; and Biography.

The New York Times Film Reviews (1913-1974), 10 vols.
Arno Press, New York.

Bound editions of all film reviews appearing in **The New York Times** arranged by date of review. Title and name index.

Readers' Guide to Periodical Literature
H. W. Wilson, New York.

7 issues per year. Period covered: 1900 on. The basic index to general interest magazines which often have film and television articles and reviews. Cumulative.

Retrospective Index to Film Periodicals, 1930-1971 by Linda Batty
R. R. Bowker Co., New York, 1975.

Designed to complement the FIAF's **International Index to Film Periodicals**. Separate sections on individual films, subjects, and book reviews. Indexes the contents of 14 English language periodicals from their beginnings through December 1971, and reviews and articles from **The Village Voice**.

PROGRAMMING GUIDES

Feature Films on 8mm, 16mm, and Videotape, 6th Edition compiled and edited by James L. Limbacher
R. R. Bowker Co., New York, 1979.

Updated edition of the master reference work for film bookers. Lists over 16,000 features alphabetically by title and includes company, release date, running time, color, format, director, principal cast and all distributors. Appended is a list of directors and their films. Supplements are published quarterly in **Sightlines** (EFLA).

Film Programmer's Guide to 16mm Rentals, 3rd Edition edited by Kathleen Weaver
Reel Research, Box 6037, Albany, CA 94706, 1980.

13,000 titles of 16mm films from Hollywood, foreign and independent releases, social and political documentaries, experimental and underground films, animations, silents, both features **and** shorts. Provides directors, date, running time, other pertinent notes, distributors and rental information.

How to Organize and Run a Film Society by Janet Weiner
The MacMillan Co., New York, 1973.

Contains valuable information, especially about organization and publicity of programs.

Manual on Film Evaluation revised edition by Emily S. Jones
Education Film Library Association, New York, 1974.

The process of evaluating a 16mm nontheatrical film, with a special section on coordinating an evaluation workshop.

FUNDING AND OTHER SKILLS GUIDES

About Foundations: How to Find the Facts You Need to Get a Grant
by Judith B. Margolin
The Foundation Center, 888 7th Ave., New York, NY 10019, 1975.
    A guide to foundation funding research.

Approaching Business for Support of the Arts
Business Committee for the Arts, Inc., New York, 1976.
    A pamphlet with practical suggestions for raising funds.

The A-V Connection: The Guide to Federal Funds for A-V Programs
National Audio-Visual Association, Fairfax, VA, 1977.
    Lists 33 federal programs and the aid that each offers. Topical headings include College Library Resources, Handicapped Media Services and Captioned Films, Adult Education — Grants to States, Metric Education, etc. With Subject Index.

The Foundation Center
888 7th Ave., New York, NY 10019.
    A resource library with regional offices providing computer services, print-outs, annual reports from foundations and corporations. Extensive material helpful to grant-seekers; the center has a well-trained professional staff.

The Grants Planner
The Institute for Fund Raising, 333 Hayes St., San Francisco, CA 94102, 1978.
    A Systems Approach to Grantsmanship. Combines background information, how-to's, and tools such as forms, worksheets and checklists and a 25-page bibliography of theoretical books, practical guides and articles on important topics to grant-searchers.

The Grassroots Fundraising Handbook: How to Raise Money in Your Community by Joan Flanagan
The Youth Project, 1555 Connecticut Ave., NW, Washington DC 20009.
Swallow Press, 1977.
    A How-to-do-it guide based on the author's experiences and extensive researching, includes case histories, sample charts, checklists, annual fundraising calendar, event timetable, and a comprehensive bibliography.

How to do Leaflets, Newsletters and Newspapers by Nancy Brigham
The New England Free Press, 60 Union Square, Somerville, MA 02143.
    Good introduction to procedure of design and layout.

Leading Film Discussions by Madeline S. Friedlander
League of Women Voters of the City of New York, 1972.
    A pamphlet of useful suggestions, includes recommended films and program ideas.

We Interrupt This Program: A Citizen's Guide to Using the Media for Social Change by Robbie Gordon
Citizen Involvement Training Project, University of Massachusetts, 138 Hasbrouck, Amherst, MA 01003.
Designed to help groups and individuals get access to the media, design press releases and public service announcements, and make effective contact with the press.

What Makes a Good Proposal? by F. Lee Jacquette and Barbara L. Jacquette
The Foundation Center, New York, 1976.
A booklet of suggestions.

What Will a Foundation Look for When You Submit a Grant Proposal? by Robert A. Mayer
The Foundation Center, New York, 1976.
Useful suggestions.

INDEPENDENT FILM AND VIDEO

Access. Film and Video Equipment: A Directory by Nancy Legge
The American Film Institute, JFK Center for Performing Arts, Washington, DC 20566.
Listings of facilities and resource centers throughout the country, broken down by region and state. Includes name of the facility, the contact person, hours, description of access policy, services and other resources available, equipment inventory and development plans.

Chicorel Index to Videotapes and Cassettes edited by Marietta Chicorel
Chicorel Publishing Co., 275 Central Park West, New York, NY 10024.
Annotated guide by title or subject with distributor and producer index. "Oriented towards programs appealing to patrons of public libraries." Emphasis on recreational aspects of the subjects. Annual, 1978.

Guide to Film and Video Resources in New England compiled by Abigail Nelson
University Film Study Center, Cambridge, MA 02139, 1978.
Lists by state. Film Services and Producers; Video Services and Producers; Broadcast TV Stations; Cable TV Systems and Video Access; Film and Video Organizations; New England State Arts Agencies; Sources of Funding Information.

A Guide to Independent Film and Video (Bulletin for Film and Video Information, Vol. II, No. 6) edited by Hollis Melton
Anthology Film Archives, 80 Wooster St., New York, NY 10012, 1976.
"To serve the information needs of independent film-and-videomakers and their audiences." Film and Videomaking; Distribution; Programming and Exhibition; Study; Funding. Includes catalogs.

The Independent Film Community: A Report on the Status of Independent Film in the U.S. 1977 edited by Peter Feinstein, prepared by the Committee on Film and Television Resources and Services.

Anthology Film Archives, 80 Wooster St., New York, NY 10012.

A review of independent filmmaking in the United States, including filmmakers, films, and funding agencies. Distribution, funding, non-commercial exhibition, preservation, study, with some attention to TV and video.

The Merc Directory

Young Filmmakers/Video Arts, 4 Rivington St., New York, NY 10002, 1977.

Paperback guide listing independently produced film and video works, distribution contact and exhibition equipment needed. From Publishing Center for Cultural Resources, 27 W. 53rd St., New York, NY 10019.

Profiles in Video: Who's Using Television and How by John H. Berwick and Steward Kranz

Knowledge Industry Publications, White Plains, NY, 1975.

A guide to organizations, schools, libraries, and others using video and a description of their products.

FILM AND VIDEO MAKING: TECHNICAL AND EQUIPMENT

American Cinematographer: International Journal of Motion Picture Photography and Production Techniques

The American Society of Cinematographers, P.O. Box 2230, Hollywood, CA 90028.

A monthly magazine covering equipment, with articles on production; oriented toward the professional filmmaker; technical and seminar information.

American Cinematographer's Manual, 4th edition compiled and edited by Charles G. Clarke and Walter Strenge

American Society of Cinematographers, 1973.

"The cinematographer's Bible." Complete information on equipment and supplies.

The Audiovisual Equipment Directory 23rd Edition 1977-1978

National Audiovisual Association, Inc., Fairfax, VA.

Annual guide to AV hardware arranged by type of equipment. Lists models, prices, features and accessories.

Equipment Loan Handbook

Young Filmmakers/Video Arts, New York, NY, 1979.

Equipment and services available to New York area filmmakers through YF/VA.

Independent Filmmaking by Lenny Lipton

World Publishing Co., Straight Arrow Books, San Francisco, CA 94107.

A complete guide to 8mm, super-8, single-8, and 16mm moviemaking covering technical as well as aesthetic aspects of films. Detailed equipment information, editing techniques, laboratory roles, etc.

Taping It Together: A Video Manual for Community Groups by Bob Matorin
The Media Project, Urban Planning Aid, Inc., Boston, MA 02116.
A comprehensive handbook written for community organizers. Concrete examples of effective video use around the country, plus suggestions, instructions and data.

DISTRIBUTION

Doing It Yourself: A Handbook on Independent Film Distribution by Julia Reichert, coordinated and edited by Amalie R. Rothschild
Association of Independent Video and Filmmakers, Inc., 99 Prince St., New York, NY, 1977.
A practical guide, with a list of film festivals and sample business forms.

Non-Theatrical Film Distributors: Sales Service Policies, revised edition, edited by Carol A. Emmens
Educational Film Library Association, New York, 1974.
Includes type of films handled, distribution method, extent of distribution, and preview policies for 137 companies. Listed alphabetically by company's name.

16mm Distribution compiled by Judith Trojan and Nadine Covert
Educational Film Library Association, New York, 1977.
Filmmakers and specialists explore the 16mm market and audience, distribution alternatives and theater showcases. Useful appendices, including an International Film Festivals and Awards list.

FILMOGRAPHIES

(This is a selected list of general and specific topic-related filmographies.)

GENERAL FILMOGRAPHIES

The American Film Institute Catalog of Motion Pictures
R. R. Bowker Co., New York, series in progress.
Encyclopedia-sized catalogs of films (features, shorts, newsreels) released in the U.S. for 10-year periods. Already published are 1921-1930 and 1961-1970. Volume I is alphabetical annotated list by film title, with year of release, copyright, production company, credits, synopsis. Volume II includes credits, literary and dramatic sources and subject index.

Famous People on Film by Carol A. Emmens
Scarecrow Press, Metuchen, NJ, 1976.
Gathers into one alphabetical listing (by individual subject) all currently available films on that subject. With brief annotations, credits. Also, a selected list of feature films on the famous. With title and subject (by occupation) index.

Film Canadiana, 1977-1978: The Canadian Film Institute Yearbook of the Canadian Cinema compiled by Marg Clarkson, supervising editor, Piers Handling

Canadian Film Institute, 75 Albert St. #611, Ottowa, Ontario K1P 5E7, 1978.

The Canadian film industry's yearbook, with listings of films produced there during 1977-78. Separate listings for films for TV, bibliography, distributors, awards, filmographies, and an overview of the Canadian industry. Thorough.

Film Evaluation Guides

Educational Film Library Association, New York.

Hard cover cumulation of EFLA evaluation cards with subject index. Supplement One 1965-1967, Supplement Two 1967-1971.

From "A" to "Yellow-Jack" — A Film Study Collection

Indiana University Audio-Visual Center, Bloomington, IN 47401.

Good selections. Includes feature, documentary and experimental work, politics and art.

Index to 16mm Educational Films — Sixth Edition 1977

National Information Center for Educational Media, Los Angeles, CA 90007.

Vol. I: Subject guide and directory of producers and directors. Vol. II-IV: Alphabetical guide to 16mm films. A large basic guide to the 16mm field, but it has many omissions (new edition 1980).

Library of Congress Catalogs

Quarterly, annual and quinquennial cumulations available. List of films filed in the Library of Congress. Directors, who it is released by, description. Very specific, but weak on independents. Good when used in conjunction with the **Index to 16mm Educational Films.**

AFRICA

Africa from Real to Reel: An African Filmography by Stephen Ohrn and Rebecca Riley

African Studies Association, Brandeis University, Waltham, MA 02154, 1976.

1300 shorts and features about Africa. Includes date, producer and filmmaker, characteristics, location, distribution, synopsis. Descriptive annotations.

Chamba Notes (See listing under periodicals.)

AGING

About Aging: A Catalog of Films, revised 3rd edition

E. P. Andrus Gerontology Center, University of S. California, Los Angeles, CA 90007, 1977.

Discusses content of films and lists distributors.

Aging by Judith Trojan

Educational Film Library Association, New York, 1974.

An annotated list of over 150 films about and for the aging.

Media Resources for Gerontology
Institute of Gerontology, University of Michigan, 520 E. Liberty St., Ann Arbor, MI 48109, 1977.
Large catalog which includes tapes/slides, videotape, audio tapes and film strips.

Past Sixty: The Older Woman in Print and Film by C. Hollenshead
The Institute of Gerontology, 1977.
Sexuality, legal and economic issues, ethnic background. Includes discussion of film contents.

ART

Films on Art compiled and edited by The Canadian Centre for Films on Art
Watson-Guptill Publishing, New York, 1977.
Source book of films on painting, drawing, prints, sculpture, architecture, photography, and archaeology. Lists films in alphabetical order, by subject, by artist. Includes distributor directory.

DANCE

Dance Film Directory: An Annotative and Evaluative Guide to Films on Ballet and Modern Dance by John Mueller
Princeton Book Co., Princeton, NJ, 1979.
Valuable for dance programmers. Basic information on distributors, choreographers, dance works, and dancers, as well as appendices on mime films, ethnic dance films, Fred Astaire, Busby Berkely.

ENVIRONMENT/LAND/FOOD CO-OPS/ENERGY

Energy: A Multi-Media Guide for Children and Young Adults by Judith H. Higgins
American Bibliographical Center/Clio Press, Santa Barbara, CA, 1979.
Illustrated, indexed, and with a bibliography, the multi-media materials section lists films by subject headings: Coal, Nuclear Energy, Gas, Oil, Solar Energy, etc. Lists by subject, title, and author. Includes a distributors directory.

Energy on Film
New York State Alliance to Save Energy, 366 W. 44th St., #709, New York, NY 10036, 1978.
A non-profit organization concerned with popularizing discussions of energy and conservation. 18 pages of films, some free.

Films on Food and Land
Earthwork, 1499 Potrero, San Francisco, CA 94110, 1979.
Includes Spanish-language films, suggestions for obtaining films, index by subject, description of films, sources and distributors. About 300 films.

Man and His Environment by Hannah C. Williams
Interstate Publishers, Danville, IL, 1972.

Intended as a supplement to **The Critical Index of Films on Man and His Environment**, available from the same publisher.

ETHNIC CONCERNS

Blacks in the America of the Seventies
Indiana University Audio-Visual Center, Bloomington, IN 47401. Published periodically.

Inexpensive rentals. Films primarily by PBS, WNET. All aspects of Black culture and life. Includes Black African Writers series.

Ethnic American Minorities: A Guide to Media and Materials edited by Harry A. Johnson
R. R. Bowker Co., New York, 1976.

An in-depth discussion of minorities, with films, books, and AV materials indexed by title. Also includes a producer/distributor directory.

Guide to Audio-Visual Aids for Spanish Speaking Americans
HEW, Public Health Service, Health Services Administration, 5600 Fishers Lane, Rockville, MD 20852.

Films and film-strips in Spanish, on such things as alcoholism, breast self-examination, etc.

Jewish Films in the United States: A Comprehensive Survey and Descriptive Filmography compiled by Stuart Fox
G. K. Hall and Co., Boston, MA, 1976.

4000 titles (features, shorts, documentaries, television specials) having anything to do, in any way, with Jews and Judaism.

FOLKLORE

American Folklore Films and Videotapes — An Index edited by Bill Ferris and Judy Peiser
The Center for Southern Folklore, 1216 Peabody Ave., P.O. Box 4081, Memphis, TN 38104, 1976.

A list of films and videotapes about diverse American folk traditions—ceremonies, art, music, humor, the South, Appalachia, etc. Brief description of film/tape, where and how to rent each.

Films on Traditional Music and Dance: A First International Catalog edited by Peter Kennedy
United Nations Educational, Scientific and Cultural Organization (UNESCO), Place de Fonteray, 75 Paris-7e, 1970.

Lists films from many countries. Descriptions, where to rent. Also has film catalogs on ballet, art, music, education, mime, opera, etc.

HEALTH

The Health Sciences and Audiovisual Resource List: 1978-1979 edited by Malcolm Brantz
University of Connecticut Health Center Library, Learning Resources Center, Farmington, CT 06032, 1978.
Three volumes. A comprehensive guide covering health materials not generally covered by other guides. Vol. I lists producers, subject index and code key for Vol. II and III. These are alphabetical listings on 16mm films, audiotapes, videotapes, slides, transparencies, records, etc. with credit information and descriptions.

In Focus: Alcohol and Alcoholism Media compiled by the National Clearinghouse for Alcohol Information
Supt. of Documents, U.S. Government Clearinghouse, Washington, DC 20402.
Includes a discussion of each film's content.

A Selective Guide to Audio-Visuals for Mental Health and Family Life Education
Mental Health Materials Center, 419 Park Ave. South, New York, NY 10016, 1979.
Comprehensive guide of films and audio-visuals from government, professional and commercial sources, arranged by subject area. Includes summary, primary audience, uses, evaluation and ordering information.

KIDS AND YOUNG ADULTS

Films Kids Like compiled and edited by Susan Rice
More Films Kids Like by Maureen Gaffney
American Library Association, Chicago, IL, 1973 and 1977 respectively.
Annotated lists of films tested with groups of children. Reports their reactions. Excellent programming resources.

Movies for Kids by Edith Zornow and Ruth M. Goldstein
Discus Books, New York, 1973.
Annotated selection of 125 features and 75 shorts of interest to children. Supplementary features list, addresses of film distributors and organizations, book and periodical listings for further research.

On the Nature of Children's Film by Maureen Gaffney
Educational Film Library Association, New York, 1980.
An extensive analysis of what makes a good children's film; specific works are cited as illustrations. This is an excellent resource for media educators, programmers, writers, and filmmakers.

Positive Images: Non-Sexist Films for Young People edited by Linda Artel and Susan Wengraf
Booklegger Press, 555 29th St., San Francisco, CA 94141, 1976.
Annotated lists of films, video, filmstrips, slides.

What to Do When the Lights Go On by Gerry Laybourne and Maureen Gaffney
Oryx Press, Suite 103, 2214 N. Central Ave., Phoenix, AZ 85004.
　　A resource for programmers and arts educators in a cookbook format with ideas for combining film and arts activities and an extensive annotated filmography.

LABOR

Films for Labor prepared by the AFL-CIO
Dept. of Education, 815 16th St., NW, Washington, DC 20006, 1970, 1975.
　　Labor history, social and economic problems, civil rights, union-sponsored programs, leadership training, political education.

Film Library Quarterly, Special Labor issue, Vol. 12, #2
Film Library Information Council, Box 348, Radio City Station, New York, NY 10019, 1979.
　　A special issue on labor films, including historic and current films.

LATIN AMERICA

Chicano Cinema Coalition Newsletter
　　Includes up-to-date information on films, sources, activities and articles dealing with concerns of the Chicano film community. The June 1979 issue includes a Chicano Cinema Filmography and a bibliography. Send self-addressed, stamped envelope to Newsletter, P.O. Box 32004, Los Angeles, CA 90032.

Latin America: Sights and Sounds prepared by Jane M. Loy
Consortium of Latin American Studies Programs Publication #5 LASA Secretariat, Box 13362, University Station, Gainsville, FL 32601, 1973.
　　A guide to motion pictures and music for college courses.

Latin American Cinema Film and History by E. Bradford Burns
UCLA Latin American Center, Los Angeles, CA, 1975.
　　Book with a filmic approach to studying Latin American history. Bibliography of books and articles of Latin American Cinema, sources for films.

Latino Materials: A Multi Media Guide for Children and Young Adults by Daniel Flores Duran and Neal Schuman
American Bibliographical Center/Clio Press, Santa Barbara, CA, 1979.
　　Includes a bibliography/filmography on Latin Culture, designed for librarians serving the Spanish-speaking community.

The New Latin American Cinema compiled by Julianne Burton
Cineaste, 419 Park Avenue South, New York, NY 10016, 1976.
　　A bibliography designed as a research guide to the achievements of politically committed filmmakers during 1960-1976; summaries of books in Spanish, Portuguese, French, and English, distributors, film journals, festival and conference publications, and films listed by country of origin.

SCIENCE

Science Books and Films
American Association for the Advancement of Science, 1515 Massachusetts Ave., NW, Washington, DC 20005.
A quarterly publication which updates **Science Film Catalog**.

Science Film Catalog
American Association for the Advancement of Science, R. R. Bowker Co., 1975.
Social sciences, pure sciences, technology (applied sciences). Listed by subject heading, alphabetically, producer/distributor directory. Published periodically.

SOCIAL CHANGE

Alternatives by Nadine Covert and Esme J. Dick
Educational Film Library Association, New York, 1975.
Annotated list of over 150 films on education, life-styles, work and religion.

American Issues Forum
Educational Film Library Association, 1975.
Annotated list of over 200 films dealing with U.S. history, government, politics, labor, business, social issues.

A Bibliography of Civil Rights and Civil Liberties by A. D. Brooks
Civil Liberties Educational Foundation, Inc., 200 Park Ave., New York, NY, 1962.
Lists books, filmstrips and films. Thorough coverage of all aspects of civil liberties. Interesting for an historical perspective.

Emancipation Film Locater edited by Emancipation
Emancipation, Box 3774, Merchandise Mart, Chicago, IL 60654.
List of films by subject area from many distributors with brief descriptions and basic information. Wide variety of films around social issues. Distributor directory.

Mobilization for Survival Audio-Visual Guide 1979-80
MFS, 3601 Locust Walk, Philadelphia, PA 19104.
List of films by subject. Distributors list.

Political Change: A Film Guide by James Morrison and Richard Blue
University of Minnesota, Audio-Visual Library Service, 3300 University Ave. SE, Minneapolis, MN 55415, 1975.
Thirty-three films, written for persons interested in the academic teaching of economic development and political change.

Reel Change: A Guide to Social Issue Films edited by Patricia Peyton
The Film Fund, P.O. Box 909, San Francisco, CA 94101, 1979.
Lists approximately 600 social issue films plus video tapes and slide shows relevant to various social issues. Includes a chapter on how to program classics and a distributor directory resource list. Annotations are based on film user comments from groups throughout the country.

War. Peace. A Film Guide
World Without War Council, 7245 S. Merrill Ave., Chicago, IL 60649, 1974.
   The arms race and the effect of nuclear war, non-violence, U.S. foreign policy. Published periodically.

THIRD WORLD (Also see listings under Africa, Latin America, and Ethnic Concerns)

A Filmography of the Third World: An Annotated List of 16mm Films by Helen W. Cyr
Scarecrow Press, Metuchen, NJ, 1976.
   Very good, comprehensive. Includes a distributor address list.

Programmers Guide to Third World Cinema
Tricontinental Film Center, 419 Park Ave. South, New York, NY 10016, 1979.
   Select list of recommended films and distributors, a bibliography of programmers' resources, and a description of Third World Cinema and its history.

WOMEN (Also see listings under Aging)

Films By And/Or About Women
Women's History Research Center, 2325 Oak St., Berkeley, CA 94708, 1972.
   Directory of filmmakers, films and distributors.

Women and Film: A Resource Handbook prepared by the Project on the Status and Education of Women
Association of American Colleges, 1818 R. St. NW, Washington, DC 20009.
   Lists a number of women's films. Also, planning a festival, reducing costs, and previewing films.

Women's Films: A Critical Guide
Audio-Visual Center, Indiana University, Bloomington, IN 47401, 1975.
   Includes films from Indiana University Audio-Visual Center and other distributors, distributors' index, bibliography, films listed by topic with commentary.

Women in Focus by Jeanne Betancourt
Pflaum Publishing, Dayton, OH, 1974. Also available from EFLA.
   Catalogs and reviews more than 90 films that are non-sexist or specifically feminist in perspective and emphasizes the work of women filmmakers. Indexes by filmmaker, theme, and distributor.

Women's Films in Print by Bonnie Dawson
Booklegger Press, 555 29th St., San Francisco, CA 94131, 1975.
   Annotated guide to 800 films. Includes American "underground" artists.

PERIODICALS

(This is a highly selective listing of periodicals emphasizing those which review films or provide updated information on new releases. More comprehensive lists of film periodicals can be found in the **AFI Factfile #1**, the film literature indices cited above, and publications of the Educational Film Library Association.)

AFI Education Newsletter edited by Annette Bagley

The American Film Institute, National Education Services, J. F. Kennedy Center, Washington, DC 20566.

For film educators. Includes model course syllabi, profiles of film archives or specialized institutions, calendar and job listings. Bi-monthly during the academic year.

Afterimage edited by Nathan Lyons

31 Prince St., Rochester, NY 14607.

Emphasis on photography. Includes reviews of artists and their work, current books and issues, a national calendar of events. 9 issues per year.

Airtime

Global Village Video Resource Center, 454 Broome St., New York, NY 10013.

Covers aspects of cooperation between independent producers and public TV. Includes activities of Global Village Media Center. 10 issues per year.

American Cinematographer edited by Herb A. Lightman

American Society of Cinematographers, P.O. Box 2230, Hollywood, CA 90028.

Oriented to discussion of technical aspects of film, equipment and books. Monthly.

The Animator edited by Bill Foster

Northwest Film Study Center, Portland Art Museum, 1219 S. W. Park Ave., Portland, OR 97205.

Useful calendar of film related activities nation-wide. Includes brief articles on independent film and video activity in the northwestern U.S. Quarterly.

Booklist edited by Irene Wood (Nonprint)

American Library Association, 50 East Huron St., Chicago, IL 60611.

Film section reviews new releases and evaluates them for use in library and community group settings.

Camera Obscura edited by J. Bergstrom, S. Flitterman, E. Lyon, C. Penley

The Camera Obscura Collective, P.O. Box 4517, Berkeley, CA 94704.

Articles, interviews and distribution information. In depth. Also covers women in film and criticism. 3 issues per year.

Center for Southern Folklore Newsletter edited by Kini Kedigh

Center for Southern Folklore, 1216 Peabody Ave., P.O. Box 408, Memphis, TN 38104.

Covers folklore and media projects nation-wide with emphasis on activity in the southeast region. Bi-annual.

Chamba Notes edited by St. Clair Bourne

P. O. Box 1231, Hollywood, CA 90028 or P.O. Box U, Brooklyn, NY 11202.

International news, editorials, interviews, announcements of activities of Afro-American, African and Third World in a Pan-African cultural context. Quarterly.

Cineaste edited by Gary Crowdus

419 Park Avenue South, New York, NY 10016.

Explores the art and politics of international cinema. Critical articles, book reviews, film reviews, and interviews on films and filmmakers, including many independents. Quarterly.

Cinefantastique edited by Frederick S. Clarke

F.O. Box 270, Oak Park, IL 60303.

Science fiction, horror and fantasy films and related media. Bi-monthly.

Cinemanews

Foundation for Art in Cinema, 1365 San Anselmo Ave., San Anselmo, CA 94960.

Formerly **Canyon Cinemanews**. Interviews with filmmakers, film reviews and news of films shown at Canyon Cinematheque in San Francisco and activities at Canyon Cinema Cooperative. Bi-monthly.

Cinemantics edited by James S. Elliot and Timothy O'Malley.

2000 Pearl, Austin, TX 78705.

Independent film and video, theory, history and criticism articles. Bi-monthly.

Cinematexas Program Notes edited by Edward Lowry

Department of Radio-TV-Film, CMA 6.118, University of Texas, Austin, TX 78712.

Analysis and research section, credits, reviews and occasional interviews relating to films shown at University of Texas at Austin. 8 issues per year.

Field of Vision edited by Robert A. Haller

Pittsburgh Film-Makers, P.O. Box 7200, Pittsburgh, PA 15213.

Emphasis on experimental, avant-garde film/video/photography/holography. Special attention to Pennsylvania artists. Quarterly.

Film and Video Makers Travel Sheet edited by Rebecca Popovich Burdick

Carnegie Institute, Museum of Art Film Section, 4400 Forbes Ave., Pittsburgh, PA 15213.

Lists works, itineraries, showcases and announcements for independent film/video makers. Monthly.

Film Comment edited by Richard Corliss

Film Society of Lincoln Center, 140 W. 65th St., New York, NY 10023.

Discusses international film and TV. News and book reviews. Bi-monthly.

Film Culture edited by Jonas Mekas

G.P.O. Box 1499, New York, NY 10001.

Forum for writings on independent, avant-garde and classical cinema. Irregular publication dates.

Film Literature: Current
Filmdex, Part II, Inc., Box 22477, SUNY A, 1400 Washington Ave., Albany, NY 12222.
Compilation of the Tables of Contents of the international periodical literature of film/TV and index of articles on those subjects from non-specialized periodicals. Monthly.

Film Library Quarterly edited by William Sloan and Emma Cohn
P.O. Box 348, Radio City Station, New York, NY 10019.
Interviews, articles and reviews of film, video and books. Emphasis on special interest areas. Useful to film librarians and community programmers. In-depth. Quarterly.

Film News edited by Rohama Lee
250 W. 57th St., Suite 1527, New York, NY 10019.
Listings, reviews and general and specific film news particularly useful to teachers, librarians and community group users of films. 5 issues per year.

Film Quarterly edited by Ernest Callenbach
University of California Press, Berkeley, CA 94702.
Articles, reviews, interviews and book reviews. Critical and theoretical, deals with various genres of film. Quarterly.

Filmmakers Monthly edited by H. Whitney Bailey
P.O. Box 115, Ward Hill, MA 01830 or 41 Union Square West #416, New York, NY 10003.
Formerly **Filmmakers Newsletter**. For commercial and independent filmmakers. Monthly.

The Independent
Association of Independent Video and Filmmakers, 99 Prince St., New York, NY 10012.
Includes information on festivals and grants, production notes, equipment access, jobs and internships, AIVF programs, and current issues relating to film/video. Geared to independents. Monthly.

Journal of Popular Film and Television edited by Michael Marsden and John G. Nachbar
Popular Culture Center, Bowling Green State University, Bowling Green, OH 43403.
TV and popular film criticism in a cultural context. Includes subject bibliographies and filmographies, interviews, poetry. Quarterly.

Journal of the University Film Association edited by Timothy J. Lyons
Department of Radio-Television-Film, Temple University, Philadelphia, PA 19122.
Geared to teachers of film courses. In-depth. Context is international and historical. Quarterly.

Jump Cut edited by John Hess and Chuck Kleinhans
P.O. Box 865, Berkeley, CA 94701.
Political, theoretical and critical articles and reviews of films and film books. 4 to 6 issues per year.

Landers Film Reviews edited by Bertha Landers

P.O. Box 69760, Los Angeles, CA 90069.
Commercial reviewing service.

Mass Media Newsletter edited by Janice P. York

Mass Media Ministries, 2116 North Charles St., Baltimore, MD 21218.
Ecumenical reviews of various areas of media. 20 issues per year.

Millennium Film Journal edited by Alister Sanderson, Vicki Z. Peterson and David Shapiro

Millennium Film Workshop, 66 E. 4th St., New York, NY 10003.
Articles by writers, critics and filmmakers. International in scope. Deals with all genres of film. 3 issues per year.

Monthly Film Bulletin edited by Richard Combs

British Film Institute Publications Department, 81 Dean St., London W1V 6AA, England.
Reviews every feature film released commercially in England and also covers selected shorts, silents and early sound films. Monthly.

News from the Film Fund

80 E. 11th St., New York, NY 10003 or 308 11th St., San Francisco, CA 94103.
Emphasis on social issue films. News on grants, projects, and current releases. Quarterly.

Previews: Audiovisual Software Reviews edited by Phyllis Levy Mandell

R. R. Bowker Co., New York.
Reviews of films for all ages. Monthly from Sept. to May.

Quarterly Review of Film Studies edited by Ronald Gottesman

Redgrave Publishing Co., 430 Manville Rd., Pleasantville, NY 10570.
In-depth theoretical and critical articles. Theme oriented. Quarterly.

re: act edited by Maureen Harmonay

Action for Children's Television, 46 Austin St., Newtonville, MA 02160.
Formerly ACT News. News stories. Deals with children's television programming. Quarterly.

Savicom Newsletter edited by Jay Ruby

Society for the Anthropology of Visual Communication, Department of Anthropology, Temple University, Philadelphia, PA 19122.
Scholarly newsletter on films and issues relating to anthropology.

Sight and Sound edited by Penelope Houston

British Film Institute, 127 Charing Cross Rd., London WC2H OEA, England and Eastern News Distributors, 111 8th Ave., New York, NY 10011.
International journal of critical, theoretical and historical film articles. Book reviews and festival reports. Quarterly.

Sightlines edited by Nadine Covert
Educational Film Library Association, 43 West 61st St., New York, NY 10023.

A quarterly magazine which focuses on a new theme in each issue. Also includes interviews, new film/video releases, listings of current events, section on children's media, and updates the Limbacher book.

Soho Weekly News, Inc.
514 Broadway, New York, NY 10012.

Weekly reviews of films opening in the New York area.

Southwestern Alternate Media Project Newsletter
1506½ Branard, Houston, TX 77006.

Forum for independent video and filmmakers. Emphasis on the southwest. Irregular publication dates.

Televisions edited by Rebecca Moore, Larry Kirkman and Gayle Gibbons
P.O. Box 21068, Washington, DC 20009.

Interviews, news of video, cable programming and public TV. Quarterly.

University Film Study Center Newsletter edited by Gisela Hoelcl
18 Vassar St., Bldg. 20, Cambridge, MA 02139.

News and reviews of current film activities and events. Emphasis on independent film. Interviews included. Quarterly.

Variety edited by Syd Silverman
154 W. 46th St., New York, NY 10036.

Major trade weekly of the entertainment industry.

Velvet Light Trap edited by W. Dixson Powell and Steven Grant
P.O. Box 3355, Madison, WI 53704.

Discusses American film, past and present. Emphasis on theme issues. Quarterly.

Videography edited by Peter Caranicas
475 Park Avenue South, New York, NY 10016.

Products and programs reviews. News and interviews. Monthly.

Videoscope edited by John Reilly
1 Park Ave., Suite 1520, New York, NY 10016.

Incorporating **Radical Software**. News on current trends, outlets for production, funding sources, and general information for the independent video producer. Quarterly.

The Village Voice
80 University Place, New York, NY 10003.

Weekly reviews of films opening in the New York City area.

Visions edited by Randall Conrad
Boston Film/Video Foundation, 38 Brighton Ave., Allston, MA 02134.

Film and Video newsletter of BF/VF. Interviews, calendar, announcements, articles on independents. 10 issues per year.

Wide Angle edited by Peter Lehman
P.O. Box 388, Athens, OH 45701.
    Each issue has a theme and carries articles and interviews. The end result is a variety of approaches to film study. Quarterly.

Wilson Library Bulletin (Cine-Opsis)
H. W. Wilson Co., 950 University Ave., Bronx, NY 10452.
    Audio visual column reviewing films for library use.

Young Viewers
Media Center for Children, 3 W. 29th St., New York, NY 10001.
    Discusses children's films and programming. Quarterly.

DISTRIBUTORS

(Film distribution is constantly growing and changing. Film distributors range from companies with thousands of titles to individuals who distribute their own films. This list is not comprehensive but is as up-to-date as possible. It will provide a starting point for contacting distributors. More comprehensive lists and updates can be found in the titles listed in our programming section, in the books cited in the subject area Filmographies, and in **Reel Change** and **AFI Factfile #6**. Quarterly updates to Limbacher are provided in **Sightlines**.)

Amanecer Films
733 N. Seward St., Los Angeles, CA 90038.
    Produces and distributes a few Chicano films.

The American Federation of Arts
41 E. 65th St., New York, NY 10021 — (212) 988-7700.
    Programs of American independent cinema, avant garde and films on arts and crafts.

Anthology Film Archives
80 Wooster St., New York, NY 10012 — (212) 226-0010.
    Distributes videotapes, and maintains archive of American avant garde cinema.

Appalshop
Box 743, Whitesburg, KY 41858 — (606) 633-5708.
    Production, training, distribution and education utilizational projects center. Produces and distributes films, recordings, videotapes about Appalachian life and culture.

Arcus
1225 Broadway, New York, NY 10001 — (212) 686-2216.
    American feature films, comedies and cartoons. Distributes to East Coast.

Association Instructional Materials (Association Films)

866 3rd Ave., New York, NY 10022 — (212) 736-9693.

Educational, entertainment, American features, classic and contemporary, children's and Walt Disney films.

Azteca Films Inc.

1500 Broadway, New York, NY 10036 — (212) 869-3666.

Spanish-language feature films; primarily from Mexico, a few from Argentina and Spain.

Bauer International

695 West 7th St., Plainfield, NJ 07060 — (201) 757-6090.

Foreign feature films, primarily France and Germany, some American classics.

Benchmark Films

145 Scarbourough Rd., Briarcliff Manor, NY 10510 — (914) 762-3838.

Educational films primarily for institutional use.

Bilingual Educational Services

1603 Hope St., South Pasadena, CA 91030 — (213) 682-3456.

Bilingual films on a wide range of social topics; emphasis on Chicano history. Also distributes other films (e.g. Disney) to bilingual market.

Budget Films

4590 Santa Monica Blvd., Los Angeles, CA 90029 — (213) 660-0187.

Large collection of shorts, also classics, contemporary films, "B" films, silent and foreign films (mainly European).

Bullfrog Films

Oley, PA 19547 — (215) 779-8226.

Small and important collection of documentaries on health issues, social sciences, environment and energy.

Cambridge Documentary Films

P.O. Box 385, Cambridge, MA 02139 — (617) 354-3677.

Production and self-distribution. A regional media resource for libraries, schools, universities and organizations.

Canadian Filmmakers' Distribution Cooperative

406 Jarvis St., Toronto, Ontario M4Y 2G6 — (416) 921-4121.

Independent Canadian production, primarily documentaries and shorts.

Canyon Cinema Cooperative

2325 3rd St., Suite 338, San Francisco, CA 94107 — (415) 626-2255.

Films, rentals, prices, graphics, subject categories and descriptive notes are all the creations of various filmmakers who contribute to the catalog. All films in the catalog are owned by the filmmaker; all films submitted are accepted.

Carousel Films

1501 Broadway, New York, NY 10036 — (212) 354-0315.
Sales catalog featuring 16mm, mostly educational, films emphasizing government, science, social studies and the arts.

Castelli-Sonnabend Tapes and Films, Inc.

420 W. Broadway, New York, NY 10012 — (212) 432-6229.
Includes works by artists: e.g. Claes Oldenburg, Peter Campus, Vito Acconci.

Churchill Films

662 N. Robertson Blvd., Los Angeles, CA 90069 — (213) 657-5110.
Collection of documentaries, shorts, and educational films.

Cinema 5

595 Madison Ave., New York, NY 10022 — (212) 752-3200.
Variety of important contemporary feature and documentary films from the U.S., Italy, Soviet Union, Spain; also a few shorts.

Clem Williams Films Inc.

2240 Noblestown Rd., Pittsburgh, PA 15205 — (412) 421-5810.
Large collection of Hollywood feature films and shorts. Other offices in Georgia, Texas and Illinois.

Columbia-16

116 N. Roberton Blvd., Los Angeles, CA 90048 — (213) 652-9364.
Hollywood 16mm feature film distribution.

Corinth Films

410 E. 62nd St., New York, NY 10021 — (212) 421-4770.
An eclectic collection of American and foreign classic and contemporary feature films. Includes a bibliography with each film listing.

Creative Film Society

7237 Canby Ave., Reseda, CA 91335 — (213) 881-3887.
Art shorts ranging from old-time comedy classics to contemporary film art.

Direct Cinema Limited

Box 315, Franklin Lakes, NJ 07417 — (201) 891-8240.
Independently produced features and shorts on a variety of topics.

Educational Media Corporation

2036 LeMoyne Ave., Los Angeles, CA 90026 — (213) 660-4076.
Current independent films on Chicano culture and history, films on nature, hunger, Native Americans and energy.

Emgee Film Library

16024 Ventura Film Blvd., Suite 211, Encino, CA 91436 — (213) 981-5506.
American historical films, silents, westerns, D.W. Griffiths, historical animation, documentary, experimental, surrealist and avant-garde films.

Encyclopedia Britannica Educational Corporation

425 N. Michigan Ave., Chicago, IL 60601 — (312) 321-6800, (800) 621-3900.
Educational collection.

Femme Films Inc.

4537 Grand Ave. South, Minneapolis, MN 55409 — (612) 824-1640.
Small collection of feminist films (the non-profit corp. of the Twin Cities Women's
Film Collective).

Film Classic Exchange

1914 S. Vermont Ave., Los Angeles, CA 90007 — (213) 731-3854.
Wide selection of silents; American, French, Spanish and German films; features
and documentaries.

Filmmaker's Cooperative

175 Lexington Ave., New York, NY 10016 — (212) 889-3820.
First film distribution cooperative, organized so that independent filmmakers could
retain total control over their films. All films submitted are accepted for non-exclusive
distribution. Approximately 500 members, 1700 films. Foreign filmmakers are accepted.

Films Incorporated

733 Green Bay Rd., Wilmette, IL 60091 — (312) 256-3200.
American features, documentaries, foreign films, creative shorts, sound filmstrips,
videocassettes. Other offices in Illinois, California and Georgia.

Green Mountain Post Films

P.O. Box 177, Montague, MA 01351 — (413) 863-4754.
Excellent selection of films and slideshows on nuclear power, energy and the
environment.

Grove Press Film Division

196 W. Houston St., New York, NY 10014 — (212) 242-4900.
A large, diverse collection of films concentrating on the avant-garde and experimental; some politically and socially relevant features; films on art and theater;
foreign and domestic.

Haymarket-Kartemquin Films

1901 Wellington, Chicago, IL 60657 — (312) 472-4366.
Produces and distributes films and videotapes on a wide range of social issues.

Hurlock-Cine World

13 Arcadia Rd., Old Greenwich, CT 06870 — (203) 637-4319.
American and international feature films.

Icarus

200 Park Ave. South, Rm. 1319, New York, NY 10003 — (212) 674-3375.
Collection of documentary films from the Middle East, Eastern Europe, Third
World. Recently acquired the Impact collection of films on Black Americans, general
issues and cultural documentaries.

Interamerican Pictures
3528 Cahuenga Blvd., Hollywood, CA 90068 — (213) 851-8110.
Produce and distribute Chicano films and videotapes.

Iris Films
P.O. Box 5353, Berkeley, CA 94705 — (415) 549-3192.
Small collection of women's and lesbian films.

Kit Parker Films
P.O. Box 227, Carmel Valley, CA 93924 — (408) 659-4131/3474.
Large selection of American and foreign classic and contemporary features, shorts,
experimental cinema; some documentaries.

Latin American Film Project (See Unifilm)

Leacock-Pennebaker
56 W. 45th St., New York, NY 10019 — (212) 840-2425.
The films of independents Richard Leacock and D. A. Pennebaker.

Learning Corporation of America
1350 Avenue of the Americas, New York, NY 10019 — (212) 397-9330.
Massive collection of educational films relevant to the humanities, values, science
and social sciences.

Lucha
P.O. Box 288, Culver City, CA.
Film production and distribution collective dedicated to issues relevant to Latin
America.

MacMillan Films
34 MacQueston Parkway South, Mt. Vernon, NY 10550 — (914) 664-5051.
First national 16mm distribution house, featuring a large collection of international features and shorts. Indispensible catalog. Other offices in California, Texas,
Illinois, Minnesota, Arizona and Ohio.

Museum of Modern Art
Department of Film, 11 W. 53rd St., New York, NY 10019 — (212) 956-4204/4205.
Carefully chosen collection of films: silents, classics, documentaries, avant-garde.

National Film Board of Canada
1251 Avenue of the Americas, New York, NY 10020 — (212) 586-2400.
Canadian film production and distribution; documentaries, shorts, children's films;
wide range of issues.

New Day Films
P.O. Box 315, Franklin Lakes, NJ 07417 — (201) 891-8240.
A distribution cooperative for feminist films on a broad range of subjects: mar-
riage, masculinity, sexism, women's roles, families, aging, etc.

New Line Cinema
853 Broadway, New York, NY 10003 — (212) 764-7460, (800) 221-5150.
Classic and contemporary American and foreign films; wide range of genres.

New Times Film Inc.
1501 Broadway, Suite 1901, New York, NY 10036 — (212) 921-7020.
Documentaries on social issues.

New Yorker Films
16 W. 61st St., New York, NY 10023 — (212) 247-6110.
Important international and U.S. feature films, shorts and documentaries, many on social issues. Excellent selection of African, Brazilian and Japanese films.

Newsreel
630 Natoma, San Francisco, CA 94103 — (415) 621-6196.
Extensive listing of films and videotapes exclusively on social/political issues. Production facilities and services, training programs. Encourages community participation. Sliding rental scale. The Southern Africa Media Center is a project of California Newsreel.

Nguzu Saba Films
1002 Clayton St., San Francisco, CA 94117 — (415) 731-7336.
Selection of children's films including African folk tales.

Northwest Media Project
P.O. Box 4093, Portland, OR 97208 — (503) 223-5335.
Distributes documentary films and videotapes, offers workshops; clearinghouse for information on film and video production in the Northwest.

Open Circle Cinema
P.O. Box 315, Franklin Lakes, NJ 07417 — (201) 891-8240.
Small selection of social/political documentaries.

Paramount Pictures
Non-Theatrical Division, 5451 Marathon St., Hollywood, CA 90038 — (213) 462-0700, (800) 421-4432.
Hollywood features, comedies; some documentaries.

Phoenix Films
470 Park Ave. South, New York, N.Y. 10016 — (212) 684-5910.
Documentaries and shorts, many by independent filmmakers. Animation, children's, non-sexist, etc.

Picture Start
204½ W. John St., Champaign, IL 61820 — (217) 352-7353.
Independent experimental, animated and avant garde films.

Pyramid
P.O. Box 1048, Santa Monica, CA 90406 — (213) 828-7577.
Educational films, documentaries, shorts and videotapes. Good selection of children's films.

Select Film Library
115 W. 31st St., New York, NY 10001 — (212) 594-4450.
American features, shorts, cartoons.

Serious Business Company
1145 Mandana Blvd., Oakland, CA 94610 — (415) 832-5600.
Good selection of independent films: avant-garde, animation, feminist, health and sexuality, children, anthropology.

Swank Motion Pictures Inc.
201 S. Jefferson Ave., St. Louis, MO 63166 — (314) 534-6300.
American features, shorts, comedies.

Third World Newsreel
160 5th Ave., Rm. 911, New York, NY 10010 — (212) 243-3210.
Political/social issue films and videotapes. Also offers production facilities and services, training programs, sliding fee scale.

Time-Life Films
100 Eisenhower Dr., Paramus, NJ 07652 — (201) 843-4545.
Educational films and videotapes.

Tricontinental Film Center, Inc. (See Unifilm)

Unifilm
419 Park Ave. South, 19th floor, New York, NY 10016 — (212) 686-9890.
1550 Bryant St., Suite 605, San Francisco, CA 94103 — (415) 864-7755.
Consolidates the film libraries of Latin American Film Project and Tricontinental Film Center with features, documentaries and shorts from/about the Third World, European and independent American productions.

United Artists-16
729 7th Ave., New York, NY 10019 — (212) 575-4715.
Features and shorts from UA, Warners (pre-1949), Monogram (1932-1947).

Universal-16
8906 Beverly Blvd., Los Angeles, CA — (213) 550-7461.
Hollywood features and shorts. A few documentaries.

Viewfinders
P.O. Box 1665, Evanston, IL 60204 — (312) 869-0600.
Subdistribute short films from Janus, Corinth and others.

Visual Communications
313 S. San Pedro St., Los Angeles, CA 90013 — (213) 680-4462.
Produce and distribute videotapes and films on Asian Americans.

Zipporah
54 Lewis Wharf, Boston, MA 02110 — (617) 742-6680.
Films by director Frederick Wiseman.

FILM USERS' NETWORK

New films are constantly being released that can be of use to you. No matter how expertly you have done your research, you may have missed a good film or been unable to locate a particular title. Despite their efforts to reach you through catalogs, reviews and ads, filmmakers and distributors have just as hard a time finding film users interested in their particular film as you do finding them.

We have set up the **Film Users' Network** to help solve this problem. Let us know what topics interest you and filmmakers and distributors will send you announcements of new releases as a free informational service.

To join the **Network**, first select up to three areas of interest from the list below. By writing in 99 you will receive materials from all subject areas. Enter the code-numbers in the spaces on the form, fill out the rest of the form and send it to Cine Information.

01 **All National Issues**
02 **Aging and Generations**
03 **Ecology, Environment, Energy**
04 **Education**
05 **Ethnic Minorities**
06 **Health**
07 **Labor**
08 **Law and Civil Liberties**
09 **Lifestyles and Sexual Roles**
10 **Neighborhood Issues**
11 **Youth and Children**
12 **Women's Issues**
13 **Black Studies**

14 **Native American Studies**
30 **Sports/Physical Education**
31 **Anthropology and Ethnography**
32 **Economy**
33 **Geography**
34 **History**
35 **Natural Sciences**
36 **Psychology**
37 **Sociology**
38 **Political Science**
41 **The Art of Film**
42 **Experimental Films**
43 **Performing Arts**

44 **Visual Arts**
45 **Foreign Languages**
50 **Religion**
60 **All International Issues**
70 **Middle East**
71 **Africa**
72 **Asia**
73 **Europe**
74 **Latin America**
75 **Puerto Rican Studies**
76 **Chicano Studies**
80 **All Features**
81 **International Features**
82 **U.S. Features**
99 **All Possible Materials**

Send to: Cine Information, 419 Park Ave. So., New York, NY 10016

I'd like to join the Film Users' Network. I've entered the code numbers of my three areas of interest in the appropriate spaces:

_____   _____   _____

If other specify _____

Name _____
Department _____
Organization _____
Address _____
City _____ State _____ Zip _____

Send to: Cine Information, 419 Park Ave. So., New York, NY 10016

I'd like to join the Film Users' Network. I've entered the code numbers of my three areas of interest in the appropriate spaces:

_____   _____   _____

If other specify _____

Name _____
Department _____
Organization _____
Address _____
City _____ State _____ Zip _____

Send to: Cine Information, 419 Park Ave. So., New York, NY 10016
        (Prepaid orders only — make check or money order payable to Cine Information)

Send _____ paperbound copies of IN FOCUS at $8.95 each _____

Send _____ hardbound copies of IN FOCUS at $17.95 each _____

                                              Sub Total _____

In New York State add 8% sales tax   _____

Add $1.00 shipping and handling fee per book   _____

Enclosed find my check or money order for: Total _____

Name _____
Department _____
Organization _____
Address _____
City _____ State _____ Zip _____

IN FOCUS EVALUATION FORM

If you would take the time to complete this form, it will greatly assist us in evaluating the usefulness of **In Focus**, and in preparing supplements. Please let us know not only how **In Focus** worked for you but also where more or different information is needed. Descriptions of your experiences using films and **In Focus** would also be valuable.

I have worked on _____ film screenings in the past two years.

These films were presented for audiences of _____ (size).

I work in _____ (type of organization).

The screenings were planned and presented by _____ (# people).

_____ (#) films presented using **In Focus**.

Skills and information evaluation:

	Areas where you were already skilled.	Areas where you were weak or needed information.	Areas where In Focus provided needed information.	Areas where In Focus stimulated new ideas.	Areas where In Focus needs additional information.
Program goals	_____	_____	_____	_____	_____
Film selection	_____	_____	_____	_____	_____
Program planning	_____	_____	_____	_____	_____
Space evaluation	_____	_____	_____	_____	_____
Publicity	_____	_____	_____	_____	_____
Running a screening	_____	_____	_____	_____	_____
Projection techniques	_____	_____	_____	_____	_____
Evaluations	_____	_____	_____	_____	_____
Film sources	_____	_____	_____	_____	_____
Information sources	_____	_____	_____	_____	_____
Sound	_____	_____	_____	_____	_____
References on film	_____	_____	_____	_____	_____
Distributors	_____	_____	_____	_____	_____

Based on your evaluation, elaborate on any information which you think would be useful to add or which would supplement **In Focus.**

_____

_____

_____

_____

_____

Check the ways you think would be most effective for us to provide you with the needed additional information:

_____ written supplement
_____ diagrams
_____ local resources
_____ consultation

_____ local or regional
training sessions
_____ local or regional
workshops
_____ national conference

Ways in which **In Focus** has been used by you/your group (check all applicable):

_____ read completely
_____ read individual
chapters
_____ reread particular
chapters
_____ used to organize a
screening
_____ on hand at screening
or meetings for
reference

_____ passed around group
_____ xeroxed specific
sections for
worksheets
_____ followed particular
procedures
_____ located/ordered
suggested resources
_____ recommended to
others

Additional Comments: _____

_____

_____

_____

_____

Name _____

Department _____

Organization _____

Address _____ City _____

State _____ Zip _____ Phone (___)_____

Return to: Cine Information, 419 Park Ave. So., New York, NY 10016